The Master of the Ladder

The
MASTER
of the
LADDER

THE LIFE AND TEACHINGS OF
Rabbi Yehudah Leib Ashlag

by Rabbi Avraham Mordecai Gottlieb

Translated and Edited by Yedidah Cohen

Nehora Press
POB 2586, Har Canaan, Safed 1330000, Israel
tel: 972-4-6923254 or 972-52-698-5931
nehora@bezeqint.net
www.nehorapress.com

Publisher's Cataloging-in-Publication data

Names: Gottlieb, Avraham Mordecai, author. | Cohen, Yedidah, editor.
Title: The Master of the ladder : the life and teachings of Rabbi Yehudah Leib
Ashlag / by Rabbi Avraham Mordecai Gottlieb ; translated and edited by Yedidah
Cohen.
Description: Includes bibliographical references and index. | Safed, Israel: Nehora
Press, 2019.
Identifiers: ISBN 978-965-7222-06-5 (Hardcover) | 978-965-7222-12-6, (pbk.) | 978-
965-7222-13-3 (epub) | 978-965-7222-10-2 (Kindle) | 978-965-7222-14-0 (pdf)
Subjects: LCSH Ashlag, Yehudah, 1886-1955--Study and teachings. | Mysticism-
-Judaism. | Cabala. | Rabbinical literature. | Spiritual life--Judaism. | BISAC
RELIGION / Judaism / Kabbalah & Mysticism | BIOGRAPHY &
AUTOBIOGRAPHY / Jewish
Classification: LCC BM723 .G68 2019 | DDC 296.7/12--dc23

לעילוי נשמת

צבי בן אברהם יעקב וחיה קלרה ז״ל

נחמה בת אברהם יעקב וחיה קלרה ע״ה

שרה בת אברהם מאיר וציפורה שפרינצה ע״ה

Dedicated in loving memory of
Tzvi Hadassi, Nechamah Dekel, and Sarah Agmon

ת.נ.צ.ב.ה

לעילוי נשמת

חנה אנט בת משה ומזל ע״ה

In loving memory of

Hannah Annette Alkaslassy

who lived a life of dedication to her family

and to the people of Israel.

ת.נ.צ.ב.ה

לעילוי נשמת

אהרון לב ופייגא לזר ז״ל

Arnold & Florence Lazar

אהרון אליעזר ושרה קוטלר ז״ל

Aaron Eliezer and Shirley Kotler

ת.נ.צ.ב.ה

Contents

cont.

Songs

> This is the book of the generations of Adam. On the day that God created Adam, He created him in the image of God. Male and female He created them and He blessed them and He called their name "Adam" on the day of their creation. (Genesis 5:1-2)

> "Adam" is both male and female and is not called "Adam" except with the inclusion of both. (Zohar)

> He created them male and female and He called their name "Adam." Each one alone is only half a body and is not called "Adam." (*Perush haSulam* on above Zohar)

Equally problematic is the use of the pronoun "He" for God. The Ari, in the Etz Chaim, states:

> There is no created intelligence that can attain God as He is, for He has no place, no border, and no name.

From this we learn that the essence of God has no gender. The word "He" does not refer to God, but to the fact that we perceive God's light as a giving energy. When God's light is perceived as a receiving energy, God is referred to as "She."

For a further discussion of the meaning of the terms "male" and "female" in the context of Kabbalah, see "The Language of Kabbalah," page xix.

Preface

*"I give thanks to God with all my heart,
I will tell of all Your wonders" (Ps. 9:2).*

When I saw that the students of the holy sage Rabbi Yehudah Leib Ashlag were departing this world, I became anxious to preserve what I could of his life and deeds.

Learning from the deeds of the righteous is in itself Torah, so I set to the task of compiling this biographical work on the life and teaching of Rabbi Yehudah Leib Ashlag, known as the Baal HaSulam.

Actually, even before I made this decision, whenever I heard my teacher, Rabbi Baruch Shalom Ashlag, tell an anecdote of his father, Rabbi Yehudah Leib Ashlag, I would write it down immediately. Equally, when the older members of the beit midrash (study hall) would meet and tell of a happening in the lives of the Baal HaSulam and of his students or discuss a saying attributed to them, I would take note of it. However, once I had made the decision to write this book, I and some of my pupils went specifically to meet with the students of Rabbi Ashlag and their descendants, and we listened to their words over many hours.

Through their words emerged the story of their lives: Lives of fortitude and holiness made up of sacrifice and dedication, all of which sprang from the desire to fulfill the will of the Creator, the Holy Blessed One.

This book, which describes the lives of Rabbi Ashlag and his students, is not about personages who lived in some remote period with whom we have no connection. It is a book about living people, some of whom I had the privilege of knowing personally. It is from such near acquaintance that I am able to attest to their great spiritual stature.

All of them walked the path of serving the Creator. It was a path that Rabbi Ashlag received from his teachers and that he himself taught.

Rabbi Ashlag's spiritual attainment cannot be simply described; however, we get glimpses of it through his writings and through his oral teachings that were recorded. Undoubtedly, he reached the highest levels a human being can reach in connection with the Creator. Rabbi Ashlag chose to use his great spiritual attainment in teaching us a path that we may learn how to serve our Creator and discover the joy of a true connection with Him.

My purpose in compiling this book was, therefore, not solely to write a factual memoir or a historical document, but to awaken our hearts.

In the Shade of the Teacher

My teacher was the holy sage Rabbi Baruch Shalom Ashlag, Rabbi Ashlag's firstborn son. Rabbi Baruch Shalom took on the mantle of sage after his father's death. I first came into his presence before I was fifteen years old. I remember the first time I saw him. It was on Shabbat (the Sabbath) at three o'clock in the morning. I went into the room where the lessons were given. Already, the students were poring over the *Talmud Eser haSephirot* [The Study of the Ten Sephirot]. The atmosphere in the room was saturated with holiness and purity; one could really feel it in the air. Rabbi Baruch Shalom entered and sat on his chair. Even before he began to teach, I had the feeling that I could seek wisdom and knowledge of spiritual matters from him. Indeed, the spiritual stature of this holy man of God was pronounced, even before he said a word. When he entered the room a spirit of great strength entered with him. His face expressed tremendous fortitude. His whole being spoke of determination and decisiveness, of great strength of will, of resolve to establish all the actions of his life according to the will of God.

Since then, I have cleaved with all my life and spirit to my teacher, never removing myself from him. He raised me as a loving father and supervised my path with great watchfulness, as a father supervises his son in all ways. He taught me all I have learned in Torah and gave me the means to understand it so that nothing that I have originates from me. All that I know and understand of the learning of Kabbalah and of the practical way of serving God, I learned from him.

Day by day, I saw Rabbi Baruch Shalom, his face filled with majesty. His ability to serve God in such an exalted way was really incomprehensible to normal human intelligence. He trod the path of faith that transcends knowledge: the way of giving to others—a way that demands great resolve. When we, his students, gazed at his face, we felt an immediate desire to dedicate our lives to God from love.

With the mercy of God, I merited to serve Rabbi Baruch Shalom and became one of the students who were closest to him. I spent many hours in his presence, and from this closeness I learned a lot—sometimes more than was possible to learn in the study sessions themselves. Being in his presence gave me an understanding, in the most concrete way possible, of what it means to be a person who truly believes in God. He considered all his ways, his words, and his thoughts, according to the one criterion: am I in accord with the will of God or not? This was the one single rule to which he adhered throughout his life.

In his last year, Rabbi Baruch Shalom related to me, more than once, the events of his life. He told me of his childhood and of the period after his marriage when he became a student in the beit midrash of his great father. He told me of his very deep connection with his father and of his affinity with him. He spoke of the texture of the relationships that the students had enjoyed with his holy father and between each other. He also told me of the many trials of his life—most of which I do not want to retell here—and how they strengthened his longing for *dvekut* (unity) with the Creator.

It is now clear to me that it was the years that I merited to spend in the presence of Rabbi Baruch Shalom that inspired me to write this book. All the explanations that I have written here spring forth from the life teaching of my teacher, the sage Rabbi Baruch Shalom Ashlag.

I would like to apologize to the reader because sometimes the topics in this book are not polished in a literary sense. For, really, I am not a writer; but I didn't want to put this holy work into the hands of professional writers, because, however good such writers may be, they are still outsiders and will see things only from an outsider's perspective, and I did not want this. Therefore, I preferred to do this work myself with the purpose of giving the reader, as much as possible, an inner view of our holy Rabbis.

Naturally, I haven't been able to convey that much of the inner spirit that permeated our holy teachers because these matters aren't easy to pass on. I couldn't pass on the day-to-day difficulties of the students in rising before dawn, in acting toward their fellow students with love, in deferring to the Rabbi. This is a whole way of life that is possible to understand in real terms only when one walks this spiritual path in actual practice.

But I have tried as much as I can to pass on the wonderful spirit that ruled in the beit midrash of our holy teacher, Rabbi Yehudah Leib Ashlag, and in that of his son, Rabbi Baruch Shalom Ashlag. I have also endeavored to clarify their principles and show how they put these principles into practice in every step of their lives.

In our generation, to my very great sorrow, the issues of how to serve the Creator have become very blurred. People who are not qualified to do so purport to teach others the way of serving God. The truth is lacking from such teachings and the resulting confusion and darkness are very great indeed.

I hope that this book will bring about a change in the thought of those who seek to come close to the Holy Blessed One. This is my real purpose in putting these matters onto paper—to show the way of serving God in its true form.

I wish to point out that while undertaking this research on the lives of our holy sages, I occasionally came across instances when the sages rebuked their students. I tried to understand the reason for these rebukes and in what way the students erred, as I wished to find guidelines for our own lives. I wished to understand how to serve the Creator truly, without compromise. One must remember, however, that the students themselves were men of great spiritual stature who served God with incredible devotion and self-sacrifice. They were of an entirely different dimension from ourselves. Even if we do not measure up to their standards, we may, nevertheless, learn from them.

Acknowledgments

I would like to take this opportunity to thank my honored father, Rabbi Shraga Gottlieb, and my dear mother, Rabbanit Rachel Gottlieb, who were faithful messengers of the Almighty and raised me in the ways of the holy Torah. They did not spare any labor or toil throughout their lives in fulfilling the will of God. May the Holy Blessed One grant them health and much joy from their children and may they merit to see success in the service of the Creator.

May we all soon merit the complete redemption when the Creator's divine light will be manifest to all.

Avraham Mordecai Gottlieb
Student of Rabbi Baruch Shalom Halevi Ashlag

Kiryat Ye'arim, Israel

Introduction

Until the coming of Rabbi Ashlag, the study of Kabbalah was closed to all but the great sages and other people of outstanding piety and virtue. But its absence had left a hole in the spiritual life of our people; the spark of true connection with the Creator was lacking. It was time to act. It was Rabbi Ashlag who opened the study of Kabbalah for all of us.

Kabbalah comprises the inner aspect of the Torah. Because it deals with the intentions of actions, which, for the most part, are hidden from us, it is called "the hidden Torah." Through its study, we learn what the intentions of our forefathers and our foremothers were in the events described in the Torah. Knowing why our ancestors acted in the way they did helps us to identify with them. Only thus can they become living guides for our own lives.

Through our study of Kabbalah, we also learn the reasons for the mitzvot. This gives us enthusiasm and joy when we fulfill the mitzvot in practice, and leads us to be more careful in our ethical behavior, as Kabbalah gives us sound principles by which the whole society may run with integrity and honesty.

The study of the Kabbalah uncovers the deep beauty and precision of the Torah so that even people who are not religious can clearly see its truth. We discover the divine logic and system through which the study of the Torah and the performance of the mitzvot pluck on the strings of our soul with complete exactitude to transform us. We begin to see how all that comes to pass in our lives, and all that took place in the lives of those who came before us, has the purpose of moving us from a state of egoism, a state in which our self-interest is dominant, to a state in which our care for each other takes precedence. It is no wonder that when Jews who were not given a religious education are exposed to this wonderful knowledge they draw closer to the religion, as the true godliness of every mitzvah becomes apparent. Non-Jews also become aware that the spiritual laws revealed by Kabbalah bring justice and sanity to the world.

In this book, I have brought two pieces of writing that particularly fill me with awe. In one, Rabbi Ashlag writes that he merited the soul of the Holy Ari, Rabbi Yitzchak Luria. In the other, he tells of a prophetic revelation he received in which God revealed Himself to him, saying, "I have chosen you to be the tzaddik and sage for all this generation in order that the crisis of humanity may be healed with a lasting salvation."

These words are evidence of the role that the Holy Blessed One assigned Rabbi Ashlag. Such a role becomes apparent only over time. Other famous sages, Rabbi Moshe ben Maimon (the Rambam), the Baal Shem Tov, and Rabbi Moshe Chaim Luzzato, all faced enormous opposition in their own generations, but over time their greatness became recognized and their light shone forth, turning the hearts of thousands of Jews to their Creator.

The psalmist says, "Taste and see that God is good" (Ps. 34:9). When we try to follow Rabbi Ashlag's teachings and that of his son, Rabbi Baruch Shalom Ashlag, we see how we are lifted above materialism to the happiness and eternity of unity with the Creator. This experience of following true teachings is, in fact, what ultimately defeated the opposition to the Baal Shem Tov, the Ari, Rabbi Moshe Chaim Luzzato, and the Rambam. Once their light was clearly manifest in the world, people who followed their teachings found that the paths taught by these sages raised them up and brought them into connection with the Creator.

For the first time in Jewish history, through Rabbi Ashlag's commentary on the Zohar, the ordinary Jew has obtained access to this central work of Judaism. Rabbi Ashlag also clarified the teachings of the Holy Ari, Rabbi Yitzchak Luria, the great Kabbalist of the sixteenth century, who described the evolution of the soul from its origin in the higher worlds until its incarnation in this world. This Rabbi Ashlag did in his major commentaries on the *Etz Chaim* of the Ari: the

Talmud Eser haSephirot and the *Panim Meirot uMasbirot.* Anyone who learns these works in depth comes to the conclusion that these are not products of Rabbi Ashlag's intellectual thought, but they are detailed descriptions of his clear perception of the processes of the spiritual worlds. He wrote:

> Chiefly, success in prophetic utterance is realized through the bringing of God's light down to those who dwell on earth. One who is able to bring the light down to the lowest level is the most successful.

Rabbi Ashlag's work is permeated with his love for God and his love for all humankind. This is a love that I cannot describe, for you can only experience it for yourself. It is for this reason that so many excerpts of Rabbi Ashlag's teachings have been brought in this book, to enable you, the reader, to begin to experience for yourself this great love. I sincerely hope this book will provide the inspiration for you to go deeper into the study of this great Torah.

Rabbi Ashlag's work is a source of enlightenment for all people: the religious Jew, the secular Jew, and the non-Jew. It comprises a revelation of the divine wisdom that has the potential to bring each one of us to fulfill the true purpose of our lives, such that we cease to work only for our own material pleasure but dedicate our efforts to serve the Creator here on earth.

It is through this service that we may bring ourselves and our fellows to a lasting *dvekut* (unity) with the Creator. And then we will witness with our own eyes the fulfillment of the prophecy: "They shall not hurt nor destroy in all My holy mountain; for the earth shall be filled with the knowledge of the Lord, as the waters cover the sea" (Isa. 11:9). Amen, may this be God's will.

Translator's Introduction

The Language of Kabbalah

Yedidah Cohen

Our physical world is made up of elements that interact with each other in time and space, and our ordinary spoken language reflects the way we perceive this world through our senses and through our intellect. However, the discussion of the sages of the Kabbalah is not centered on the physical world, but on the ways that God reveals Himself to us and on our awareness of Him.

In particular, Kabbalah examines how God reveals Himself to us through the words of the Torah and in the events the Torah describes. Through the teachings of the sages of Kabbalah, but particularly those of the Holy Ari, we learn that the different levels of our awareness of God accord with different worlds of consciousness, which we refer to as the higher spiritual worlds. These worlds are arranged according to how closely they align with God's nature, which is that of unconditional giving of true goodness.

The sages tell us that the spiritual worlds are created one from another like an impression is created from a rubber stamp, such that every element in a lower spiritual world has its corresponding component in a higher spiritual world.

In exactly the same way, our physical world may be seen as an impression taken from the spiritual world above it. Thus everything that exists within the physical world, whether discerned by our senses or even created by our imagination, has its root within the higher spiritual worlds. Indeed, every element of this physical world is a branch that stems from its specific root in a higher spiritual world.

The relationship between the elements of our physical world (the branches) and their roots in the higher spiritual worlds was clearly perceived by the sages of the Kabbalah and of the Talmud. Thus, by referring to an element in this world, when they were really intending the spiritual root from which it derives, the sages of the Kabbalah found a ready-made language that they could use to describe any particular consciousness they perceived.

Thus the language of Kabbalah, called the "language of the branches," is made up of the same words that comprise our ordinary, everyday language, but it uses these words differently. The language of Kabbalah does not refer to the way things appear to us in the reality of this world, but to their spiritual roots. So words or phrases that we read in the books of Kabbalah, particularly in the Zohar, although they conjure up images of this world, are, in fact, describing elements that relate to awareness of God. Indeed, the images evoked by these words often mislead us, because we may mistakenly attribute meanings pertaining to the physical world to writings that really relate to an entirely different realm of consciousness. Throughout the centuries, this has been, and remains, the greatest source of error regarding the works of Kabbalah.

Our great sages throughout the ages, who have been able to perceive the spiritual worlds directly, have had a living connection with Kabbalah and have been spiritually nourished by its truths. But for the ordinary person who lacks such direct perception, the language of Kabbalah proved an insurmountable barrier. It was Rabbi Ashlag who first opened up the code to this language in his seminal work on the Kabbalah of the Ari, the *Talmud Eser haSephirot*, and in fact, wrote more than one dictionary of the language of Kabbalah.

As we learn Kabbalah, we find its language embedded in all texts, including the written Torah, the prayer book, the Haggadah, the Talmud and all aspects of the Oral Law. As our proficiency with this language grows, texts from all these sources reveal new and deeper meanings.

One of the features of this language of the branches is the singularity of each branch, which is to say that each branch relates to only one root in the spiritual worlds and not to any other; and one branch cannot be exchanged for any other. This leads to many instances in which the material under discussion seems disturbing to us in a human sense. For example, the term "male" in the language of the branches actually means "the aspect of giving." Thus, when, in the Torah, God is referred to as "He," the term is not assigning a gender to the Creator, but it implies that His light is emanating in the aspect of giving. Similarly, the term "female" should be translated as "the aspect of receiving" and God's light is then termed "the Shechinah." When we know the true usage of these terms, we no longer consider such texts or our liturgy as sexist or patriarchal. It is important for us to remember that whenever we come across passages in the Zohar or in other Kabbalah texts that seem disturbing to us, we need to first translate them from the language of the branches into our spoken language. Only then can we see what they are really saying, because our habitual usage of the words gives rise to misleading images within us.

Another feature of the language of Kabbalah is its succinct nature. Frequently, we find one short phrase being used to describe a whole state of consciousness. The sage, in using that phrase, expects the reader to summon up within himself an appreciation of that specific spiritual state, which he is then going to discuss within a particular context.

One example of such a phrase is "affinity of form." This refers to a situation in which two people, or two spiritual entities, share the same desire. This phrase is most frequently used in the context of our relationship with God. The sages of Kabbalah teach us that the Creator is good and desires only to give good unconditionally to all created beings. When we, likewise, wish to give to our fellow or to God without needing or expecting anything back, simply giving unconditionally, we are in affinity of form with the Creator. This is because we are acting with a similar desire to the Creator's desire. Understanding the full meaning of such phrases, which abound in Kabbalah writings, requires a patient step-by-step building of our understanding of the texts.

Our understanding of the texts requires, not just intellectual work, but also inner work, as the subject matter is always the relationship of the soul with the Creator. Our study is on the texts, but our relationship with the texts and hence our understanding of them is intensely personal. As our understanding grows, we slowly integrate these teachings into our lives.

Since the subject of this book is the life and teachings of a great Kabbalist, much material from the wisdom of Kabbalah has been included. Inevitably, this has involved the use of the language of Kabbalah. This has posed a particular problem as the translation required is now not only from Hebrew into English, but also from the language of the branches into our spoken language! I have endeavored to explain words and phrases as they first appear in the text for the reader who is unfamiliar with them, trying not to disturb the flow of thought too much, but of necessity these short explanations are limited. Furthermore, even phrases and terms with which the reader feels familiar often take on a different meaning when used in Kabbalah. For example, the term "Torah and mitzvot" should be interpreted in the widest possible sense as the receiving of divine wisdom together with its practical, conscious application, rather than a narrow definition of ritual acts carried out without intention. For this reason, a comprehensive glossary is provided at the back of the book, and the reader is encouraged to refer to it, even for terms of which he feels he knows the meaning.

If you would like to go deeper into the language and concepts of Kabbalah as they refer to our own consciousness, then I recommend the books *In the Shadow of the Ladder: the Introductions to the Kabbalah by Rabbi Yehudah Lev Ashlag* and *A Tapestry for the Soul: the Introduction to the Zohar by Rabbi Yehudah Lev Ashlag*. Details on these books can be found on the Nehora Press pages at the end of the book.

My plea to my fellow Jews in particular—and this plea does not exclude others reading this book—is to learn Hebrew. Jews everywhere, throughout history, taught their children *lashon hakodesh*, the holy tongue. Nuances of meaning, subtleties of harmonies, are simply not translatable. The soul resonates with the holy language. It is never too late, and even a little goes a surprisingly long way.

Acknowledgments

Apart from issues of language, I have been involved with much work of editing and collating material that has emerged since the Hebrew publication of the original work, *HaSulam*, and which has been included in this book. I cannot thank Rabbi Avraham Mordecai Gottlieb enough for his patience and promptness in responding to every query, and for his eager support in bringing to the English-speaking world at least a hint of the beauty and deep refreshment to the spirit waiting for all who are inspired to follow the teachings of Kabbalah, as taught by Rabbi Yehudah Leib Ashlag and his son Rabbi Baruch Shalom Ashlag.

My deepest appreciation and heartfelt gratitude are extended to Shoshana Rotem for her clear-sighted editing so freely given, which has made an immeasurable difference to the accessibility of the material in this book. My thanks are also extended to Reuven Goldfarb, Dr. Susan Jackson, and Elina Shcop Nascek for linguistic help. My thanks are also given to Avraham Loewenthal for his unwavering belief in this book and his encouragement when my own spirits flagged.

No words are adequate to express my thanks to my sisters, Chana Kotler and Elizabeth Topper, to my chevrutas and to my family who have so supported me throughout the period of bringing this work to fruition. I owe a debt of thanks to my chevruta, Shalom Siegal z"l, who believed in my work and never hesitated to say so. I would also like to thank Yossi Dabush for his steadfast care and support, without which it is hard to envisage how this work would have been completed.

As I write these words, my heart goes out in thanks to HaShem, who gave me this privilege of working with these texts, and I most humbly acknowledge His gift to me. I pray I may be worthy, in even the smallest measure, of my great teachers, Rabbi Yehudah Leib Ashlag and his son Rabbi Baruch Shalom HaLevi Ashlag, whose boundless love for their Creator and whose love and service for all humanity shine forth in their every deed and word.

Yedidah Cohen

Tsfat, Israel

The Master of the Ladder

וְהִנֵּה סֻלָּם מֻצָּב אַרְצָה, וְרֹאשׁוֹ מַגִּיעַ הַשָּׁמָיְמָה.

And behold! A ladder is set on the earth,
and the top of it reaches the heavens.

Genesis 28:12

Chapter One

Foundations

One evening in 1892, in a suburb of Warsaw, a seven-year-old boy was lying in bed when suddenly a book fell off the bookshelf, hitting him on the head. The boy picked it up and started to examine it. His father, hearing the sound, came in, and seeing the book in his son's hand, took it from him, saying, "This is a book for angels, not for you," and replaced it on the shelf. But the boy argued, "If it has been printed, it must be meant for everyone." "No," insisted his father, "it is not for you." But the boy's curiosity had been aroused, and he started to study it. It was a book of Kabbalah and its light illumined his heart.

The child was Yehudah Leib Ashlag.

Masha Rachel, Yehudah's mother, was a firm educator. When her children were naughty she never punished them there and then, because she felt herself swayed by her own anger. So she would wait some days before mentioning the wrongdoing to the child, and then she would punish him in order to educate him. Such was the young Yehudah's careful upbringing, and it must have influenced the formation of his unusual personality.

Yehudah's father, Rabbi Simchah HaLevi Ashlag, was a chasid of the sage Rabbi Meir Shalom of Kalozhin, the grandson of the Holy Jew of Peschischa. When he went to visit the sage, Rabbi Simchah took his son with him, and thus began the connection between the great sage and the young student.

Batsheva Reichbard, one of Rabbi Ashlag's daughters, tells of her father's childhood:

> Until the age of ten, my father was an only child. He was exceptionally gifted. To some extent, his parents spoiled him, but they took care to ensure that he was brought up nicely. They made him go to bed on time, but he would only pretend to be asleep. Once his parents slept, he would get up, light a lamp, and study until dawn.

As a youth, Yehudah Leib studied in the yeshivah (seminary) of the Gur Chasidim, which was located in Warsaw. There he breathed the atmosphere of Torah. His perseverance and diligence in his Torah studies were exceptional. He slept very little. He would not allow his body to dictate how much sleep he got but fought with himself to subdue its demands so he could progress on the pathway to unity with God. His brilliance in his Torah studies was such that by the time he was fourteen years old, he was proficient in the Talmud with all its commentaries.

Rabbi Baruch Shalom, Rabbi Ashlag's son:

> My father began to study Kabbalah when he was still young. Since he did not want anyone in the yeshivah to notice, he would pull pages from the book the *Etz Chaim* [Tree of life] of the Ari, and slip them between the leaves of his Talmud. When someone came up to him, he turned over the page and continued learning the Talmud.... .

Once, Rabbi Ashlag said of himself that by the age of fifteen he was so devoted to the attribute of truth that he was incapable of telling a lie. His work on his attributes was continuous. He always exerted himself to behave as if he were in the presence of a great king.

Rabbi Azriel Chaim Lemburger, one of Rabbi Ashlag's assistants:

> One time, our teacher, Rabbi Ashlag, told me, "At eleven years of age, I began to learn books that taught *musar* [ethics]. I did not move from one book to the next until I had put the first into practice and it had become second nature to me. By the age of eighteen, I was already an *Adam* [man]."

The meaning of the concept "Adam" is explained by Rabbi Shimon Bar Yochai in the tractate *Yebamot* in the Talmud: "You are called 'Adam,' whereas those who serve false gods are not called 'Adam.'" This statement is explained by Rabbi Ashlag:

> The name "Adam" is from the phrase *Adameh laElyon*—"I will resemble the Most High" (Isa. 14:14). A person who seeks to emulate God in His mercy and in His compassion is called "Adam."

Rabbi Azriel Lemburger's father, Rabbi Moshe Baruch Lemburger, told him that he once heard Rabbi Ashlag say of himself that by the age of twenty-four, he no longer had any desire to receive for himself alone.*

So the young Yehudah Leib continued to progress in the knowledge of Torah, working on his virtues with intense labor, but with modesty and without outward show. On reaching the age of nineteen, he was appointed to the rabbinate by the great rabbis of Warsaw. At that time—the early years of the twentieth century—the Polish authorities required rabbis to know Russian in order to obtain their rabbinical certificates. This did not bother Rabbi Ashlag at all; he learned the Russian language within a short period and received his certification. For the next sixteen years, he served as rabbi and *dayan* (judge) in the rabbinical court of Warsaw, which, at that time, was a great center for Torah learning. During this period, Rabbi Ashlag published his first book, *Sichot Chaim* (Living Discourses) that told of the works and teachings of the sage of Morgalintzia.

Family

When he reached the age of twenty in 1906, Rabbi Yehudah Leib Ashlag married Rivkah Raiza Abramovitz of the nearby town of Porisov, to whom he was distantly related. She was then sixteen years old. Together they had eleven children, of whom eight survived: Rabbi Baruch Shalom Ashlag, Rabbi Ya'acov Ashlag, Rabbi Shlomoh

---

* "To receive for oneself alone" is a term in the Kabbalah of Rabbi Ashlag. It means to supply the demands of the ego to enhance our selfish love. See Glossary page 333.

Binyamin Ashlag, Rabbi Moshe Menachem Aharon Ashlag, Sara Bodchek, Batsheva Reichbard, Devorah Weitzman, and Menuchah Verdiger.

Rabbi Ashlag's daughter, Batsheva Reichbard, continued her story:

At that time in Poland, it was the custom for the young married Talmudic students to be supported by their fathers-in-law, if the father-in-law was a man of means. This left the young scholars free to carry on with their intensive study of Torah. So my mother's parents, who were very wealthy, supported the young couple in Porisov. However, the behavior of their son-in-law seemed very strange to them. He would arise every night at one o'clock to serve the Creator. This was unlike a normal householder who would rise at dawn. My father was totally engrossed in Torah and in prayer; he did not pay attention to anything else. My grandparents began to show their displeasure openly and tried to turn my mother against her husband. My parents suffered greatly from this opposition so they decided to leave Porisov and move to Warsaw.

In Warsaw, my father continued his study of Torah and his practice of intense service to God. From time to time, he would travel to his teacher, the sage of Kalozhin, with whom he would stay for three months at a time, completely engrossed in his learning, before returning home.

In practice, all her life, my mother was the one who financed the household. She took care of the children's needs and of their clothing; she even found the money for their dowries herself. Later on, she helped sell my father's books. She did everything on her own, because even though her parents were wealthy, they did not wish to help at all. My father never held money in his hand and never knew what a coin was.

Their poverty was immense. Rabbi Baruch Shalom Ashlag:

At that time in Warsaw, when it came to the festival of Succot, no one built his own private *succah* [festive booth] but would join in building one large succah that was used by the whole community. Only the men sat in the communal succah, and my mother would send in food for her husband via one of the children. However, the fact was, there was hardly anything to eat. Since my mother did not want their great poverty to be known to all, she used to make a tremendous effort to get a little extra money to buy good food, so she could send a nice portion to my father in the succah. My father, who knew the real situation, would taste just a tiny bit and then send the whole portion back home so that the children could have something to eat.

Batsheva Reichbard:

At the Shabbat table at which my father presided, there was absolute quiet, even awe. My revered father would sit at the head of the table like a burning flame; the holiness of Shabbat burning within him as if he were an angel of God. Are there people like this today who sit at the Shabbat table with absolutely no interest in food but with mystical unity with God gushing through their veins? Food, for my father, was only a means by which to fulfill God's commandments. Aside from this, it held no interest for him. All of the children, from the very youngest to the eldest, knew not to talk, not to say anything, so as not to disturb our father. Even children as young as a year old already understood they should be quiet. If a child was late for the Shabbat meal, his place was not kept for him.

The disciples would come to my father's holy table, at which point he would give a discourse on the Torah, his entire being burning with the fire of holiness.

In the Shade of his Teachers:
The Sages of Kalozhin, Porisov, and Belz

In his youth, Rabbi Ashlag was a disciple of the sage of Kalozhin, Rabbi Meir Shalom Rabinovitz.* Rabbi Ashlag would come every night at two in the morning to learn with his teacher. He once related that the

---

* Rabbi Meir Shalom Rabinovitz was a grandson of the Holy Jew, Rabbi Ya'acov Yitzchak Rabinovitz, the founder of the Peschischa dynasty of Chasidism.

holy Sage would be awake the whole of the Shabbat eve, pacing up and down in his room, filled with the love of God, saying one sentence throughout the night, *HaShem Hu HaElohim, Ein Od Milvado!* "The Lord is God, there is none other than Him" (Deut. 4:35).

The sage of Kalozhin, Rabbi Meir Shalom, died in 1903 and was succeeded as sage by his son Rabbi Yehoshua Asher of Porisov. However, Rabbi Ashlag did not immediately adopt the son as his sage. Only three years later, following a dream, he made his decision. He saw, as in a vision, Rabbi Meir Shalom sitting with his son the Rebbe of Porisov, and he, Rabbi Ashlag, sitting between them. The sage of Kalozhin, Meir Shalom, pointed to his son and told Rabbi Ashlag to go to him. From then on, Rabbi Ashlag became a disciple of the sage Rabbi Yehoshua Asher of Porisov.

Among the disciples of the sage of Porisov, there were, broadly speaking, two types of people: those for whom the propensity to search within themselves for their inner truth was developed, and those for whom it was not. The sage of Porisov related to each individual according to which group of people he belonged. He taught those of his disciples who were less spiritually developed according to the generally accepted way of practicing Torah, which is the practice of *Torah shelo l'shmah* (Torah that is practiced, not for its own sake).*

However, among the disciples of the sage of Porisov, there were also a handful of people who understood the real meaning of working on oneself. These, the Sage instructed in the true path: the way of giving unconditionally to God. Among this handful of disciples was our teacher, Rabbi Yehudah Leib Ashlag. These, the Sage taught according to the chasidic schools of Peschischa-Kotzk, and it was in this method that Rabbi Ashlag was educated. These are schools of chasidut that emphasize modesty, learning, and strict adherence to the halachah coupled with a clear, honest introspection that tolerates no self-deception.

Rabbi Baruch Shalom related that the sage of Porisov would keep his real disciples at a distance, not spoiling them or flattering them. The closer the student really was to the Sage, the more he pushed him

---

* See Glossary, page 332.

away. When the sage of Porisov gave out food at the *tisch* (chasidic gathering), he would routinely skip over Rabbi Ashlag, telling him, "I do not give to you!"

In general, people look for honor; they imagine that they are working spiritually, but they are not really prepared to invest their entire lives to the point of self-sacrifice for the sake of their inner work. To such people, the sage of Porisov gave the honor they were looking for. But those disciples who sincerely wanted instruction on how to follow the path leading to affinity of form* with the Almighty, and were prepared to give their all for this purpose, weren't interested in honor or flattery. On the contrary, they found such approbations repulsive since they knew that such praises kept them from knowing the truth about themselves—indeed, accolades would serve only to keep them at a distance from the Creator. So the sage of Porisov would test the students by treating them with disdain to see if they would stay or if they would get insulted and leave.

The sage of Porisov would often take Rabbi Ashlag with him on his visits to the great sage Rabbi Yissachar Dov of Belz. On one occasion, the sage of Porisov expressed his conviction to Rabbi Ashlag that the sage of Belz had a soul whose root originated in the spiritual world of Atzilut.** It was through his great deference to the sage of Porisov and to the sage of Belz that Rabbi Ashlag made great progress in his spiritual life at this time.

Rabbi Baruch Shalom:

When my father was eighteen years old, the sage of Porisov once took him to spend Shabbat with the sage of Belz.

On the eve of Shabbat, when the sage of Belz, Rabbi Yissachar Dov, was about to make Kiddush [welcoming the Shabbat with

---

* Affinity of form implies acting with the same desire. The Creator desires only to benefit the created beings unconditionally. When we act similarly we attain affinity of form with Him. However, this is extremely hard to achieve, as the ego, our inbuilt nature, opposes such giving. Therefore the students needed much instruction on this path. See Chapter Five, The Path, page 57

** The highest spiritual world we, as human beings, can attain. See Glossary, page 321 and see also Rabbi Ashlag's Works, page 340.

the sanctification of the wine], it was suddenly discovered that one of the children was missing. The members of the household quickly searched for the child. When they found him outside, they brought him to the Shabbat table. The Belzer Rebbe reprimanded the little child severely, and even as he did so, he raised his cup and began to make Kiddush.

After the meal, the Porisover asked Rabbi Ashlag what he thought about the Kiddush that the sage of Belz had made. The young Rabbi Ashlag was astonished and asked, "How could the Rebbe make Kiddush without any preparation, and after dealing out such a severe reprimand?" The Porisover answered him, saying, "This is the greatness of the sage of Belz; nothing separates him from his unity with God."

This is only a tiny example. Even with much more serious incidents, the rabbi of Belz would not budge, not by even a hair's breadth, from his unity with the light of God.

Then Rabbi Baruch Shalom Ashlag added:

And in truth, so we saw with my esteemed father, Rabbi Ashlag. He didn't require any preparations for study or for prayer.... Does a person have to prepare to breathe?

Rabbi Azriel Chaim Lemburger was told of a similar incident by Rabbi David Mintzberg, one of the first students of Rabbi Ashlag:

One Shabbat eve, Rabbi David was present at the house of Rabbi Ashlag following the service of *Kabbalat Shabbat* [the special hymns with which we welcome the Shabbat]. Only when Rabbi Ashlag was preparing to make Kiddush did Rabbi David leave to go home.

When Rabbi David got downstairs, he found the father of one of Rabbi Ashlag's students furiously angry, on his way to shout at the Rabbi because he was drawing his dear son near to the "errant" way of learning Kabbalah, the study of the innermost aspect of the Torah. So Rabbi David went up again to the apartment to defend the honor of his holy teacher. But he found this to be unnecessary as he saw his teacher rebuking the father.

Then, without missing a beat, the Sage started to make Kiddush. Rabbi David saw, with his own eyes, that all the Rabbi's acts and words were taking place while in total unity with the Holy Blessed One, and that nothing moved him from this unity.

On *Shvat* 7, 5667 (January 22, 1907), Rabbi Ashlag's first son, Baruch Shalom, was born. As he grew, his father would take him along on his journeys to the sages of Porisov and Belz for his education.

Rabbi Baruch Shalom Ashlag told:

Once, I traveled with my esteemed father, Rabbi Ashlag, to Galicia to visit the sage of Belz, Rabbi Yissachar Dov, of blessed memory. While we were staying with him, the First World War broke out. We stayed a while at the Belzer Rebbe's because all the roads were blocked; madness and chaos reigned. No one knew what the next day would bring. There was no organized transport at all. After some time, the Belzer Rebbe told us we could journey to our destination. There did not seem any logical way to find a safe passage back to Warsaw, but my father had total trust in the words of the holy Sage, so we set out. And it happened that we found a train of soldiers with which we returned to Warsaw.

It was this great faith in his teacher that was to stand by Rabbi Ashlag in an experience that was to change the course of his whole life.

Chapter Two

The Work Begins

It is customary among the great tzaddikim to conduct themselves so that their own spiritual achievements and experiences are kept hidden. Accordingly, in the last year of his life, Rabbi Ashlag requested his devoted assistant, Rabbi Moshe Baruch Lemburger, to make a pile of his personal papers and burn them. However, others who were present contrived to save the papers from the fire.

Among these papers is a piece of writing in which Rabbi Ashlag describes his thoughts and feelings when he had the merit to receive the great light of God, the *Or d'Chochmah*. This is the great light that God wants to give us according to His purpose in creation. A person receives the *Or d'Chochmah* only when he has finished his personal *tikkun* (rectification of his soul). At the time of the redemption, however, all humanity will receive this great light.

In this document, we have a record, unique in Jewish spiritual literature, of the development of the tzaddik on his receiving the *Or d'Chochmah*—an experience of enlightenment while in affinity of form* with the Creator. It was an experience that was to change the direction of Rabbi Ashlag's life.

Rabbi Ashlag starts by asking a question: He wants to know what his service to God now consists of. So he sets out to visit his teacher, the Rabbi of Belz. But when he arrives at the beit midrash, he finds

---

* Affinity of form means that Rabbi Ashlag is acting with a similar desire of giving unconditionally as is the Creator. Rabbi Ashlag is not receiving this great enlightenment to gain anything for himself but only in order to give pleasure to the Creator, who wishes to give to Rabbi Ashlag.

that the Sage's response to him in his state of enlightenment is not encouraging. Rabbi Ashlag finds himself in a quandary: on the one hand he believes in his experience; on the other hand, he has faith in his rabbi. Perplexed, Rabbi Ashlag has to resolve this seeming contradiction for himself.

[Since Rabbi Ashlag set down this experience in a note he clearly intended for his own use, it is written both in an enigmatic style and with content that is only alluded to. For example, in the original Hebrew, Rabbi Ashlag refers to himself mostly in the third person, not wanting to use the word "I." For the sake of clarity, I have translated the whole piece in the first person, even though an aspect of Rabbi Ashlag's reticence and modesty is lost.

Regarding content, Rabbi Avraham Mordecai Gottlieb has provided us with a detailed commentary on this manuscript, helping us to understand the allusions. This commentary follows Rabbi Ashlag's original manuscript. My advice to the reader is to read it, marvel, but not worry if you don't understand it. Y.C.]

Parashah Metzorah 5679 (April 1919)
A great principle caused me some doubt: Can a person be spiritually alive without giving service to God? Or is it possible that the desired service to God may be expressed by giving glory to God and by thanking God?

At that time I had no desire to go to the Sage; yet I went and journeyed without desire and even without connection [with the Rabbi of Belz], for I went to see if the Prime Cause would manifest there again.

At the very moment that the Sage saw my reality, he knew that I was coming.

Remember this amazing thing: Even when I was not connected [with the Rabbi of Belz], the moment my feet moved outside, I was filled with wondrous glory and great delight.

I arrived there in the middle of the prayer. It happened that when the prayer was over, the Sage looked for me among the crowd, which was not at all according to his custom. Mockingly, he asked, "It seems you have come to receive blessings on leaving the hidden wisdom?" And I didn't understand.

But actually, even while I was still in my house, I had wondered: How is it possible to grasp the fact of the light's ceasing after Seder night that makes it possible to start counting the omer, so that one can prepare oneself for the Receiving of the Torah? What use is the light of a candle at noontime?—Because the state had happened to me that the Scripture describes in these verses: "I will keep My loving-kindness for him forever, and My covenant is certain for him, and I have established his line forever, and his throne to be as lasting as the heavens" (Ps. 89:29–30); and, "But My loving-kindness I will not withdraw from him and I will not betray My faith" (Ps. 89:34)—in every possible way.

This is what the Sage hinted to me in his parting blessing. Because really I received his blessing in a state of consciousness similar to that which is present on the first day of Pesach. Later on in the morning, I felt that the Sage was alluding to me when he said that these spiritual states are like death and parting.

Following the prayers, he gave me the Kiddush cup of wine, wondering at me that I had not left any over from the Kiddush of the Sabbath eve. After that, he said that a lion has no need to fear; a bear has need to fear, but not a lion, he has no need to fear. I was distressed by his words.

At the time of the third Sabbath meal, following the afternoon prayer, I felt a little doubt concerning him, and I was ashamed.

After the *Melavah Malkah* [a special gathering in Chasidic circles following the end of the Sabbath], I felt tremendous sorrow. Chiefly, I wondered, are my ways acceptable to God or not? Since they are acceptable to God, why are they not acceptable to my teacher? Can it be possible that God would give me so much praise and my teacher not, but he even denigrates me somewhat?

I couldn't sleep all that night. I pondered my ways to see if they were mistaken in any way. I wondered, am I fooling myself? Is it possible that the aspect, concerning which there is nothing else higher in reality, really isn't present? Therefore, I went over again in my mind, hundreds of times, these three names of God that were shining so brightly, and I couldn't see any possibility at all that I could incline after something that was outside holiness. This being the case, it was impossible to deny what I could taste in my mouth and feel in actual physicality.

Yet my faith in my teacher was strong, and since this state was not pleasing to him, there must be some defect. So I pondered my ways yet again and I found them to be beautiful. And so it went on, round and round, all through the night.

Then I made a clear agreement with myself to listen carefully to my teacher's words on the matter. If he well recognizes these paths in spirituality according to their quality and their measure, yet he decrees not to use them, then I will immediately obey.

When I arrived at the Sage's doorway, I felt him stand up from his chair, and he began to pace this way and that; and I was alarmed, for I knew with certainty that he was doing this spiritual work for my sake. This carried on for about half an hour until I was nearly fainting from the tremor and the dread, and from the sound of his sighs caused by his inner work at such an extremely high level at that time. Then he opened the door and asked me into his room. He asked me, what do I want? I couldn't open my mouth. But he said to me, as if he were answering his own question, that I must arouse in him what I want from him. So I blurted out that I want to receive the light of revelation in the right way.

Then the Sage sat on the chair and expounded the Torah of "one for the sin-offering and one for the burnt-offering" (*Parshat Metzorah*). He said that it seemed to him that he had expounded this Torah on that Shabbat afternoon especially for me. After that, he asked me if I felt his persecution of me during the Shabbat, and he said to me that it is not correct to go either with enlightenments or with words [transitory stages of holiness].

Then he told me the Torah on: "When I lay down at night, I sought Him whom my soul loves, I sought Him, but did not find Him" (Song of Songs 3:1). [1] He asked me if I understood. But I didn't understand. So he told it to me a second time. But I told him that I didn't understand at all.—And really, I couldn't understand the issue of the night because the sun was shining for me.—Then he said, "Search here well and you will find because here is to be found this whole secret."

Then my teacher said to me, "Have you forgotten what I have taught you several times, that it is forbidden to use any enlightenment?" He began to tell me that same teaching concerning the seed from which much good springs because of the way the wheat is sown.

Then I could no longer refrain for I knew that the light I had received was eternal, and it was like a kosher animal that is eaten. I interrupted his holy words—which is the first time in my entire life that such a thing happened to me—and I said to him, "Was it not so that the honored Rabbi had already promised me according to the Scripture that we read on Rosh HaShanah, 'And Abraham said, "I have sworn it"' (Gen. 21:24)?" At that moment, he stood up from his chair and said, "I have no more strength."

Explanatory teaching on this article: (*Rabbi Ashlag's original words are in bold.*)

Rabbi Ashlag had come to a state of *dvekut* (unity) with the Creator, may He be Blessed, and was in a conscious state of receiving the great light of God, the *Or d'Chochmah* [the great light that God wishes to give all created beings at the fulfillment of creation]. It is from this perspective that he asks a question:

A great principle caused me some doubt: Can a person be spiritually alive without giving service to God? When a person is in unity with God, actually experiencing His great light, there is no spiritual work for him to do. **Or is it possible that the desired service to God may be expressed by giving glory to God and by giving thanks to God?**

At that time, I had no desire to go to the Sage—the Rabbi of Belz. Rabbi Ashlag had no desire to go to his Sage because the Sage had already warned him not to attract the great light, the *Or d'Chochmah.*

Yet I went and journeyed without desire and even without connection to the Rabbi of Belz. His lack of connection with the Rabbi of Belz occurred because he was not in the same conscious state as that of the Rabbi of Belz. **I went to see how the Prime Cause would manifest there again.** Rabbi Ashlag went to see how the Creator would join his conscious state, which was completely illuminated with the *Or d'Chochmah*, with that of the Sage of Belz.

At the very moment that the Sage saw my reality he knew that I was coming. The Rabbi of Belz saw the inner spiritual state of Rabbi Ashlag with his divine insight even though he had not yet arrived physically. **Remember this amazing thing, that even when I was not connected with the Rabbi of Belz, nonetheless, the moment my feet moved outside, I was filled with wondrous glory and great delight.** That is, once Rabbi Ashlag made the move to go to his Rabbi, he was filled with great joy because his great love for his Rabbi was founded on faith, which is the consciousness of giving. And it was this that brought him to this joy.

I arrived there in the middle of prayer. That is to say that the other members of the beit midrash were in a state of consciousness that is associated with lack—a state that arouses prayer. But Rabbi Ashlag was completely filled with light and was thus not in a state of lack so he could not connect with the prayer.

It happened that when the prayer was over, the Sage looked for me among the crowd, which was not at all according to his custom. Mockingly, he asked, "It seems you have come to receive blessings on leaving the hidden wisdom?" The Rabbi of Belz uses the language of separation to Rabbi Ashlag because of the difference in their conscious states. The Rabbi of Belz was in the state of consciousness that is characterized by faith and giving. This state of consciousness attracts the light that is called the *Or d'Chassadim*. This light is the joy of giving. It pertains to the Tikkun of Creation [the state of correcting the vessels of receiving]. Rabbi Ashlag, on the other hand, was in a state of receiving the *Or d'Chochmah*, the great light that pertains to the Purpose of Creation. Hence the separation between them.

And I didn't understand. From his perspective, Rabbi Ashlag couldn't see any separation, as he was not receiving the light for himself alone, God forbid, but his receiving of the light was solely with the intention of giving pleasure to the Creator.

Such receiving of the light, which is only received for the sake of giving pleasure to the Giver, is considered as pure giving. Rabbi Ashlag is receiving the great light that God intends all created beings to receive at the *gmar hatikkun* (the perfected state of creation). He has finished the *tikkun* (rectification) of his own vessels of receiving, and he has no desire to receive for himself alone. He is receiving the light only in order to give the Creator the pleasure of fulfilling His Purpose of Creation.

But actually, even while I was still in my house,—Rabbi Ashlag here hints at his state of consciousness, that he had attained the *Or d'Chochmah*, the light of wisdom, according to the scriptural phrase, "the house will be built through wisdom" (Prov. 24:3)—**I had wondered: How is it possible to grasp the fact of the light's ceasing after Seder night?** The Ari teaches that the light of the *Or d'Chochmah* is manifest to the full on the first night of Pesach [Seder night]. [2] This light is the spiritual light of Chochmah. But it does not remain for the second night of Pesach.

On Seder night the light comes from God irrespective of the spiritual state of the souls. But it does not remain, as the Creator wants us to rectify ourselves by doing our own work. Therefore, this high light leaves, and we start the work of counting the omer—the fifty days of preparation from the second day of Pesach until the Receiving of the Torah on the festival of Shavuot. So Rabbi Ashlag asks: **How is it possible to grasp the fact of the light ceasing after Seder night that makes it possible to start counting the omer, so one can prepare oneself for the Receiving of the Torah? What use is a candle at noontime?** In other words, the lights of rectification that come into the vessels of the counting of the omer are minuscule compared to the mighty light that Rabbi Ashlag had attained as a permanent state of consciousness.

Because the state had happened to me that the Scripture describes: "I will keep My loving-kindness for him forever, and My covenant is certain for him, and I have established his line forever and his throne to be as lasting as the heavens" (Ps. 89:29–30); and "My loving-kindness I will not withdraw from him and I will not betray My faith" (Ps. 89:34). Rabbi Ashlag had reached his complete tikkun. He had merited to attain the light of Chochmah of the world of Atzilut, and now the framework of evil had no power over him at all since his entire being was directed to receiving the light of God only with the intention of giving pleasure to the Creator. **In all possible ways.** This implies that whatever the situation, Rabbi Ashlag's state of dvekut with the Creator could never leave him. It had become eternal.*

This is what the Sage hinted to me in his parting blessing above. Because really I received his blessing in a state of consciousness similar to that which is present on the first day of Pesach. When the Rabbi of Belz blessed Rabbi Ashlag, he hinted to him that this was a blessing of parting as he had become separated from him in his consciousness.

Later on in the morning, I felt that the Sage was alluding to me when he said that these spiritual states are like death and parting. The Sage of Belz hinted to him that the spiritual levels that Rabbi Ashlag had attracted to himself could bring him to spiritual death, similar to that which occurred at "the shattering of the vessels."**

Following the prayers, he gave me the Kiddush cup of wine, wondering at me that I had not left any over from the Kiddush of the Sabbath eve. The Kiddush cup of wine hints at the *Or d'Chochmah,* the high light associated with the Purpose

---

* As the Rambam teaches, "The Knower of all secrets testifies for him that he will never again revert to his foolishness." (*Hilchot Teshuvah* 1)

** The "shattering of the vessels" was an event in the evolution of the spiritual worlds wherein certain vessels inadvertently attracted to themselves more light than they were able to receive only for the sake of giving pleasure to the Creator. As a result they received for themselves alone—the spiritual equivalent of death and separation. A similar event occurred with the sin of Adam who, by eating from the Tree of Knowledge, intended to rectify the entire creation. But Adam did not have the capability of maintaining his intention that his receiving of such a huge light would be only for the sake of giving benefit. Thus, when he ate from the Tree of Knowledge, he brought separation on himself.

In a similar way, the Rabbi of Belz was concerned that the great light illuminating the soul of Rabbi Ashlag could bring him to fall, even though his intentions were pure.

of Creation. The view of the Rabbi of Belz was that one should not receive all the light, symbolized by drinking all the wine. But Rabbi Ashlag was sure that he was acting correctly since his receiving of the light had the sole intention of giving.

After that, he [the Rabbi of Belz] said: A lion has no need to fear; a bear has need to fear, but not a lion, he has no need to fear. The "lion" refers to Rabbi Ashlag, whose middle name "Leib" means a lion, and the "bear" refers to the Sage of Belz whose name was Yissachar Dov; "Dov" means a bear.

The Belzer Rebbe is speaking with sarcasm, saying that it appears that Rabbi Ashlag is not afraid of any defect happening in his work; the proof of this being that he receives the light of the Purpose of Creation. Whereas he, the Belzer Rebbe, does not draw to himself such great lights and is satisfied with the light of the Tikkun of Creation, which is expressed by faith in God and the fear of being separated from Him.

I was distressed by his words. Rabbi Ashlag saw that his teacher did not agree with his spiritual state. He could not understand why this should be since his receiving of the light was with the sole intention of giving benefit.

At the time of the third Sabbath meal following the afternoon prayer, I felt a little doubt concerning him. I wondered if my teacher had actually apprehended these high spiritual states, **and I was ashamed.**

Following the *Melavah Malkah* [a special gathering in Chasidic circles following the end of the Sabbath], **I felt tremendous sorrow. Chiefly, I wondered, are my ways acceptable to God or not? Since they are acceptable to God,** and the proof of this is that God had given Rabbi Ashlag such great divine lights, **why are they not acceptable to my teacher? Can it be possible that God would give me so much praise and my teacher not, but he even denigrates me somewhat?**

I couldn't sleep all that night. I pondered my ways to see if they were mistaken in any way. I wondered, am I fooling myself? Maybe I am not receiving the light solely with the intention of giving benefit to the Creator, **and that aspect, concerning which there is nothing else higher in reality, really isn't present?** Therefore, I went over again in my mind, hundreds of times, these three names of God that were shining so brightly. These are the aspects of the left-hand line, the right-hand line and the middle line of the light of Chochmah, **and I couldn't see any possibility at all that I could incline after something that was outside holiness,** that is, that I could possibly receive this light for myself alone. This being the case, it was impossible to deny what I could taste in my mouth and feel in actual physicality.

Yet my faith in my teacher was strong, and since this state was not pleasing to him there must be some defect. So I pondered my ways yet again and I found them to be beautiful. Rabbi Ashlag again found that his receiving of the great light of Chochmah was entirely for the sake of giving benefit. **And so it went on, round and round, all through the night.**

Then I made a clear agreement with myself to listen carefully to my teacher on this matter. **If he well recognizes these paths in spirituality according to their quality and their measure** that is, if he knows them entirely, **yet he decrees not to use them, then I will immediately obey.**

When I arrived at the Sage's doorway, I felt him stand up from his chair. The Rabbi of Belz attracted the great light of the Purpose of Creation to himself and he began to pace this way and that, using the right-hand line and the left-hand line, and I was alarmed, for I knew with certainty that he was doing this spiritual work for my sake. This carried on for about half an hour until I was nearly fainting from the tremor and the dread; from the sound of his sighs caused by his inner work at such an extremely high level at that time. All this, the Rabbi of Belz did in order to show Rabbi Ashlag that he himself did know the light of Chochmah to a full measure.

Then he opened the door and asked me into his room. He asked me what do I want? I couldn't open my mouth. But he said to me, as if he were answering his own question, that I must arouse in him what I want from him. So I blurted out that I wanted to receive the light of revelation in the right way.

Then the Sage sat on the chair and expounded the Torah of "one for the sin-offering and one for the burnt-offering" (*Parashah Metzorah*). These are the sacrifices of which neither the priests nor the owners of the animals, eat any portion. The Rabbi of Belz is here telling him that he must give up this great light. He said that it seemed to him that he had expounded this Torah on that Sabbath afternoon especially for me. So that Rabbi Ashlag would know that he should offer up this great spiritual attainment as one offers up incense on the altar, and burn it entirely, exactly as these particular sacrifices were burnt in the Temple.

After that, he asked me if I had felt his persecution of me during the Sabbath, and he said to me that it is not correct to go with enlightenments or with "words." That is, one should not remain with spiritual stages that are temporary, because sooner or later the person has to let go of these particular spiritual stages in order to carry on with his spiritual work. It was more correct to attract the *Or d'Chassadim*, the light that comes through desiring to give loving-kindness and faith, which is a permanent light.

Then he told me the Torah on, "When I lay down at night, I sought Him whom my soul loves; I sought him, but I did not find him" (Song of Songs 3:1). He asked me if I understood. But I didn't understand, and he told it to me a second time. But I told him that I didn't understand at all.—And really, I couldn't understand the issue of the night, because the sun was shining for me.—"Lying down" implies the light of the Tikkun of Creation, which is a lesser light, whereas Rabbi Ashlag felt the *Or d'Chochmah*, the great light of God, to the utmost. Then he said, "Search here well and you will find because here is to be found this whole secret. A person has to agree to use only the lights of the Tikkun of Creation, the *Or d'Chassadim*, which are lesser lights, even if he has the ability to attain the much greater light of the *Or d'Chochmah*, which pertains to the Purpose of Creation. This he only receives if it is God's will that he do so, even when his receiving of such great light is only for the sake of giving benefit. He does not attract it for himself.

Then my teacher said to me, "Have you forgotten what I have taught you several times, that it is forbidden to use any enlightenment?" And he began to tell me that same article concerning the seed from which much good springs because of the way the wheat is sown. Sowing the seed implies both letting go and tikkun, as seed needs to rot for new wheat to germinate from it. Likewise, in spirituality, we need to let go and start afresh to allow the new to come forth.

Then I could no longer refrain. I knew that the light I had received was eternal. Rabbi Ashlag knew that all he had received was for the sake of giving, and from its essence, he knew that it was eternal. And it was like a kosher animal that is eaten and not, God forbid, like a non-kosher animal, from which it is forbidden to eat. I interrupted his holy words—which is the first time in my entire life that such a thing happened to me—and I said to him, "Was it not so, that the honored Rabbi had already promised me, according to the Scripture that we read on Rosh HaShanah, 'And Abraham said, "I have sworn it"'" (Gen. 21:24)?" The inner meaning of this verse implies a total commitment to dvekut that has come through complete purification and cleansing and which is not liable to cease.

At that moment, he stood up from his chair and said, "I have no more strength."

The end of this manuscript is missing. However, it is clear from subsequent events that Rabbi Ashlag accepted the way of the Rabbi of Belz. The turning point came in the night when he made a clear agreement with himself to let go of the great light of the Or d'Chochmah if he saw that his teacher knew this light himself, and yet did not approve.

We know that when Rabbi Ashlag planned to leave Poland for Israel, the Sage of Porisov warned him that in the Land of Israel he would lose his spiritual lights. But Rabbi Ashlag answered him calmly, saying that he was not looking for spiritual lights but for work. This answer is in accordance with the above teaching of the Sage of Belz.

Even though Rabbi Ashlag had finished his own personal tikkun and was in permanent dvekut with God, all the souls of the world have yet to reach their tikkun. Since all the souls together form the one soul that God created, they are mutually dependent on each other. Therefore, no tikkun can be totally complete in itself until the *gmar hatikkun* (the rectification of all the souls). This is why the Rabbi of Belz had warned Rabbi Ashlag not to attract to himself such great lights, as humankind has not yet reached the *gmar hatikkun*.

Thus, Rabbi Ashlag achieved dvekut with God permanently and eternally. Yet the Sage of Belz taught him to let go of the great lights of the *Or d'Chochmah* and to attract instead the joy of giving unconditionally, the light that comes through faith, the *Or d'Chassadim*. This choosing of the light of faith, even when God's great light is manifest, constitutes a further step on the tzaddik's spiritual journey.

For most of us, not yet having achieved the stage of the tzaddik, our faith in God is the only way we have of connecting with Him, as His light is concealed from us. It is a choice we have to make again and again on a moment-to-moment basis as we move into a consciousness of faith and out of it again. Faith in these circumstances is an act of giving to God as we cannot see or sense His presence.

Yet the giving of such faith cannot be considered as an entirely free choice when God's light is concealed from us, as in this circumstance, we don't have any other way of staying connected with Him. In contrast, when a person is actually receiving the high light of God's revelation as Rabbi Ashlag was, he can choose the path of faith as a totally free and open choice.

By choosing the lesser light of faith over that of the greater light of the *Or d'Chochmah*, the tzaddik demonstrates that he values the ability of giving to the Creator even more than he values that of receiving from Him. Furthermore, choosing the light of faith at such a time adds an additional value to all the previous work the tzaddik undertook when such a choice was not available to him. Previously, he was obliged to render all his service to God in faith, in the absence of divine revelation. Now the tzaddik demonstrates that even if God's light had been revealed to him, he would still have chosen to give to God in faith, rather than receive even the highest of divine lights.

This lesson of choosing faith—even while in the presence of the revelation of God's light—changed the direction of Rabbi Ashlag's life and influenced all his subsequent work. Indeed, its mark can be seen on all of Rabbi Ashlag's writings, and in his instruction to his own students, when they too reached these high levels of holiness. (See the letter to Rabbi Joshua Horovitz, page 82.)

It is for such a person, who, acting entirely with the modality of faith, foregoing even the greatest possible joy, that the highest lights of all are revealed, as the Scripture says, "not so my servant Moses, in all my house, he is faithful" (Num. 12:7). Such a person becomes a limitless channel of light for others.

Completion of Tikkun

Rabbi Azriel Chaim Lemburger tells of an incident he heard from Rabbi David Mintzberg, one of Rabbi Ashlag's closest pupils in Jerusalem:

> When the Sage of Porisov was already advanced in years, he was approached by his three greatest disciples, one of whom was Rabbi Ashlag. They told the Sage, by way of a hint, that they had finished their personal inner work for their self-rectification. The Sage asked them, "And what do you intend to do?" The other two students stayed silent, but our holy teacher answered, "I intend to find other work for myself." Then the Sage of Porisov responded, "It is true that you have finished your tikkun, but only you (and he pointed to Rabbi Ashlag) may take on pupils."
>
> When they were outside the Sage's room, the other two students turned to Rabbi Ashlag saying, "After all we have been through, laboring so hard, what, to start all over again?! We have nothing left to look for in this world; we have finished all our work." And indeed, within less than a fortnight these two pupils of the Porisover Rebbe passed away. But our holy teacher gathered a band of young students around him and began to give over the teachings.

"Finishing their *tikkun*" implies that these disciples had achieved the purpose for which they were born into this world; they were already in a state of continuous dvekut with regard to every action, every movement, even with every word that they uttered. All came from the great love for God that burned in their hearts.

Rabbi Ashlag studied the wisdom of Kabbalah until he was familiar with the writings of the Ari, the Zohar, and the writings of Rabbi Moses Cordovero. Quietly, he began teaching lessons on these works to a band of young men who were dedicating their lives to serving God. They would start their study at one o'clock in the morning. Rabbi Ashlag made the condition that the students were not to reveal to anyone they were learning from these books or that he was giving over such lessons.

The holy Sage of Porisov died on the 19th of *Tishrei*, on the fifth day of the festival of Succot, the day on which, by tradition, Aaron the High Priest is the spiritual guest in the succah. This day is also the *yarzheit* (anniversary of the passing) of the Holy Jew of Peschischa, who was the great-grandfather of the Porisover Rebbe and the founder of the school of chasidism that Rabbi Ashlag adhered to. So Rabbi Ashlag, and later, his son Rabbi Baruch Shalom, always held a large gathering in the succah on that day.

When Rabbi Ashlag's granddaughter, Rachel Levi, gave birth to her firstborn son, she asked her grandfather to name the child. He told her that he would do so on the day of the *Brit* (the circumcision ceremony at which a Jewish male child receives his name). When the day arrived, Rabbi Ashlag told her that the name of the child was to be Yehoshua Asher, naming him for his own spiritual father, the Sage of Porisov.

"Walk modestly with your God" (Mic. 6:8)

Rabbi Baruch Shalom used to tell us that his father had the custom of awakening every night and learning until dawn. If he started to drowse, he would punish his body by putting his feet in icy water. He preferred to suffer physically rather than fall asleep.

Rabbi Baruch Shalom also told of an incident that involved the members of the congregation in Warsaw. They noticed the presence of this holy man in their midst and started to admire him. When Rabbi Ashlag saw this, he acted to put a stop to such admiration. He wanted all his deeds to be carried out according to the principle of "walking modestly." So when he got to the beit midrash and heard the men praising him, he got up and said in a loud voice, "Do you think that I just follow my animal instincts like you do and spend all my nights asleep? I awaken the dawn and the dawn does not awaken me! And not just this night, but every single night…!" When the people heard this, they grew angry and immediately lost their reverence for him because they all understood him to be a man of great pride.

Rabbi Azriel Chaim Lemburger related that he heard the following from the Rabbanit, Rivkah Raiza, the wife of our holy teacher:

> The Rabbi was hidden from the world completely. The world did not recognize him at all because he was modest in all his ways. But I knew him, and I can tell you that at one o'clock in the morning when he got up to study, he would put sharp stones from the oven in his shoes, or he would put his feet in a bowl of water with ice in it so that he wouldn't fall asleep.

Batsheva Reichbard, the daughter of Rabbi Ashlag, added:

> My holy father was a very strong man physically, and actually needed a lot of sleep. However, he did not give in to his body and would employ every possible tactic in the world so that he would awaken at one o'clock in the morning. I remember many times, when, as a youth, my brother Rabbi Baruch Shalom would stay up until one o'clock in the morning in order to awaken Father for his daily work and learning.

We must ask ourselves, how is it possible to achieve such a high level of dedication to spiritual work? But it all hinges on one thing: the more a person considers the Creator to be important, the more he or she is ready to sacrifice in order to do the Creator's will. Thus the purpose of our spiritual work is to be able to hold the Creator in high esteem, and it is here that we need to focus our work, whether we are occupied in prayer, in study, or indeed in any situation in which we find ourselves. Each of us needs to pray that God should help us and grant us the capacity to believe in His greatness.

Rabbi Moshe Mordecai Shultz

As a youth, Rabbi Moshe Mordecai studied with Rabbi Ashlag in the yeshivah of Gur. Among the chasidim of Gur, Rabbi Moshe Mordecai later emerged as one of the more important of the disciples, sitting at the table of the sage of Gur, Rabbi Avraham Mordecai Alter. Gur, at that time, was a great center of the Chasidic movement. Before the Holocaust, it had more than one hundred thousand adherents.

In due time, Rabbi Ashlag received Rabbi Moshe Mordecai as a pupil and *chevruta* (study partner). He was outstanding. Rabbi Ashlag made one request of him: not to divulge anything of their learning to anyone, but to continue to go to the beit midrash of Gur as before.

Rabbi Moshe Mordecai cleaved to our teacher with all his heart and soul, but he simply could not refrain from telling the chasidim of Gur about him. For the first couple of months, Rabbi Moshe Mordecai managed to restrain himself, but on the third month, while he was waiting with the other chasidim for Rabbi Avraham Mordecai Alter to come, he stood up, banged on the table, and cried out, "My fellow Jews, why are you asleep? We have such an important and holy Jew in the world! If you want to see him you must come with me." Naturally, these words provoked a great storm among the chasidim. When Rabbi Ashlag heard what had happened, he immediately packed up and went to live in another city. But from that moment, all the persecutions that he suffered began.

Rabbi Moshe Mordecai used to carry out ascetic practices in order to negate his bodily appetites. When this became known to Rabbi Ashlag, he instructed him to desist from these practices, because such practices increase a person's pride.

Later, Rabbi Ashlag wrote on this issue to one of his students, Rabbi Levi Krakowski:

Cheshvan 17, 5687 (1926)
I received your letter of the 13th day of *Tishrei*, in which you wrote, "I know that I need to undertake external ascetic practices, to a great extent, in order to rectify the external aspects of myself." And I say to you that you do not need ascetic practices, neither do you need to correct the external aspects of yourself. Who taught you this new Torah? This has arisen only because you are not cleaving to me as previously and therefore you are tending strange vineyards.

However, you should know that you have no more loyal friend than I. And I counsel you that you should not, in any way, rectify the outer aspects of yourself, but only the innermost aspect of yourself. For only the innermost aspect of yourself is ready to receive tikkun. The cause of the innermost aspect of a person becoming spoiled is because of the sins that heap up. These come from the will to receive for oneself alone, the signs of which are the ego and pride. And this ego is not afraid of all the ascetic practices in the world! On the contrary, it loves them, because it, together with pride, is strengthened by such ascetic practices.

If you want to purge away your sins, you have to deal with the negation of the ego instead of carrying out ascetic practices. That is to say, you need to feel for yourself that you are the lowest and worst of all the inhabitants of the world. One needs to learn and have great wisdom in order to understand this. You have to test yourself, each time, to check that you are not deceiving or misleading yourself. It is also helpful to humble oneself in actual practice before one's *chevruta* [study companion].[3]

Explanation: Firstly, we need to arrive at a spiritual state wherein each of us lives a healthy and natural life in which we develop healthy and good self-esteem, and in which we feel happy with ourselves. This spiritual state is called the "right-hand line" or the line of faith.

In order to acquire this state, we need to work on our faith that God created the world as a whole entity. This wholeness includes each of us as an individual. Each one of us needs to believe that all our qualities are ultimately good and full of worth, and that we have good and positive virtues, some of which already have expression as good, while others are still only potentially good. Only once this right-hand side is well established can we then come to the left-hand line. The left-hand line consists of self-criticism and of truth, in which each of us endeavors to see where we really are; where we are still far from God in our thought, in our action, and in our speech.

Each of us needs to learn that the whole purpose of our spiritual work is to come to love our fellow. Gradually, we begin to perceive that we are far from this, until finally, at the end of a very gradual process, we see just how far away we are from this love of our fellow in reality.

But of course, this is a very gradual process because we are not talking about information, but about a feeling. One cannot come to a feeling of genuine lowliness until the healthy self-esteem of the right-hand side is well established. Furthermore, such a true feeling can manifest only when each of us, as an individual, has attained free choice, that is to say, we have achieved insight into, and control over, our will to receive for ourselves alone in all its manifestations, and despite this, we still fall!

Since the rule is that we judge everybody else mercifully, we must assume that when other people stumble and fall, it is because they are unconscious or have no free will in the matter. Only the individual can know regarding himself that he is in separation from the Creator, and when he realizes that he is, in some way, choosing this, then he feels himself to be worse than his fellow human beings. Ultimately, he comes to feel that he is the worst person in the world.

An ascetic practice that does not increase one's pride, but works to help let go of one's will to receive for oneself alone, is the practice of exile and begging for alms. This was an ascetic practice undertaken by many of the chasidic masters.

It is told that Rabbi Ashlag and Rabbi Moshe Mordecai took upon themselves this practice of exile; taking no money but begging for their basic needs. They started off together, wandering from place to place. But Rabbi Moshe Mordecai, who was a respected Jew in Warsaw, could not bear to beg, and after a while returned to his home. Not much is known of this period of Rabbi Ashlag's life.

Rabbi Moshe Mordecai remained in connection with our holy teacher, whom he loved and revered with all his heart, throughout his life. After Rabbi Ashlag left Poland for the Holy Land, they constantly communicated by letters. From those that have come to us, and from the copies of letters that Rabbi Ashlag wrote back, we can see a beautiful fabric of love and unity woven between them in true service to God. These letters testify to Rabbi Moshe Mordecai's very high spiritual stature. Once, Rabbi Ashlag wrote that he had spent two days and a night just to understand what Rabbi Moshe Mordecai had written!

Rabbi Ashlag's letters to Rabbi Moshe Mordecai differ in character from those he wrote to his other students. The young Yehudah Leib and the young Moshe Mordecai had sat together on the study bench, and over the years they had developed a common language of reference between them. Rabbi Ashlag shared his thoughts and feelings with Rabbi Moshe Mordecai in a way that he didn't with others.

Rabbi Moshe Mordecai made many efforts to leave Poland to join his teacher and companion in the Land of Israel, but for different reasons was unable to do so.

Rabbi Ashlag returned once to Warsaw after he had already emigrated to the Holy Land. At this time, he too tried to organize a visa for Rabbi Moshe Mordecai to get to Israel via Beirut.[4] Unfortunately, he was unsuccessful. Rabbi Moshe Mordecai Shultz perished with his family in the Holocaust, as did most of the chasidim of Gur. May his memory be for a blessing.

Fish for the Sabbath

Rabbi Baruch Shalom Ashlag related that despite the family's extreme poverty, his father was very particular about obtaining fish for the Sabbath table. It happened one time in 1915 that Rabbi Ashlag was unable to obtain fish for the Sabbath. Then he heard that fish were to be had from the Vistula River where it flows in a part of Poland that was, at that time, under German rule. Despite all the dangers, he went, accompanied by a translator, and when he got there he was allowed to get fish from the river.

One needs to ask, What is this about? Of course, a person should take pains to supply the necessities for the Sabbath, but why did the Rabbi go to such extreme lengths?

To examine this we will look at a parable that Rabbi Baruch Shalom used to tell:

When Levi met his old friend Reuben, he asked him where he was living. Reuben told Levi his present address. On hearing the answer, Levi's eyes grew round with surprise, "Surely, that's where Simon, the infamous criminal, is living. He must be making your life a misery!"

Reuben replied, "I really don't know what you are talking about. I have no complaints at all about my good neighbor, Simon. I don't know why you are telling such stories about him!"

Levi grew astonished, "But Simon's wickedness is known to everyone. Tell me, how do you manage between you?"

Reuben replied, "Whenever I go to the grocery store, I ask him if he needs me to bring him something from there, also when I go to the vegetable store. Actually, whenever I go anywhere I always ask him if there is something I can do for him. I try to fulfill his needs and even give his wants priority over mine."

Levi laughed, "Now I understand. Since you serve him with all your heart, of course he doesn't make trouble for you! But try, just once, to do something that is contrary to his will, then see what will happen...."

When we keep Torah and mitzvot in order to receive a reward, either in this world or in the next world, then our will to receive for ourselves alone—our ego—doesn't bother us at all; on the contrary, it encourages us to fulfill the mitzvot in the best possible way. Our ego feels content because it is profiting through our acts. We find we have great strength available for us to call on, as our ego participates in our work. We are able to do many good deeds with wonderful energy.

But when we want to fulfill Torah and mitzvot for the Torah's own sake, then our will to receive for ourselves alone starts to oppose us and begins to wage war on us. The wickedness of our selfish love becomes obvious in that it doesn't want to give anything to the framework of holiness, meaning, it doesn't want us to give to God unconditionally, and it wages war over even small issues.

Concerning this, the Sages said: "The greater a person is, the greater is his evil inclination." [5] Therefore, Rabbi Baruch Shalom taught that when we try to serve God truly, through giving unconditionally, we face an inner battle over doing even simple acts for God. The ego becomes very smart and questions, "Who is God that I should listen to His voice?" or "What does this service give to you?" These are the questions that the archetypes of the ego within us—the Pharaoh of Egypt and the wicked son of the Pesach Haggadah—ask.

This opposition by the ego occurs only when a person wants to fulfill the Torah and mitzvot because he believes in God as the cause of all and because he has faith in Him. His own ego battles with him over the smallest thing, because he is ignoring its desires and doesn't bother about fulfilling them.

Look at what is written: "I remember God and I sigh when I see every city built, standing on its hill, but the city of God is cast down to the depths." [6] Explanation: "A city" (עיר) has the same letters as the word ער meaning "awake." The person who wants to serve God unconditionally wonders, "Why is it that I have energy when I awaken to serve God when my service is on the basis of self-serving, but when I awaken to do God's work to serve Him, simply because He is the root of all, then I don't have any energy and it feels like ashes in my mouth?"

When a person wants to serve God in the true way—the way of giving unconditionally—then his will to receive for himself alone becomes as subtle as a human being. On every possible occasion, it will ask the person searching questions, simply to turn him aside from his spiritual work.

In this case, the sages, commenting on the Scripture, "God saves man and beast" (Ps. 36:7), advised, "Though being subtle in knowledge as Adam, yet they place themselves like the beast in humility." [7] In other words, if you wish to serve God, just carry on like the beast; just carry on fulfilling the mitzvot and doing good deeds out of faith without listening to the subtle wiles of the ego.

Now we can see why these holy men were diligent in fulfilling even the smallest of acts, even going to greater lengths than an ordinary person would. An ordinary person would not undertake such difficult journeys just to obtain fish for the Sabbath!

The Revelation of the Hidden

In the year 1918, a hidden Master Kabbalist came into the life of Rabbi Ashlag, one who opened the gates of holiness and purity in the wisdom of Kabbalah to him. He wrote of this to his cousin, Rabbi Abraham Mendel Bronstein:

> *Tevet* 10, 5688 (January 3, 1928)
>
> … I shall describe to you everything that happened from beginning to end through which I merited this wisdom by virtue of the great mercy of God.
>
> On the twelfth day of the month of *Cheshvan*, on a Friday morning, a certain man came and introduced himself to me. It became clear to me that he was wondrously wise in Kabbalah and also in many other disciplines. As soon as he started to speak, I began to sense his divine wisdom. All his words had a wondrous quality to them, a sort of glory. I really trusted my feelings in this regard. He promised to reveal the true wisdom to me. I studied with him for three months, meeting him every night after midnight in his home. Mostly, we talked about matters of holiness and purity. On every occasion, I would implore him to reveal a secret from the wisdom of Kabbalah to me. He began to tell me chapter headings, but he never explained any concept fully. So I was left with tremendous yearnings. Then one time, after I had greatly implored him to do so, he fully explained a concept to me and my happiness knew no limits.
>
> However, from that time I began to acquire a little ego, and as my self-assertion increased, so my holy teacher began to distance himself from me. But I did not notice this happening. This continued for around three months, on the last days of which I could no

longer find him in his home at all. I searched for him, but I could not find him anywhere.

Then I truly became aware of how he had become distanced from me. I was extremely sorry and began to mend my ways. Then in the morning of the ninth day of the month of *Nisan*, I found him and apologized profusely for my behavior. He forgave me and related to me as before. He revealed to me a great and deep teaching on the subject of a ritual bath that is measured and found to be too small. I once more experienced tremendous joy.

However, I saw that my teacher had become weak. I stayed at his house and the next morning, the tenth day of *Nisan*, in the year 5679 [1919], he passed away, may his memory shield us and all Israel. There are no words to describe the greatness of my sorrow, for my heart had been full of hope to merit this great wisdom of Kabbalah, and now I was left naked and with nothing. I even forgot at that time all that he had taught me on account of my extreme sorrow.

From then on, I prayed with all my heart and soul with untold longing. I did not rest a single moment of the day until I found favor in the eyes of my Creator, may He be blessed. Then, the merit of my holy teacher and his Torah stood by me and my heart was opened to the higher wisdom ever increasingly, like a flowing spring. Through the mercy of the Holy Blessed One, I also remembered all the deep teachings that I had received from my late teacher, may his memory be for a blessing. Blessed be He who has kept me alive and sustained me! How can I, poor in deeds as I am, have any way to thank Him? From the beginning, God knows my poverty, that I have neither intelligence nor wisdom to thank and praise Him for His mighty goodness. However, who can say to Him what He should do, or how He should act?

My holy teacher was a successful businessman and known throughout town as an honest trader, but no one at all knew that he was a Master Kabbalist. He did not give me permission to reveal his name.

Rabbi Azriel Chaim Lemburger:

> This letter was discovered, by the help of God, by Rabbi David
> Mintzberg while traveling in Poland. Rabbi David arrived in
> Warsaw in the middle of the night when the city was completely
> dark, and he searched for a place to stay. Suddenly, he saw a light
> shining from one of the houses. He knocked on the door and
> entered. There sat an elderly Jew learning the Talmud. It trans-
> pired that this Jew was the very cousin to whom our teacher, Rabbi
> Ashlag, had written this letter! When the cousin heard that Rabbi
> Mintzberg was a disciple of our holy teacher, he immediately took
> out the letter and showed it to him.
>
> Thus the letter was found by Divine Providence. But if you
> think that this letter made any impression on Rabbi Mintzberg,
> then you are wrong.

The disciples of Rabbi Ashlag did not look for miracles or wondrous signs to help them serve God. Their deference to their teacher
was based on faith. The attribute of faith belongs to a paradigm of
consciousness that requires giving and is, therefore, more in affinity
of form with the Creator than receiving verification. The students did
not search for signs or proofs in order to verify the greatness of their
Sage; they looked for ways to give to their teacher and to the Creator
unconditionally.

Chapter Three

From Warsaw to Jerusalem

R abbanit Rivkah Raizah Ashlag: [1]

In the year 1921, Rabbi Ashlag told me, "I have nothing more to do in this world; I have already rectified that which was laid on me to rectify." Hearing this, I cried and said, "What shall I do if you leave me, and the children are so little?" Then he said to me, "There is only one possibility through which I will not depart this world, and that is if we go to the Land of Israel." I protested, "After all that you have achieved here! Now, when you have become a famous rabbi in Warsaw and a spiritual teacher for many pupils, you want to lose all this and go to a desolate place?!" He told me, "Only in Israel do I still have work to do in this world. If I don't go to Israel, then I will be in the same situation as were my two companions, the pupils of the Rabbi of Porisov, who no longer had anything left to rectify." When I heard these words, I understood their meaning and became extremely alarmed. Then the Rabbi told me, "If we decide to emigrate to the Land of Israel, we have to travel immediately."

They had no money. So the Rabbanit began making arrangements to obtain money. She was then heavily pregnant, but, notwithstanding, began packing suitcases, getting ready to emigrate. They left Poland on the eve of the month of *Elul*, 5681 (September 1921). While on board the boat, she gave birth to her daughter, Batsheva.

Sara Bodchek, Rabbi Ashlag's daughter:

My parents left in so much haste that they couldn't take all the children with them because they didn't have enough money to pay for all the tickets. So they had to leave me and some of the other children with relatives. Only later, I joined them.

Rabbi David Mintzberg:[2]

Before they left for Israel, Rabbi Ashlag went to see the Sage of Porisov to say goodbye. The Sage was concerned at the prospect of the journey. He told Rabbi Ashlag, "You should know that in the Land of Israel you will lose every spiritual stage." But Rabbi Ashlag answered him, calmly, "I am not looking for spiritual lights. I am looking for work." And they parted in peace.

The family arrived at the port of Jaffa on *Chol haMoed* (the intermediate days of) Succot. They then traveled to Jerusalem on donkeys—the only means of transport they could afford—and made their home in the Jewish Quarter of the Old City. Sadly, not long after their arrival in the Holy Land, they heard that two of the children who had been left behind in Poland had died—a boy of thirteen named David, and a daughter named Brachah.

Trying to Remain Concealed

On arriving in Israel, Rabbi Ashlag's first thought had been to hide his spiritual stature. He preferred to make his living working as a craftsman so as not to make use of the Torah for personal gain. He had brought tools with him from Warsaw with which to prepare parchment for Torah scrolls and also equipment for the manufacture of soap. But despite his proficiency in these skills, the work did not go well, and the business did not succeed.

Jews who had known Rabbi Ashlag as a *dayan* (judge) in the rabbinical court in Poland began to arrive in Jerusalem, and Rabbi Ashlag found he could no longer hide his stature of learning in Torah.

Disappointment in the Jerusalem Kabbalists and Opposition

Rabbi Yehudah Tzvi Hirsch Brandwein: [3]

> When Rabbi Ashlag had still been in Poland, he had heard that there were Kabbalists in Jerusalem, and he had even heard of a yeshivah where the students learned Kabbalah. He wished to see how this yeshivah organized its studies. As he had arrived in Jerusalem during the festival of Succot, Rabbi Ashlag was particularly interested in learning the *kavanot** the Jerusalem Kabbalists practiced when shaking the lulav and etrog [as used on this festival]. So he hurried to Yeshivah Beth El in the Old City. But when he arrived, he was disappointed to find it closed. On asking the janitor why it was locked up, Rabbi Ashlag was told that the yeshivah was on holiday for the whole month of *Tishrei* [the month of the festivals]. This came as a great surprise to him because the concept of a holiday was unknown among the orthodox Jews of Poland.

Initially, Rabbi Ashlag had thought he would be able to join with the Jerusalem Kabbalists. But he found the reality very different from his expectations and was bitterly disappointed. He wrote about the type of study he found:

> Since I had been wasting away, so confined in the constrictions of the city of Warsaw in Poland where I had nothing in common with my surroundings, I had anticipated delight in settling in the Old City of Jerusalem, may it speedily be rebuilt, Amen. However, when I arrived and met with the people, I clearly saw their spiritual poverty, their ignorance and their foolish ways, defiling and trampling the soul of our Temple. "For as the sound of the thorns under the pot, so is the laughter of the fool, and this too is vanity" (Eccles. 7:6). They vilify God, the Torah, and the people of Israel. Here there is no clear voice in the wisdom of Kabbalah. There is no understanding, neither is there any knowledge or logical argument at all. They just see Kabbalah as a collection of words and

---

* Specific intentions based on the directions in which the lulav and etrog are shaken.

names with no parable and its solution, only literal words. These people regard it as a merit to simply prattle pieces of text exactly as they are written, in the perfect faith that these are holy words, and that by reciting them we are fulfilling the Purpose of Creation! They believe that when more people will occupy themselves in reciting these texts just as they are written, in complete faith, then immediately the Messiah will come because they think that the entire *tikkun* [rectification of the world] will be completed in this manner and nothing else will be necessary!

Then I met the more famous of them. These are men who have spent years learning the Zohar and the writings of the Ari to the extent that they are able to recite the books of the Ari by heart to a wondrous degree, and they are known as holy men. I asked them if they had learned with a teacher, one who had attained the inner meaning of these matters. But they replied, "God forbid! There are no inner meanings. Only the words as they are written were handed down to us. There is nothing more to say on the matter." I asked them if Rabbi Chaim Vital had grasped the inner under-standing of these matters, and they answered me that certainly he had not grasped any more than they had! I then asked them concerning the Holy Ari himself, and they answered that even he didn't know any more of the inner meanings of the words than they did! All that the Ari had known, he had passed to his student, Rabbi Chaim Vital, and so it had reached them.

I laughed at them exceedingly, because if the Ari had neither known nor understood the connection between matters, then how was it possible that the matters were connected in his heart? They answered that the Ari received the connection between matters from Elijah the prophet, and only he knew their inner meanings because he was an angel. At this point, I poured out my anger on them because I had no more patience to be in their company.

When I see the stupidity that has found roots in nearly all those who occupy themselves with this wisdom at this time, then I cry, "Woe to the ears who hear this! 'Would you seduce the Queen, and I am in the house?'"(Esther 7:8). The Zohar itself has already spoken out bitterly on the deceit with which these men sin in their souls when they say there are no inner meanings in the Torah. The holy Zohar itself addresses this, saying that if the purpose of the Torah is simply to tell stories and chronicles of history, then these are also to be found in the stories of the other nations of the world. The sages further say that those who think like this are blaspheming. (See Zohar, page 42.)

What would the sages of the Zohar say if they were to see the spiritual culture of these sinning men, men who deny that there is any wisdom or logical argument in the words of the Zohar or in any aspect of the innermost part of the Torah, the true wisdom itself? Even regarding the secrets of the Torah, they say no knowledge or rational thought is revealed in this world—only reams of text. They have dared to have their way with the Queen, the holy Shechinah, in the innermost aspect of the palace of the King! Woe to them, because they have caused evil to their souls.

The sages of the Talmud said, "The holy Torah puts on sackcloth and laments before the Holy Blessed One: 'Your children have made of me a harp for them to play on for their entertainment.'"[4] These people don't even make the semblance of a song from the Torah, just words that appall every listener until he is filled with anger and contempt. Even while acting so despicably, they request the reward of the zealous, as they say that what they are doing is done with perfect faith. On such people the Scripture states, "And the Lord said, 'Forasmuch as this people draw near, and with their mouth, and with their lips, they honor Me, but they have removed their heart far from Me, and their reverence of Me is a commandment of men learned by rote; therefore, behold, I will again do a marvelous work among this people, even a marvelous work and a wonder; and the wisdom of their wise men shall perish, and the prudence of their prudent men shall be hid" (Isa. 29:13-14).

This is the reason that the first Temple was destroyed and Satan is still dancing among us—even now, in the generation when the footsteps of the Messiah can be heard; even at this time, when the secrets of the Torah will be secret no longer. And the jealousy for the Lord of Hosts comes like a fire within me that cannot be extinguished. There has come within me such an awakening to reveal the garment in which the Torah is clothed in such a measure so they will know that there is wisdom in Israel.[5]

Zohar

(58) Rabbi Shimon said: Woe to the man who says that the Torah's purpose is to tell literal stories and stories of people like Esau and Laban and such like. For if this were so, even in these times we could make a Torah out of the words of ordinary people—even nicer stories than these.

If the purpose of the Torah were to demonstrate the affairs of the world, well, the rulers of the world have more excellent matters than those in the Torah. Then we could follow them and make a Torah from them in the same way.

But all the words of the Torah are high matters and are of the highest inner meanings.

(59) Come and see! There is a higher world and a lower world and they are weighted in the same weight. Israel, below, is equivalent to the higher angels, above. Of the higher angels, it is written, "He makes His messengers as spirits" (Ps. 104:4). But when the messengers come down to this world, they are clothed in the garb of this world, for if they were not clothed in the garb of this world, they could not survive in this world, and the world could not tolerate them. And if the angels need clothing, how much more does the Torah, which created the angels and all the worlds, and which only exist through her?

The Torah came down to this world. If it were not clothed in the garments of the world, which are the stories and words of ordinary people, the world could not tolerate it.

(60) Therefore, the story that is in the Torah is but the garment of the Torah. Whoever thinks that this garment is the Torah itself and there is nothing other is crazy and will not have any portion in the next world. Because of this, David requested, "Open my eyes and I will look in the wonders of Your Torah" (Ps. 119:18), that is to say, look at what is beneath the garment of the Torah.

(61) Come and see! There is a garment which appears to all, and those silly people, who, when they see someone dressed nicely, looking splendid in his appearance, don't look further but judge the person according to the splendor of his garment. They consider the garment as the body of the person and consider the body as if it were the soul.

(62) Likewise for the Torah: it has a body, which consists of the commandments of the Torah. This body is dressed in garments, which are the stories of this world. Foolish people of the world look only at this garment, which is made up of the stories of the Torah. They don't know more and don't look to see what is beneath this garment.

Those who do know more don't look at the garment, but at the body beneath the outer garb. The wise men, the servants of the High King, those who stood at Mount Sinai, look only at the soul within the Torah, which is the chief aspect. It is the Torah itself. In the future to come, they will look on the innermost aspect of the soul of the Torah.

......

(64) Woe to those wicked who say the Torah is only a collection of stories. They are looking at the garb and no more. Happy are the righteous who look in the Torah as is fitting. Wine cannot sit except in a jug; so the Torah cannot dwell except in this garment. Therefore, we need to look only at what is beneath the garment. All the words and all the stories are garments.[6]

Those who were known in Jerusalem at that time as "Kabbalists" were men who were held in esteem by the community; thus, Rabbi Ashlag's rebuke of them aroused great opposition.

However, we need to remember that anything that is truly holy often arouses opposition and hostility. Today, who remembers the opponents of the Baal Shem Tov or of Rabbi Moshe Chaim Luzzato? The holy wisdom and its standard-bearers remain in their full glory, whereas those who opposed and vilified its proponents are lost without trace.

Rabbi Pinchas Brandwein:

Once, Rabbi Ashlag told my father, Rabbi Ya'acov Mordecai, who was his pupil, that the furor against him was no less than that faced by Rabbi Chaim Vital in his time. Many times he hinted to my father that he went through the same tribulations as had beset the Ari and his disciples.

Rabbi Shmuel Mintzberg:

Rav Michel Tukachinsky, the headmaster of the Etz Chaim School, lived near Rabbi Ashlag. He belonged to the circle of Lithuanian Jews and was renowned for his tremendous learning. He was always astonished at the opposition directed against our teacher. He told my father [Rabbi David Mintzberg], "I don't understand why they raise such an uproar against such a worthy and holy Rabbi as Rabbi Ashlag! He doesn't allow sleep to come to his eyes, but sits all day and all night studying the Torah and in service to God. Certainly, he is of the greatest of our generation."

A Jew by the name of Rabbi Zundel Hagar, who was a chasid of the Sage of Levov, lived at that time in Jerusalem. He had studied with Rabbi David Mintzberg for three years when Rabbi Mintzberg presented him to Rabbi Ashlag. At that meeting, Rabbi Ashlag told Rabbi Zundel, "At this time, it would be possible to bring many students under the wings of the Shechinah, but this does not suit the evil inclination. Therefore, he arouses dissension and persecution against us."

A few years later, Rabbi Ashlag wrote to Rabbi Moshe Yair Weinstock, from London:

Adar II 10, 5687 (March 14, 1927)
My dear Moshe Yair, I have received your letter written on the 22nd day of *Adar*, wherein you express your sorrow that your new understandings in the Torah do not find a welcome. Well, I also suffer sorrow on this issue, and in my opinion to an even greater extent than you do. But "hope for the Lord, and keep your heart in good courage" (Ps. 27:14).

Please give my best wishes to Rabbi Yoseph Weinstock on the birth of his son. May he and his household be blessed with all good from the Source of all blessings.

Concerning what you wrote, you did well not to go, but now is no time for modesty since most of the book [*Panim Meirot uMasbirot*] is already published, and whatever is going to be revealed is considered as already revealed. Therefore, you can publicize the book as much as you like.

For my part, I would like to know what impression it makes on the leaders of the Jerusalem community, who ban anything new in Torah and reject the new in favor of the old. When they look at my books, they have two possible paths: Either to say there is nothing here that is new at all because everything I wrote is already written in the writings of the Ari—this, actually, is the truth—or to say that all my words are baseless suppositions, and why didn't the earlier rabbis mention one single word of what is written in my writings, and who knows whether one can trust such a man who wants to create a new system in Kabbalah such as our forefathers recoiled from? They hang all their dubious acts on this peg. Lately, their words are burdensome for me, so I would like to know how they consider the book. Maybe you could find this out for me at the first possible opportunity, since, of all the group, you are closest to them.

The truth is, as I tell you, that I did not add anything at all to what is written in the writings of the Ari. My intention is simply to remove stumbling blocks from those who are limping and blind, so maybe they will also merit "to see the goodness of God in the land of the living" (Ps. 27:13).

It would be a good thing if you learned my books well, before they are revealed to the outside world, so you can show my detractors every single matter, how it is written and explained in the writings of the Ari, may his memory be for a blessing.

...

Yehudah Leib [7]

Chapter Four

The First Band of Pupils

On arriving in Israel, Rabbi Ashlag settled down to his Torah study at the Chayei Olam Yeshivah, situated within the walls of the Old City of Jerusalem. This began a very hard time. He received one lira a month as a stipend from the yeshivah. His family had only bread with oil to eat; occasionally they had some vegetables, and very rarely on the Sabbath, meat.

At first, Rabbi Ashlag changed his dress to the traditional Jerusalem garb, but when he saw how removed the Jerusalem Kabbalists were from the true way of serving God, he went back to the dress of the Jews of Poland.

Rabbi Pinchas Brandwein:

When our Rabbi began learning in the yeshivah, the other students would see him studying the holy Zohar in this way: He would read a small amount in the book, then he would rise. Striding up and down the hall of the yeshivah, pacing from corner to corner, he was engrossed in thought and deep concentration for a long period of time, sometimes as much as several hours. Then he would read a little in the book, and again pace up and down for several hours, completely caught up in the ideas aroused by the holy work.

When the other students saw this, they were amazed. They were not used to seeing people study the Zohar in such depth and with such intent of understanding.

The students were quite accustomed to seeing people trying to fathom the intricacies of the Talmud for hours on end, but as for the Zohar and the works of the Ari, they had never seen anyone attempt to penetrate their deep meanings. After a while, the students began to ask the Rabbi questions, requesting him to enlighten them on matters of the service of God. Gradually, his deep knowledge in the wisdom of Kabbalah became known.

It was at this time that Rabbi Joshua Horovitz, who also attended the yeshivah, met Rabbi Ashlag and pleaded with him to accept him as a student. Rabbi Ashlag told him that if he would gather together a group of suitable people he would establish a *shiur* [regular lesson].

Rabbi Menachem Yoseph Weinstock:

My revered father was descended from the sages of Lelov. He was an important member of the Chayei Olam Yeshivah at the time of Rabbi Ashlag's arrival there. Even as a child, my father showed tremendous industry, and didn't take time away from the learning of Torah. His knowledge of the holy Zohar was prodigious, and he had the ability to stand for several hours reciting whole passages of the Zohar by heart.

When our teacher, Rabbi Ashlag, arrived at the Chayei Olam Yeshivah, my father was only twenty-two years old. However, when Rabbi Ashlag saw that my father was so diligent in his learning, he invited him to be a *chevruta* [study companion] with him. Rabbi Ashlag had been an accredited rabbinical judge for many years in Warsaw, so they studied aspects of the *Shulchan Aruch* together. This was typical learning in the subject of *halachah* [Jewish law] for an accredited rabbi. However, after some weeks of studying, during which Rabbi Ashlag discerned that Rabbi Weinstock had both the ability and the desire to learn the inner aspect of the Torah, they decided to establish a regular shiur learning the Zohar.

Rabbi Ashlag lived in the Old City of Jerusalem, whereas my father lived in the district adjacent to Meah Shearim, but the distance [about an hour's walk] did not trouble him. Every night he would come to the holy Rabbi at the hour of one o'clock and learn with him for eight hours straight until nine in the morning. More than once, my father risked his life when coming and going. From that time on, my father was utterly devoted to the Sage, who, on his part, equally loved his pupil.

At first, my father hesitated to tell my mother where he was learning, and she innocently thought he was going to the synagogue in their neighborhood. But when she noticed that on rainy nights my father's clothes were soaked right through—and this happened often—he told her the truth, that he was going to learn with a rabbi in the Old City.

One time, my mother moved the hands of the clock backward so that my father would wake up an hour later because he was very tired and she felt sorry for him; but after that time, he begged her never to do so again, because she could not estimate how much damage he had incurred in that one hour in which he had not met with his Rabbi.

After learning some weeks with Rabbi Ashlag, my father told Rabbi David Mintzberg about the lesson, and then Rabbi Mintzberg joined them. Following that came Rabbi Yehudah Tzvi Brandwein, Rabbi Joshua Horovitz, and Rabbi Moshe Baruch Lemburger. These five men formed Rabbi Ashlag's first group of pupils.

Rabbi Avraham Brandwein:

My father, Rabbi Yehudah Tzvi Brandwein, lived in the same building as Rabbi Ashlag. Even before he had heard of Rabbi Ashlag, he used to rise in the middle of the night to learn Kabbalah. When it became known to one of the Jerusalem Kabbalists, Rabbi Asher Zelig Margoliot, that Rabbi Ashlag was living in the Old City, he advised my father to connect with him as quickly as possible. So began the wonderful association between my father and the holy sage, Rabbi Ashlag.

Rabbi Zalman Lemburger:

At about the same time that Rabbi Ashlag arrived in the Holy Land, my father, Rabbi Moshe Baruch Lemburger, suddenly, and in a miraculous way, became beset with all sorts of difficulties and contradictions in his service to God. He could not find any solution to them. He was full of perplexity and doubt, until, one day, Rabbi David Mintzberg told him, "One who can relieve you of all your doubts has just arrived in the country." From then on, he came to Rabbi Ashlag as both student and attendant, and cleaved to him and his way.

From these stories, we see how the hand of God wove together this holy band, each coming from a different direction. Rabbi Moshe Yair Weinstock, through his *chevruta* with the Rabbi; Rabbi Moshe Baruch Lemburger, through the difficulties in his inner work; Rabbi Yehudah Tzvi Brandwein, on the recommendation of Rabbi Margoliot; Rabbi Joshua Horovitz, because he sought a teacher in the inner work; and Rabbi David Mintzberg, through his friend, Rabbi Weinstock.

Rabbi Menachem Yoseph Weinstock:

The shiur was founded on a daily basis, meeting every night in Rabbi Ashlag's apartment at one o'clock in the morning and lasting until nine o'clock. The Rabbi usually taught from the holy Zohar, but occasionally taught from the *Etz Chaim* of the Ari.

In these shiurim, my father generally sat at the right-hand of the Rabbi, with Rabbi David Mintzberg on his left-hand side.

My father wrote down all that he heard from our holy Rabbi so that he would be able to review the learning. Slowly, other exceptional students, such as Rabbi Yosel Weinstock and Rabbi Shia Tzeinvirt, joined the band.

Rabbi Baruch Shalom, Rabbi Ashlag's firstborn son, was also present in the shiurim, even though, being only fifteen years old, he had not yet been accepted as a student. He was given the job of making the coffee for the members of the shiur. It was very noticeable that he took an inordinate amount of time serving it out, thus maximizing his time in the room.

The Shiur

Through the good offices of the organization *Or HaSulam*, we have recently been able to listen to some rare recordings of some of the later shiurim that Rabbi Ashlag conducted with the students. What follows is the translator's impressions:

> The most distinctive aspect of the recordings is Rabbi Ashlag's voice. It is wondrously clear. Although he is talking quietly, it rings out, filled with joy. This joy is palpable. It permeates everything he says. Listening to it, I feel the reality of the saying of the sages of the Mishnah: "Rabbi Meir says, 'Whoever occupies himself with Torah, for the Torah's own sake, will merit many things…. The secrets of the Torah are revealed to him and he becomes like an overflowing spring, like a river that does not cease.'"
>
> The lessons are conducted as follows: first, Rabbi Ashlag reads the text of the Zohar in Aramaic, the language the Zohar is written in, then he explains its meaning according to the Sephirot. The discussion is held mainly in Yiddish with a lot of Hebrew words sprinkled in. From the content, we can see that the companions do not have a fixed version of the text of the Zohar; there were various versions extant at the time, and Rabbi Ashlag himself decides which variant of the text is correct by meditating on it. Then he proceeds to explain it.
>
> We see the interaction between the Sage and his pupils. Although the pupils are respectful, they do not hesitate to ask questions. Sometimes, when they don't understand, they repeat the same question more than once. There is a very clear sense of active participation between Rabbi Ashlag and the students as companions in learning, in deciphering and understanding the text, even though one is the teacher and the others, the students. However, it is Rabbi Ashlag whose opinion is decisive.
>
> Rabbi Ashlag answers the students' questions carefully and with patience, checking in with them again and again, *"Hayvanta?"* Did you understand? If not, he explains again. It is clear that his explanations are for the benefit of the pupils. He displays a gentle kindness toward them. His voice is filled with love.
>
> Listening to these tapes made an enormous impression on me. I understood more clearly, more than any words could tell me,

why it was that the students devoted their lives to their teacher, his writings, and the work. The clear light of God that shone from the Sage is palpable, even after all these years, preserved on these tapes. The extraordinary love he showed the pupils clearly shines through.[1]

Rabbi Yehudah Leib Ashlag as Sage (*Admor*)

After some months, it was clear to all the students that they had the privilege of being in the presence of a man who had a living connection with God. Here was a special soul who had been sent from heaven to teach them the way to *dvekut* (unity) with God. At this point, the students decided to accept Rabbi Ashlag as sage (*Admor*).

All the students came from a chasidic background, so this was a natural step for them to take on their journey. From this time onward, the relationship between the students and Rabbi Ashlag went beyond studying. They joined with the Sage in holy meals (*tisch*) on Shabbat and festivals. These were meals eaten together in complete silence. During the course of these meals, Rabbi Ashlag would teach the inner meanings of the Torah while in dvekut with God.

The teachings that were given over by the Sage at the *tisch* form an immense body of learning that complements Rabbi Ashlag's written works. After the festival or Shabbat ended, several of the students, but most notably, Rabbi Baruch Shalom, would write down all they had heard from the Sage. It is in these talks that Rabbi Ashlag elucidated the intimate connections that exist between the formal learning and its application in daily practice.

These oral teachings are preserved in the collection *Shamati*, (I Have Heard) and form the basis of Rabbi Baruch Shalom's work, known simply as the *Sefer haMa'amarim* (The Book of Essays). This is a collection of essays that Rabbi Baruch Shalom wrote in his later years for his students. It is one of the most penetrating spiritual texts ever written, giving practical guidance on how to progress in our service to God.

Since any action that is not carried out for our own self-benefit is against our inborn nature, it follows that putting Torah and mitzvot into practice on an unconditional basis is extremely hard. It was for this reason that the sages of the Mishnah have taught, "Make for yourself a Rav, acquire for yourself a friend." [2] By accepting Rabbi Ashlag as their sage, the students took upon themselves the relationship of the disciple to the chasidic master. By nullifying the will of the ego in deferring to the sage, and by giving unconditionally to him and to the other companions, they cultivated attitudes they could then apply in their service to the Creator.

Traditional chasidic practices such as *shiri'im* (eating from the Rabbi's plate) were used as effective means in carving out a space for holiness amidst the tumult of the ego's desires.

Rabbi Ashlag would also direct the students individually on their service to God. Some of this direction is preserved in the students' notebooks, which have been published in the work, *HaShem Shamati Shemecha*, (Oh God, I have heard your fame) and in the letters that he wrote to them when away from them.

Opposition

At first, Rabbi Ashlag requested that the existence of the holy band of students that met at his house each night should remain secret. But once opposition to his work began to be expressed, he said it was now permissible to tell others about the group of students and the lessons.

At about this time, troubles also began in the students' homes. Sometimes it was the wives who opposed their husbands' learning with the Sage; other times, opposition arose from the students' parents or parents-in-law. Occasionally, opposition even expressed itself in the throwing of stones. All the students suffered in this respect to a greater or lesser extent.

Rabbi Avraham Brandwein:

Once a Jew, by the name of Moshe Stern, told me that he went with his son to Rabbi Ashlag's home. While speaking to the Sage, he suddenly heard a loud noise caused by large stones falling on the house. Many windows were broken and the upset in the household was immense. But the Sage himself remained unmoved. He knew that in order to give out his work he would have to overcome many obstacles. This was one living example of the opposition that arose against the great light that our teacher brought to the world.

It is not difficult to understand the opposition of the students' families. The wives and families had been educated according to conventional Judaism, and even though the sacrifice of the students by studying every night certainly placed a heavy burden on the wives, they would have been more able to support their husbands if they had understood the importance of the work their husbands were doing. But their husbands were pioneers; they were treading out a path that had never been traveled before. Moreover, it was a path not valued by the society around them or even deemed necessary. Indeed, the parents and wives thought their sons and husbands had been led astray.

Rabbi Avraham Brandwein:

> Once, the wives and the mothers-in-law of the students banded together and came to create havoc at Rabbi Ashlag's house. They shouted at the Rabbi that if he did not stop teaching, they would break all his windows! He told them calmly, "If you break all my windows, it will cause only your own harm because I have it in my power to say one word with which to mend everything and then all the world will see my great strength!" At these words, the women became frightened and went home.
>
> Rabbi Baruch Shalom asked the Rabbi what he meant by that. He replied: "If I were to say one word to the glazier then all the windows would get fixed!"

From the above, it might appear that the relationships between husband and wife among the students were not carried out on the basis of "Love your neighbor as yourself." But, despite their opposition to their husbands' study and to their devotion to the Sage, the wives supported their husbands faithfully in the management of the families and in the upbringing and education of their children. For their part, the husbands believed they could be doing no greater good to their families than continuing their deep connection with the Sage. An appreciation of the husbands' real care for their families can be gained from the following, related by Rabbi David Mintzberg's son:

> My mother had serious mental health problems to the extent that she was hospitalized frequently in the mental hospital. My father was left to look after the children and had to cope with all the difficulties of life alone. However, he never contemplated divorce; on the contrary, whenever my mother came home, he would look after her with the greatest love. Of all the students, my father was one of the only ones not buried next to the Sage. He asked to be buried next to his wife, because he said, "All that I have achieved in holiness is only through her merit."

Two Friends Who Never Separated

Despite the formation of the band of students around him, Rabbi Ashlag never forgot his friend and disciple, Rabbi Moshe Mordecai Shultz, who had stayed in Warsaw. Their correspondence continued over many years and remained a major element in Rabbi Ashlag's life.

Here is an excerpt from a letter, written not long after Rabbi Ashlag arrived in Jerusalem:

> *On the 3rd day of Chanukah 5682 (1921), Old City, Jerusalem, may it speedily be rebuilt:*
>
> To my dear colleague and friend of my heart, may his name, Moshe Mordecai, shine out forever,
>
> I received your letter and I have to tell you how much your letter stirred up deep longing for you within me, as you did not let me know about your personal situation in detail. How are things at home? How is your health and the health of your family? How are you managing with earning your living? How is your service of God? Is it a time of light or a time of shadow? What is the order of your conduct at home when eating, drinking, sleeping, studying Torah and serving God? Have you

lessened in your inner work? And how does your wife relate to your work?

Where did you spend the high holidays and Succot? Were you at Gur or at home? How do they receive you in Gur now, and do you still have arguments with them? What form does the opposition take now and what are the consequences? Do you have study companions, and what is the form of your connection with them, and in what depth? I would like to know all the changes that have happened to you since I parted from you. Let me know even the smallest detail.

How happy I would have been if I had found an answer to all these questions in your letter now, and how sorry I am to have to wait another eight weeks until my letter gets to you, and until an answer is received from you, saying, "I am here."

You must always remember that we are bound with everlasting bonds of love, to the extent that everything that happens to you happens to me, too. What can the weight of the physical or the geographical distance be considered, that they can make a boundary or a divide between us? After waiting almost four months, from the 9th of *Elul* until yesterday, the 2nd day of Chanukah, during which time I had hoped to enjoy what you had written, imagine how sorry I felt, when what was laid before me was a long letter full of analogies and hints from which I could not learn anything. What fault did you find in me that I should not know of your state? You must know that whatever affects you, affects me also.

Why did you not notice that you wrote to me only in hints and allusions in which I could not find you? For God's sake, from now on, when you write me something, write simply, as a man speaks to his neighbor who is not a prophet, writing so that there is no place to err or to mistake the meaning. Don't look at the beauty of the language, but on the ease of understanding, and in particular, do not mix allusions or hints into your language. You need not fear that any stranger will read your letters as my address is known in the post office and they bring me my letters directly to my home and no one else has access to them.

When you write your new understandings in Torah, clarify them to me without nouns or names of entities such as those that are found in books. Just use the simple language of the human being. I, for myself, am careful to clarify issues that come to my sense using our spoken language in the simplest way, for this is the best and truest way to clarify something. If I were to wrap matters in names, such as those used in books, it awakens within me a desire to know the thoughts of the books, and then inevitably my thought is distracted from my purpose. I have discovered this to be the case.

Apart from this, I have found that when I find something in a book that relates to my method, my pleasure makes me prone to mix falsehood with truth. Therefore, when I come to clarify some matter that I need, I am careful not to thumb through the pages that are either prior to what I need or after. I just look at what I need, so that I don't get tempted to use allusions. This ensures that I will always be present in purity to find a truth, without mixing in anything that is external to me. Only then "can the palate taste" (from Job 12:11).

… (*rest of the letter is missing*)

Yehudah Leib

Chapter Five

The Path

So what were they all striving for? What was it that called forth this extraordinary dedication of both student and teacher? What is the secret they were trying so hard to uncover, the secret that lies at the heart of the Torah and of the entire practice of Judaism?

The Zohar informs us, "The Torah, the Holy Blessed One, and the soul are one." Rabbi Ashlag and his students longed for God. They longed to serve Him, to purify themselves, and come to dvekut with Him. How could they do it? How could they forge such a path and make it their own?

The path that Rabbi Ashlag taught his students is not one he invented. He received this path from his teachers, who themselves, received it in an unbroken tradition stretching all the way back to our forefathers, Abraham, Isaac, and Jacob. It was not a completely unknown path within Judaism, but being trodden by the individual, it was not recognized as a way of serving God by the wider community. But its time had come.

The students' study of Kabbalah; their connection with the Sage; the *tisch*; the ongoing struggle to keep going despite sleeplessness and poverty; the difficulties in uniting such very different and fiery individuals into a cohesive group, all came together in the elements of this inner path of service to the Creator.

What does this path consist of?

Here are the elements of this path of service to God that were given orally to the students by Rabbi Ashlag and recorded by his son, Rabbi Baruch Shalom:

+ To believe that there is a Creator who supervises the world.

+ To choose the path of faith. Even though the conscious state of faith is less valued by us than is certainty or knowledge, nevertheless we choose to walk in faith.

+ To believe that faith, which is an act of giving, belongs to a higher paradigm of consciousness than does knowledge, which is received.*

  There are two different modalities of faith:

  (1) We choose to use our faith rather than our desire for knowledge because we have no alternative if we want to connect with the Creator.

  (2) We choose the consciousness of faith, even when we receive a revelation from God. In this situation, we no longer **need** to use faith as a means to connect with the Creator as we are in a state of receiving direct knowledge of God. Nevertheless, we choose the way of faith.

+ To give our faith to God unconditionally, and not for the sake of receiving anything from Him.

+ To attribute our inner work to God, and to believe that God accepts our service in whatever form our service appears.

+ To know that when our work is directed toward our own selfish use, after all the successes that we imagine we will be able to attain, it will be within our power to benefit only ourselves. This is not the case when we are working for the love of God. Then our work benefits everyone.

+ To give praise and thanks for the past. It is on our praise and thanks for the past that our future depends. According to the

---

* See Glossary for explanation of the terms "faith (emunah)", "above", and "knowledge."

58

measure that we offer thanks, so we value that which we receive from Above. In this way, we know to keep the help we receive from the Creator and not lose it.

- To place our emphasis on our wholeness—the right-hand line*—in our daily lives. Even if we have only the smallest grasp of spirituality, we need to be happy to have merited that God has given us the thought and the desire to do something in spirituality. [The meaning of spirituality being the desire to benefit either God or our fellow unconditionally.]

- To spend time considering the truth about ourselves—the left-hand line**—and for this, half an hour a day is sufficient. This implies that we need to make an accounting for ourselves as to how much we give preference to our love for God rather than to our selfish love. According to the measure that we see our own deficiencies in our service to God, so we can pray to God that He should bring us closer to Him, truly.

It is only according to our work in **both** lines that we can progress.

- In our inner work, we can distinguish three modalities:

    (1) To yearn to complete our soul, restoring it to its root. This is the modality of Israel.

    (2) To understand the ways of God and the subtle meanings of the Torah; for if we do not know what Our Master commands, how can we serve Him? This is the modality of Torah.

    (3) To yearn to attain the Holy Blessed One, that is to say, to cleave to Him in full consciousness. This is the modality of the Holy Blessed One.

---

* The right-hand line is the consciousness of happiness and wholeness that since God is running the world and He is perfect, then, since He created me, I am also perfect just the way I am. Likewise, all that happens to me is similarly good. Staying in this consciousness of happiness and thankfulness, while experiencing the vicissitudes of life, is a work of faith. See also Chapter Sixteen, The Foundation of a Just Society, 219–235.

** The left-hand line is the consciousness of truth. This requires the ability to face the reality of our selfish love and the bitterness of the separation from the Creator that it causes us. This is the consciousness that leads us to prayer.

It is best that we should yearn for the commands of the King, the modality of Torah, for that is the middle line. [*1]

We talked in the last chapter about the opposition the students faced from their families regarding their connection and study with Rabbi Ashlag. But the truth is, the worst opposition any of us faces when trying to tread this path in practice comes from within ourselves. The moment our ego discovers that we are in earnest in our intention of coming to dvekut with the Creator, it starts to fight us every inch of the way.

Rabbi Baruch Shalom:

> One night, Rabbi Moshe Yair Weinstock told my father that he wanted to go to the *mikveh* [ritual bath], whereupon my father told him, "The inner meaning of the mikveh is hinted at in the verse: 'And when the ark traveled, Moses said, "Arise, O God and scatter all Your enemies, and all those who hate You will flee before You"'(Num. 10:35). The Hebrew word for mikveh is מקוה. The same letters, rearranged, make the word קומה, meaning "arise." This implies that the mikveh is the restoration of God's holy name through which our enemies will be scattered.
>
> At that, Rabbi Moshe Yair turned to go, but the Sage called him back, saying, "When you go to the mikveh, have the thought that you are one of those who hate God and that you should be shattered before him!"

Explanation: In each one of us, there are two powers: a power that requires much self-sacrifice, that leads us on in faith, by giving to our fellow and to God. And opposing it is our selfish love that does not allow us to work with all our heart and soul for God. This selfish love of ours is an enemy of God; it strenuously opposes the idea that we should put God first.

"May your enemies be scattered," means, let our inner enemies be shattered, whereupon these forms of our will to receive for ourselves alone will not be able to achieve anything.

---

[*] To look at these three modalities in depth, see the letter to Rabbi Shmuel Ashlag, page 76

Chapter Six

Treading the Path

In 1924, Rabbi Ashlag moved from the Old City to Givat Shaul, an outlying neighborhood of Jerusalem, where he was appointed to act as the local rabbi and *moreh tzedek* (one who has the authority to give decisions on practical aspects of Jewish law). His house quickly became a focal place for the pupils. He gave the *shiurim* (lessons) in the Torah of Kabbalah from two o'clock in the morning until nine o'clock.

The pupils lived either in the Old City or in the Meah Shearim district of Jerusalem, and the way to Givat Shaul was rough and difficult. There were a few houses as far as the old Sha'arei Tzedek hospital, but after that, there was only wasteland over which wild dogs and jackals prowled at night. But the students did not let the danger deter them. Even when the way from Jerusalem to Givat Shaul became perilous because of marauding Arabs, they persevered, leaving their homes every night at one in the morning. Neither the fear nor the bitter cold in the winter stopped them from being present at the shiurim.

Rabbi Avraham Brandwein:

> My father, Rabbi Yehudah Tzvi, would wake Rabbi David Mintzberg and Rabbi Joshua Horovitz, and they would go together, meeting up on the way with Rabbi Moshe Yair Weinstock and Rabbi Moshe Baruch Lemburger, who lived in the area of Meah Shearim. They would walk together as a band from the Old City to Givat Shaul.

Rabbi Menachem Yosef Weinstock:

At that time, I was only a child, but I remember that every Shabbat my revered father, Rabbi Moshe Yair, would take me to Givat Shaul on two separate occasions. We went once in the morning and once for the third meal. It was a long way from Meah Shearim to Givat Shaul, but to my father, the way seemed short. It wasn't only on Shabbat that my father went on foot: each night he walked there, for at that time we had hardly anything to eat, and no one had money for a car.

The British police was informed about the group of chasidim who made their way every night after midnight to Givat Shaul. Once, the police warned them that a hyena had been spotted on the roads, but they paid no heed. Their only desire was to get to the house in Givat Shaul.

Rabbi Shmuel Mintzberg:

Once, when the students were on their way back from Givat Shaul, the British officer in charge of the prison stopped them and called them into the courtyard of the prison. They didn't know what he wanted from them and were afraid. He lined up a row of police and soldiers opposite them and told them, "Do you see these men? I see these Jews going to Givat Shaul every night. Learn from them what it means to be determined!"

Rabbi Baruch Shalom:

Once my mother came to my father and asked, "Why is it that all the other heads of the *yeshivot* [seminaries] have so many pupils, whereas you have only a few?" He answered her, "Believe me, the Master of the Universe has even fewer pupils than I have."

The Beit Midrash

One of the students, Rabbi Avraham Ashkenazi, used to relate how the pupils held Rabbi Ashlag in tremendous awe. Awe of the teacher was not an abstract concept for them, but each felt this awe in accordance with his own disposition.

Not everyone who wanted could come and learn. Rabbi Ashlag chose his students with great care and permitted only those who were capable of working to overcome their natural egoism to enter his classes. As a prerequisite, they had to have achieved great proficiency in Talmud and in halachah. All the students were men who had already attained some aspect of the tzaddik themselves, in that they had some direct perception of the higher spiritual levels. Rabbi Ashlag did not agree to teach anyone who did not fully accept his teaching on how to apply the principles of serving God, in the way that he himself had learned them from his teachers.

It is clear that Rabbi Ashlag's teachings did not stem from intellectual considerations of the material, but from his deep connection with and clear grasp of the inner meanings of the Torah. His pupils related that they had to struggle much harder to understand the lessons with the Sage than they had to struggle over a tractate in the Talmud with all the commentaries! Rabbi Ashlag dwelt on every idea until he had explained it clearly, defining every principle and penetrating every concept until there could be no room for doubt.

Only the closest of his students were allowed to join the Sage in prayer, and no one who did not belong to the group was permitted to join for any reason whatsoever.

Later on, the Sage consented to give shiurim twice a week to young men on the book *Mesilat Yesharim* (The Path of the Righteous) by Rabbi Moshe Chaim Luzzato and on the *Reishit Chochmah* (The Beginning of Wisdom) by Rabbi Eliahu De Vidash (a student of the Ari and Rabbi Moshe Cordovero).

At that time, Rabbi Ashlag's first book on the *Etz Chaim* of the Ari, *Panim Meirot uMasbirot* (Illuminating and Welcoming Revelations) had not yet been published, so he usually taught directly from the *Etz Chaim*, explaining the principles of the Ari's system. After the lesson, Rabbi Yehudah Tzvi Brandwein would go over the shiur, and the students would discuss it among themselves.

Sometimes, before a shiur, the Sage would be speaking with his students, and they thought he was talking about some aspect of this physical world. Then, the Sage would say something in particular, and the students suddenly understood that he had not been talking about some aspect of the physical world at all. Instead, he was relating to the physical world as a branch that stems from its spiritual root, and it was of this spiritual root that he had been talking all along.

Many times, after Rabbi Ashlag had finished the lesson—which had already lasted about six hours—he would go outside the beit midrash into the courtyard, where he would continue to speak on the service of God for several hours more.

Rabbi Baruch Shalom reported that on Shabbat eve the students did not sleep at all, but studied all through the night, even though their exhaustion was very great.

Rabbi Ashlag did not receive visitors. The only people who went into his study were his wife and his assistant, Rabbi Moshe Baruch Lemburger, and they, only for very short periods. Occasionally, the other students would enter in order to request individual direction regarding an aspect of their service of God. He would instruct each according to his own spiritual level and according to the root of his soul. When he spoke, it was only in order to help the student. No other words were said.

To the outside world, Rabbi Ashlag appeared as a regular person. It was not possible to discern any outward sign of internal effort that he made; no expression could be seen as extraordinary. Indeed, no aspect of his connection with the Master of the Universe was apparent. All was hidden away inside of him.

At this time, Rabbi Itzia Meir, who had been the Rabbi of Porisov's attendant, arrived from Poland. He became very close to Rabbi Ashlag, participating in the shiurim, and even waiting on him. Once, the Sage asked him what payment he would like for attending him. Rabbi Itzia Meir answered that he would like to go with the Sage to the mikveh. The Sage agreed. When they came to the mikveh, Rabbi Itzia Meir saw that from the time Rabbi Ashlag entered the courtyard of the mikveh until he left, only three minutes passed! When he asked the Sage why he had hurried, he answered, "In the mikveh, it is forbidden to think on matters of holiness, and for me not to think on holiness, even for one minute, is worse than if they were coming to slaughter me... ."

A student who joined the band at that time was Rabbi Yosel Weinstock. He became very attached to the Sage, and took upon himself the work of distributing his books.

Rabbi Pinchas Brandwein:

Rabbi Yosel's entire life was given over to our holy Sage. Everything he did or spoke revolved around him. Rabbi Yosel would not talk on any matter unless it was connected with our teacher, and only if he had made sure that his dress was properly arranged first. He even sold much of his household furniture in order to help finance the printing of the books.

Rabbi Baruch Shalom Ashlag

In the year 1924, Rabbi Ashlag married off his first-born son, Rabbi Baruch Shalom, and from then onward, Rabbi Baruch joined the shiur as one of the regular students. He cleaved with all his heart and soul to his holy father. Slowly, quietly, and with modesty, he absorbed the Torah of his father until it became part of him. His spiritual connection with his father strengthened and grew until he himself attained spiritual heights. He never looked for appreciation or honor, but hid his attainments.

Rabbi Baruch's deference to his father was really extraordinary. It can happen that a son who is constantly in his father's presence may not value his father appropriately, but this was not the case with Rabbi Baruch Shalom. Right until the last days of his life, whenever he mentioned his holy father, it was always with awe and trembling. However, the reader should not get the impression that Rabbi Baruch Shalom was a man who was humble and self-effacing by nature. The opposite was the case: Rabbi Baruch Shalom was a man with clear opinions that he held forcefully, but he deferred to his holy father wholeheartedly.

The Students

Rabbi Ashlag's students were the cream of Jerusalem. All of them were great in the study and practice of Torah. The foremost was Rabbi Baruch Shalom HaLevi Ashlag, Rabbi Ashlag's firstborn son. The other members of the holy band were Rabbi Yitzchak Agassi, Rabbi Joshua Sendar Horovitz, Rabbi Mordecai Cla'ar, Rabbi Yehudah Tzvi Brandwein, Rabbi David Mintzberg, Rabbi Moshe Baruch Lemburger, Rabbi Levi Yitzchak Krakowski, Rabbi Moshe Yair Weinstock, Rabbi Shlomoh Binyamin HaLevi Ashlag, Rabbi Yoseph Wershevsky, Rabbi Shia Tzeinvert, Rabbi Yosel Weinstock, Rabbi Meir Kuperberg, and Rabbi Zundel Hagar. The students who came from Tiberias were Rabbi Menachem Edelstein and Rabbi Avraham Ashkenazi. Students who joined in the period when Rabbi Ashlag lived in Tel Aviv were Rabbi Benjamin Sinkovsky and Rabbi Aharon Shemesh.

Some of the students came from distinguished families and traced their lineage back to the Baal Shem-Tov. But Rabbi Ashlag did not consider lineage as anything to be proud of; on the contrary, he considered it an impediment to spiritual growth. In order to uproot any pride that might stem from such connections, he sent these students to work as laborers in the building trade. This was in the year 1925. Those involved were Rabbi Baruch Shalom, Rabbi Yehudah Tzvi Brandwein, and Rabbi David Mintzberg; he sent Rabbi Moshe Baruch Lemburger to sell wine.

In a letter to his son, Rabbi Baruch Shalom, the Sage writes:

Erev Succot 5688 *(1927)*

... You have written requesting that I accept you as a pupil. You also surmised that maybe I am not satisfied with you since I already have sufficient pupils.

This is the truth that I tell you: You are heavier on me than are the others because you have more lineage than the others possess. Surely you have heard that the sage Rabbi Elimelech of Lizensk did not want to accept students who had lineage, on any account. Indeed, Rabbi Naphtali of Ropshitz poured out many entreaties and tears before Rabbi Elimelech, but nothing helped until any stench of pride that he took in his lineage had completely dissipated. He cried out, "What am I to blame if my father had a great lineage?" Only when Rabbi Elimelech recognized the truth in his words did he accept him as a pupil.

This matter should not come as a surprise to you. Most people would think that someone with a great spiritual lineage is closer to God than is a simple person, as he has seen the good deeds of his father since he was a child; and what is learned in infancy becomes more fixed in the heart.

But the matter is as follows: within each single action of God's work two opposites are to be found, as I have explained at length in previous letters. It is the case that the created being is composed of both body and soul, which are opposite to each other. As a consequence, within any attainment, whether large or small, there are two mutually opposing forms. Therefore, we have two main modes of serving God: (1) through prayer and supplication, (2) through praise and thanksgiving. It is obvious that these modes have to be conducted to the ultimate extreme.

In order to become whole in the matter of prayer, a person has to feel the closeness of God to him as being essential to him; he needs to feel that he is like a limb that is not functioning properly. Then he can cry bitterly and pour out his whole heart to God.

But when he is working on giving praise and wholehearted thanksgiving to God, a person has to feel the closeness of God as being extra, excessive, like something that does not belong to him at all. "O Lord, what is Man that You should know him? The son of Man that You should consider him" (Ps. 144:3)? Then the person can certainly give praise and thanksgiving to His great name completely, because He chose him to be among those who wait on Him, to serve Him.

It is an immense task for a person, who is composed of ego and soul, to perfect himself in these two opposite feelings so that they should be fixed in his heart on a permanent basis, simultaneously.

That a person should feel lowly and distant—and that consequently, the goodness of God to him is excessive—is immeasurably more difficult to attain than the feeling of the closeness of

God when in prayer. Most people who fail, stumble only on this aspect. And you should know that the one who has lineage is further away from attaining the feeling of lowliness than is the simple person, since he feels the goodness of God for him as a matter taken for granted. Check this out, for it is true.

...

Yehudah[1]

Torah and Work

Rabbi Ashlag preferred that a person should work for his living. It is much healthier for the person and more useful for the development of his soul not to sit all day and learn, but rather work for a certain number of hours a day, and learn Torah when he is free. Naturally, there are students, blessed with extraordinary qualities, who are exceptions to this rule, but the majority of people benefit from work.

The Companions

The group of pupils who gathered around the Sage became a holy band like those of earlier generations, such as the original chasidim of Gur and Kotzk, whose way was dedicated to coming to *dvekut* (unity) with the Creator.

The sages of the Talmud consider the possibility of dvekut with the Creator as follows:

Rabbi Chama the son of Rabbi Chaninah asked, concerning the injunction: "You shall walk after the Lord your God" (Deut. 13:5), how is it possible for a human being to walk after the Divine Presence, when the Scripture states: "For the Lord your God is a consuming fire..." (Deut. 4:24)?

The answer is by adopting the attributes of the Holy Blessed One: Just as God clothes the naked—as it is written, "And the Lord God made coats of skin for Adam and his wife, and He clothed them," (Gen. 3:21)—so you clothe the naked. Just as the

Holy Blessed One visits the sick—as it is written, "And the Lord appeared to him [Abraham] in the oaks of Mamre..." (Gen. 18:1), [when he was resting after the circumcision]—so you also visit the sick. Just as God comforts the mourners, as it is written, "And it was after the death of Abraham that God blessed Isaac his son..." (Gen. 25:11)—so you should comfort the mourners. Just as God buries the dead—as it is written, "And He buried him [Moses] in the valley..." (Deut. 34:6)—so you bury the dead. [2]

We are, therefore, in dvekut with the Creator when acting in a merciful and loving way to our fellow unconditionally—that is, without expecting anything back—just in the way that God is compassionate unconditionally, for "God is good and does good to all." [3]

When we exert ourselves to let go of our selfish love, and instead, turn our energy to giving love to our fellow man, we are preparing the ground for ourselves to acquire a new nature, a nature of love and compassion. This new nature of compassion and understanding takes the place of our original egoistic nature.

Thus it was that on many occasions, Rabbi Ashlag emphasized how important it was for the members of the beit midrash to develop brotherly love between themselves and to express this love in real ways as a means of overcoming all obstacles on their path of serving the Creator. He wrote in a letter to the students:

> I understand that you are not putting much effort into the *tikkun* [rectification] of the will to receive for oneself alone, as it is expressed through the mind and through the heart. Nevertheless, do the best you can, and the salvation of God comes in the twinkling of an eye. But the most important way that stands before you today is through all of you uniting in fellowship. Make greater and greater efforts in this, for the effort involved in this can compensate for all lacks. [4]

And in a letter written to Rabbi Moshe Yair Weinstock:

> Therefore, I surely remind you again, at this special time, of the urgency of the matter of loving your companions, on which all the

merit of our existence depends, and which will give the measure of our success, which is near to us. Therefore, turn aside from all of your other business that seems so important, and place your deepest attention to consider new ways and true ways of connecting your hearts together as one complete heart, so that you shall fulfill the Scripture, "and you shall love your neighbor as yourself" (Lev. 19:18) in simplicity. [5]*

My Soul Shall Be as Dust

All the students had the ability to be fiercely critical, not of others, but of themselves. Their criticism was not that of a general self-censure, but a penetrating inquiry into the details of their lives in their search for the truth.

In the Talmud, Raba said, "A person should know himself, whether he is a complete tzaddik or not." [6] Therefore, Rabbi Ashlag taught his students that a person should check himself every day: Have I left off using my will to receive for myself alone or not? Do I love my fellow or not? These matters need to be actually tested in reality. If I love my fellow human being, then I have to consider him or her, at least to the same extent that I consider myself.

Likewise, Rabbi Ashlag encouraged the students to question whether they truly had faith in God. A person of faith thinks, speaks, and acts as is fitting for one who is in the presence of the King of Kings; he does not do whatever he likes, or speak just how he likes, or allow his thoughts to dwell on whatever occurs to him. The student needs to ask himself, "Do I live like this or not?"

Rabbi Ashlag said on one occasion, "When my pupils are in a period of spiritual descent, they do not fall into appetites such as desiring honor, but into lowly, simple desires, like eating and so forth." He explained the matter as follows: Whoever treads on the true path aspiring to affinity of form with the King and criticizes himself on a

---

* For a deeper understanding of the importance of forming groups of like-minded companions and ways in which we can work and support each other in our service of God, see Afterword: Love of Friends, page 297–312

daily basis, merits to see the truth about himself. He sees that he is very far from unity with God and how lowly is his strength in overcoming his basic nature of selfish love, which desires just to receive pleasure. For the will to receive pleasure and joy opposes, with all possible urgency, a person's attempts to love his fellow; neither will it allow him to serve God unless it gains something for itself. So when any of the students experienced a spiritual descent, they felt so low, they didn't think about honor and suchlike, they just fell into simple desires.

On account of their fierce self-searching, the students had a natural feeling of humility. Indeed, they needed great faith that they had anything that would enable them to feel good about themselves. Regarding this perception of theirs, Rabbi Ashlag taught that whatever one perceives through the desire for faith is true, whereas whatever is perceived through the desire for certainty stems from the will to receive for oneself alone and is, therefore, misleading. So, whoever, in his own view, sees that he is lowly, and only through faith believes that he has perfection, then the truth is that he really is whole. But whoever sees himself as being perfect, but believes himself to be lowly only to fulfill the requirement of holding oneself to be humble, then, said our Sage, since the vessel of faith is actually the true vessel, he really is lowly!

The sages of the Talmud put it this way: Rabbi Yehudah said in the name of Rav, "One who wears the *talit* (prayer shawl) of a sage, but is not, in fact, a sage, is not brought into the presence of the Holy Blessed One."[7] The light of God cannot be revealed in one who is filled with his own self-importance and feels himself to be the origin of his own merits. Actually, it is to one who feels himself to be naked and in need of rectification that the light of God reveals itself and heals his wounds.

The Talmud illustrates this through the following parable:

In the future, on the day that the Holy Blessed One gives His mercy to the children of Isaac, He will make a feast for the righteous.

After they eat and drink, they give the cup of blessing to Abraham, our father, to bless with it. But Abraham says, "I cannot bless, because Ishmael also came forth from me." Abraham turns to Isaac, saying, "Take it and bless!" But Isaac says to them, "I cannot bless, for from me came forth Esau." Isaac says to Jacob, "Take it and bless!" But Jacob says to them, "I cannot bless, for I married two sisters in their lifetimes, and in the future, the Torah will forbid me to do so." Jacob says to Moses, "Take it and bless!" Moses says to them, "I cannot bless, as I did not merit to go into the Land of Israel, neither in my lifetime nor in my death." Moses says to Joshua, "Take it and bless!" Joshua says, "I cannot bless, for I did not merit to beget a son." Joshua said to David, "Take it and bless!" David said to them, "I will bless! For me, it is fitting to bless, as it says, "I will raise the cup of salvation and I will call on the name of God" (Ps. 116:13). [8]

Rabbi Ashlag asked: Did David have so much pride, to the point that he said, "I will bless"? God forbid! On the contrary, David said of himself, "But I am a worm and not a man; a reproach of man, despised by peoples" (Ps. 22:7). How, then, could he say, "Yes, I will bless"? It was because he felt so humble that he could give the biggest thanks of all.

Journeys

From time to time, the Sage and his pupils would make journeys together to change their routine and to let the heart wonder and be excited at the blessings of God. The trips brought joy into the hearts of the pupils and encouraged fellowship and brotherly love among them.

Once, Rabbi Ashlag, Rabbi Baruch Shalom, Rabbi Brandwein, and Rabbi Horovitz went on a journey to visit the cave where Rabbi Shimon Bar Yochai and his son had hidden, and where they had received the wondrous teachings that became the Zohar. The cave is to be found in the village of Peki'in, situated high in the hills of the Galilee. From Peki'in they traveled to Meron, where Rabbi Shimon and his son, Rabbi Elazar, are buried. The Sage and the pupils rode on horses, as in those days there were no other means of travel in that area. After praying at the graves of these two holy tzaddikim, they left Meron and journeyed on to Safed, where they visited the tiny room in which the Holy Ari (Rabbi Isaac Luria) studied and where he received teachings from Elijah the prophet. The Sage said, "From such a small room came forth such a great light to the whole world."

Rabbi Baruch Shalom:

> Once it happened during Pesach in the year 1926, that no fish were to be had in Jerusalem. My father heard that it was possible to obtain some fish in Jericho, but the way there was dangerous because of bandits who held sway on the roads. Despite this, my father decided to travel to Jericho to get fish.
>
> We left on Friday morning, my holy father, accompanied in the car by Rabbi Joshua Horovitz, Rabbi Brandwein, and myself. As we left, we took some matzot, some oranges and lemons, and a *talit* with us.
>
> It was close to Shabbat when the car broke down and we were still on the road. All our efforts to get it going were in vain. Shabbat was approaching, and we had no way to leave the place. So we had to stop for Shabbat in the police station in an Arab village, Khan Al Khamer, close to Jericho. When our families in Jerusalem saw we had not returned, they informed the British police. The police searched for us, and when they found us, they informed the families of our whereabouts.
>
> This Shabbat was quite amazing. My father, the Sage, spoke on the inner meanings of the Torah and on extremely deep issues concerning the service of God. Who cared that we only had one *talit*? In the morning we wrapped it around all of us! Who cared that all we had to eat were some oranges and lemons? On this fruit, we made our three meals.
>
> When Shabbat ended, we made our way back to Jerusalem. The whole city was astir, for they had been deeply worried about us.
>
> The following day, when some of us went with a tow truck to get the car back, we found, to our complete astonishment, that the car was perfectly able to move on its own!

Return to Poland

In 1925, Rabbi Ashlag traveled to Poland to fetch the children who had been left behind. On that visit, he also tried to bring his student, Rabbi Moshe Mordecai Shultz, to Israel, but without success. Rabbi Azriel Chaim Lemburger relates (having heard it from Rabbi David Mintzberg):

> In Poland, Rabbi Ashlag met once again with his revered teacher, the Sage of Porisov. When the Sage of Porisov saw him, he immediately stood up to receive him, as he knew Rabbi Ashlag's great spiritual stature. Then he untied Rabbi Ashlag's sash and tied it around his own loins in order to show his great love for him.

Ever since the end of the First World War, Rabbi Ashlag had been warning that the Jews of Europe were in grave spiritual and physical danger. Before he left Poland in 1921, he had tried to talk to the leaders of the communities on the necessity of learning the Zohar, but the rabbis saw his words as surreal and did not relate to what he said. Furthermore, his contention that all the Jews should leave the Diaspora as quickly as possible and emigrate to Israel met with even greater opposition. Citizens' rights had, for the first time ever, just been granted to the Jews of Poland, and with this fact, the threat of annihilation appeared unrealistic.

In 1925, when Rabbi Ashlag returned to Poland, he repeated his warnings, but to little avail.

The Letters

There were periods in which Rabbi Ashlag wrote many letters to his students. These letters are filled with instruction and enlightenment for anyone who seeks the truth.

In some of these letters, we find that the Sage cuts with a sharp knife to the soul of his students. He does not use velvet gloves, but uncovers the naked truth, even when it is hard and bitter. Only by making the rottenness obvious can one hope for rectification.

In a reply to a letter written to him by Rabbi Moshe Mordecai Shultz, dated *Sivan* 1, 5682 (May 28, 1922) Rabbi Ashlag writes:

With regard to what you wrote to me in your last letter, that I hide my face from you and consider you as an enemy: you mean that I am behaving to you as one who hears of his friend's reproach, yet is silent; furthermore, that I don't carry the burden [of the pain of sins] together with my companions.

And in truth, I will acknowledge that you are right. I don't feel the pain [of sins] that you feel at all. On the contrary, when these same defects are revealed and become obvious, I am glad and rejoice over them. I mourn for and regret those defects that have not yet been uncovered and may yet be revealed. For a defect that is still hidden is beyond hope of rectification. But its coming to light is a great salvation from God.

For this is a general rule: a person cannot give out anything he doesn't have within him; [or anything of which he is unaware.] If [the defect] were to be revealed now, there is no doubt that it would be completely uprooted. But it is hidden.

Therefore, I am happy in the defects' emergence from their holes; for if you place your eyes on them, they will become like a heap of bones. In this, I have no doubt, not even for a moment, for I know that we have more on our side than they have on theirs. [The forces of holiness are stronger than the forces of uncleanness.]

However, if one sits with one's arms folded, then the time is lengthened and the despised ants [sins] are hidden, and no one knows even where they are. On this, the Scripture says, "The fool folds his hands, but then eats his flesh" (Eccl. 4:5).

We can learn from the Scripture on the war against Amalek: "And when Moses raised up his hand, then Israel prevailed, but when he let his hands drop, Amalek prevailed" (Ex. 17:11). If a person lets his hands drop, then the defects hold sway, but if a person strengthens in his faith, just as Moses raised his hands in faith, then straightaway all that needs to come to light is revealed and then Israel prevails "in all the mighty hand, and in all the great awe, which Moses wrought in the sight of all Israel" (Deut. 34:12).

So, "Whatever you find within your power to do, do" (Eccl. 9:10), and when the full measure [of the defects are revealed] then the Scripture will be fulfilled: "The wicked are overthrown, and are not" (Prov. 12:7), and then comes everlasting light and joy.

I remember the words that I spoke with you on the first day of Rosh HaShanah last year when we were coming home from my honored father's house after Kiddush, and you told me of the very troubling thoughts that befell you that you saw in your siddur [prayer book] during the morning prayer. And I became very happy for you indeed. And you asked me, "Why are you so happy?" And I answered you as above: the revelation of the wicked aspects of ourselves that were buried—even though they are not yet completely overcome—nevertheless, their coming to consciousness needs to be considered as a very great salvation indeed— a salvation that was caused by the holiness of the day. [9]

In many letters, Rabbi Ashlag notes that despite any physical distance from the pupils he is, in fact, extremely close to them in spirit. He encourages them to hurry the work of throwing off their will to receive for themselves alone (selfish love) as quickly as possible and to increase the love of friends among them. The importance of working on our love of friends as a means of overcoming our natural egoistic tendencies is a recurring theme.

The immense spiritual stature of Rabbi Ashlag is reflected in these letters. His entire world was filled with the love of God and it was his constant concern to serve God in all possible ways.

We bring here two examples: The first is a letter written by Rabbi Ashlag to his brother, Rabbi Shmuel Ashlag, instructing him on the correct approach to the service of God. It contains a wonderful discussion on why the soul incarnates and the correct way to approach spiritual work.

Parashah Vayigash, Tevet 6, 5687 (December 11, 1926)
To my dear brother, the honored Rabbi Shmuel,
.... With all this, I will write to you of what the path of the middle line in the service of God consists so that you should always aim for the right-hand line and the left-hand line.

There are some people who walk a path, but end up worse off than the person who sits and does nothing. That is one who deviates from the way. Indeed, the true way is a very thin line on which the person continues to tread until he comes to the inner palace of the King. Everyone who begins to walk this line requires tremendous care not to incline either to the right of the line or to its left, not even by so much as a hair's breadth. If in the beginning, the person deviates by so much as a hair's breadth, even if subsequently he were to go in a truly straight line, he could not come, by any means, to the palace of the King, because he does not tread a true line, as envisaged here:

beginning of the work — the palace of the King

This is a completely true analogy.

I will explain the middle line to you; it accords with the inner meaning of the text: **"the Torah, the Holy Blessed One and Israel [the soul] are one."** [10] For the purpose of the soul's coming into the body is that she should merit, while still clothed by the body, to return to her Root and unite in dvekut with her Creator, may He be blessed, as it is written in the Scripture: "... to love the Lord your God, to walk in all His ways, and to unite with Him in dvekut" (Deut. 11:22).*

So you see that the final purpose of the soul is to come to dvekut with God, in the same dvekut that she had before she became clothed in the body.** However, one needs great preparation for this, that is, to "walk in all His ways." And who can know the ways of God, may He be blessed?

But this is the inner meaning of the Torah, which has 613 paths within her, so that one who walks them, will, in the end, purify himself, so that his body [ego] will no longer form an iron barrier

---

* "... to love the Lord your God, [this is the aspect of Israel]; to walk in all His ways, [this is the aspect of Torah] and to be united with Him in dvekut [this is the aspect of the Holy Blessed One]" (Deut. 11:22).

** See Glossary for the meaning of the body in Kabbalah.

between himself and his Creator, as it is written: "And I will remove the heart of stone from within you" (Ezek. 36:26). Then the person will become one with the Creator, exactly as he had been united with Him before the soul became clothed by the body.

We find that there are three aspects involved: (1) **Israel,** which refers to the person who labors to return to his Root; (2) the **Holy Blessed One,** the Root for whom he yearns; (3) the **Torah,** which has 613 paths through which a person may purify his soul and his ego. It is to this purification that the sages of the Talmud were referring when they called the Torah "medicine," as it is written: "I created the evil inclination, I created the Torah as its medicine." [11] However, in truth, these three elements, the Torah, the Holy Blessed One, and Israel, are one. Thus, in the end, every worker for God must attain them as being one, single, and united [Echad, Yachid, uMeyuchad].* They appear as separate entities only to the extent that a person's service to God is incomplete.

I will help you understand, somewhat, and a little you will see, but the whole you will not see, except through God's saving grace.

Know that the foundation of the soul is part of God on high. Before its coming into the body, the soul is in unity with God, as is a branch with its root.

The Holy Ari teaches that God created the worlds because it was His will to reveal His holy names:** that He is Merciful and Compassionate. [12] For if there were no created beings, there would be none to whom He could show compassion. Look here well, for these matters are very deep.

However, a little according to the power of my pen: Considering attainment, it is clear that whatever is unattainable we cannot

---

* *Echad:* that God is One, indivisible, with a single desire of giving goodness to the created beings.

Yachid: We need to believe that everything that happens to us, whether we perceive it as good or as bad, is only motivated by the one, single desire of giving good.

Meyuchad: We can now see, in full consciousness, that all that occurs is actually good.

For a fuller explanation see *A Tapestry for the Soul,* Lesson Six. (See Nehora Press pages at end of book.)

** A name of God is a vessel for His light.

know by name. The Zohar states: "The entire Torah is composed of the names of the Holy Blessed One."[13] The attainment of these names of God is the reward of the soul, which therefore comes into the body. It is only through the means of the body that the soul is able to attain the names of the Holy Blessed One. According to its attainment, so is the measure of its stature.

We can take as general principles: (1) The life-force of a spiritual being accords with its direct knowledge of God. (2) A living being in the physical world feels himself [to be an individual entity] because he is composed of both intelligence and physical aspects.

Since spirituality accords with direct knowledge of God, the measure of spiritual stature is the greatness of that knowledge, according to the Scripture: "A man shall be commended according to his wisdom" (Prov. 12:8). A living being that is only spiritual has direct knowledge [of God], but does not possess feeling at all. Understand this well.

Now we can understand the reward of the soul: Prior to the soul coming into the body, she was like a small point, even though she was united with her Root as is a branch with respect to the tree. This aspect of the soul is designated, "the Root of the soul and her world."

If the soul had not come into this world in a body, she would have had only her world; that is to say, her part in the Root. However, the more the souls merit to walk in all the ways of God—whose ways are revealed in the 613 paths of the Torah, which embody the names of God in actual reality—then her stature grows according to the measure of the names of God that she has attained.

This is the inner meaning of what the sages say at the conclusion of the Talmud: "The Holy Blessed One bequeaths 310 worlds to every tzaddik."*

---

* Rabbi Yehoshua ben Levi said, "In the future, the Holy Blessed One will bequeath ש"י [shai, in gematria, 310] worlds to each and every tzaddik. As it says, in the Book of Proverbs, "That I may cause those who love Me to inherit יש (yesh—substance) that I may fill their treasuries." [Both yesh, יש and shai, ש"י have the numerical value of 310.] (End tractate Uzkin)

Explanation: The soul is made up of two aspects of the tzaddik: the higher tzaddik and the lower tzaddik, in the same way that the body is divided at the navel into two halves, from the navel and above, and from the navel and below. These two aspects: the higher tzaddik and the lower tzaddik, enable the soul to merit both the written Torah and the oral Torah, which together make 620 [twice 310]. This is the inner meaning of the 613 mitzvot of the Torah, which, together with the seven rabbinically ordained mitz-vot, make up the number 620.*

The Ari, in his work the *Etz Chaim*, states that the worlds were created solely in order to reveal the names of the Holy Blessed One. Look there well, and you will understand:

> Then it arose in His undifferentiated will to create the worlds and to bring forth the created beings; bringing to light the per-fection of His works, **His names,** and His attributes, for this was the reason for the creation of the worlds. [14]

Now you see, that since the soul descended to be clothed in this polluted material of the body, she can no longer return to her Root to unite with it as comprising her entire world, as she had before coming into this world. But she is obliged to grow her stature 620 times greater than she had when in her Root.

This is the inner meaning of the perfection of all the lights that the soul attains. These lights are called, "Nefesh," "Ruach," "Neshamah," "Chayah," and "Yechidah." Indeed, the soul's vessel for the highest of its lights, Yechidah, is designated by the name "Keter" כתר, which has the numerical value of 620.**

Now you see that the 620 names of God—which are attained through the practice of the 613 mitzvot of the Torah together with the seven mitzvot instituted by the sages—correspond to the

---

* There are 620 letters on the two tablets of stone. This number hints at the 613 mitz-vot of the Torah, plus the seven additional mitzvot added by the Rabbis. All other mitzvot ordained by the Rabbis are not additional to those given on Mount Sinai, but are elucidations or derivatives of the 613 mitzvot of the Torah.

** כתר: according to the numerical value of the letters in the system of gematria, 200=ר; 400=ת; 20=כ.

five aspects of the soul: Nefesh, Ruach, Neshamah, Chayah, and Yechidah. This is because the vessels for these five lights of the soul are formed from the 620 mitzvot. The soul's lights, Nefesh, Ruach, Neshamah, Chayah, and Yechidah, are the essence of the light of the Torah that is within every single mitzvah. Thus we see that the Torah and the soul are one.

The inner meaning of the light of the *Ein Sof* (The Infinite) that is clothed in the light of the Torah is the Holy Blessed One. This is the light within the 620 mitzvot. Understand this well, for this is the inner meaning of what the sages have said, that the whole of the Torah consists of the names of the Holy Blessed One, as I have explained. For the Holy Blessed One is the general aspect, and the names are the individual vessels for the light. These vessels are attained according to the steps and levels of the soul, who does not receive her light all at one time, but only in gradual stages, slowly, slowly, one stage after another.

From all this, it will become clear to you that, in the end, the soul is destined to attain all the 620 holy names of God and acquire her full stature, which is 620 times greater than that which she had before she came into the body. The measure of her stature is apparent from the 620 mitzvot in which the light of the Torah is clothed—the Holy Blessed One being the general aspect of the light of the Torah.

So here you have explicitly that the Torah, the Holy Blessed One, and Israel are one in complete actuality. Meditate well on these matters, for they are not metaphors; they are the simple, literal truth. Happy are you if you understand what is before you.

We will return to the matter in hand: Before a person has completed his service to God, it seems to him as if the Torah, the Holy Blessed One, and Israel are three separate entities:

Sometimes a person yearns to fulfill his soul and return it to its Root. This is the aspect of Israel.

Sometimes a person wants to understand the ways of God and the inner meanings of the Torah, for "if a person does not know the commands of the King, how can he serve Him?"[15] This is the aspect of Torah.

And sometimes a person yearns to attain the Holy Blessed One; that is to say, he yearns to cling to Him in full consciousness. Then he is sorrowful only over this aspect, and he does not feel sorrow with respect to the attainment of the inner meanings of the Torah, or regarding returning his soul to its Root as it was before it came to be clothed in the body.

Therefore, one who walks the true line in preparation of serving God needs to constantly check himself to see if he is yearning for each of these three modalities equally. For the end of the action depends on its beginning. If he finds he is yearning more for one aspect than for the others, then he is inclining away from the true path. Understand this.

It is best that you grasp as your purpose to yearn for the commands, the mitzvot of the Lord, for if one does not know the paths of the Lord and the mitzvot of the Lord, which are the inner meanings of the Torah, how can one serve Him? This is the surest of the paths—the middle path of the three.

This is the inner meaning of the request: "Open for me an opening the size of a needle, and I will open for you a doorway as a gateway to a hall."[16]

Explanation: The opening of a needle is not for entering or for leaving, but to bring the thread through for sewing and for working. Likewise, a person should long for the commands of the King so he can serve Him with his work. Then, "I will open for you a doorway as a gateway to a hall (אולם)," which is the inner meaning of God's holy name in the verse,

"ואולם חי אני וימלא כבוד ה' את כל הארץ"

"ואולם [However,] as I live, and all the earth will be filled with the glory of the Lord" (Num. 14:21).

Yehudah Leib [17]

Most of the letters that Rabbi Ashlag wrote were written to students who were very advanced in their spiritual consciousness. These letters are not understandable by the ordinary reader without help. The following letter written to Rabbi Joshua Horovitz is an example of such a letter. As you will see from the content, the student has already achieved the state of being able to give unconditionally, and is thus in the first stage of the tzaddik. But he needs guidance on how to progress to the stage of receiving for the sake of giving, the final stage of the tzaddik, which involves being able to receive revelations of the light of God in the right way.

The letter is presented first in its original format and is followed by a detailed commentary.

London, *Parshat Pinchas* 5687 (July 14, 1927)
Dear Rabbi Joshua,

I am present here, with these, my words, to reveal my heart to you openly. I feel shame that the companions are not longing for my forthcoming return home as they should. I think about you, that at any rate, you are the best of them since you are not able to write to me and pour out your heart; therefore you need more of a welcome than the others require. Since this is so, I will think that you miss me more than the others do, and so I will talk and be refreshed.

On the other hand, let us discuss the gains that you have acquired in all your time with me. It is still not clear whose fault it is, but whatever the cause, your hope is weaker and needs strengthening.

From my side, I cannot help you with this, I may only clarify for you that the blame is not in me, only in you alone. It is because of the lack of your *dvekut* [unity] or your weakness of faith and such like. So all my prayers on your behalf cannot help you, because you have not yet understood how to bring forth your dvekut in actual practice.

Therefore I will give you a complete introduction and you should keep it and it will benefit you.

When a person finds favor in the sight of God, and God is calling to him to cling to Him, may the One be blessed, then it is understood that the person is completely ready for this call with all his heart and all his being. For if this were not the case, God would not have invited him to His banquet. And if the faith in his heart is like a stake that cannot be moved, then he understands the true call and he recognizes his place for eternity. And so he acts and eats and receives the presence of the King and is not concerned that he will lessen in his faith because of this, God forbid, since his connection with Him and his faith in Him are complete.

The sages said, "The Scripture, 'And fear the Lord your God,' (Deut. 6:13) means to include oneself with the sages." [18] To include oneself means to unite in true unity. Happy are those who can tolerate this.

You can see the truth of these words within yourself because when the time came and you were worthy for me to join with you, I did not miss the time by waiting until you could come to my house, but I was instantly with you. Even though you did not see my physical form, you felt my love and the exaltation of the holiness in the depths of your heart.

What was there left for you to do, but to hurry and come before me with love? And the desire does its own work. So you acted— sending feelings of love, uplift of spirit, and joy to my ears, the whole way from your house to Givat Shaul in true longing.

But once you came up to my house and saw me, the joy and the love started to diminish. That was due to your lack of faith in me. Consequently, this incurred a corresponding [lessening in my revealing] of my direct love for you, because I reflected back to you, as water reflects the face.

This was the first defect between you and me: in your doubting [my love] you immediately went out [of the connection with me] and became distanced from me according to the precise measure [of that thought]. For that is the nature of every spiritual entity: the matters are woven at tremendous speed so that pregnancy and birth occur in proximity. So once you entertained such a thought in your mind, immediately you gave birth to straw. That is to say, you doubted yourself and your pleasant and lofty thoughts of me and thought that they had been exaggerating my level; maybe I am not at this high level? Then that became so for you, God forbid. Then, of necessity, I became separated from you. So I gathered together all my work and my toil as a deposit to wait for a better time.

When that time occurred, I came back to you as previously, but you repeated your former actions, more or less. Sometimes you wanted to hear me speak on this explicitly as one speaks to his fellow, no less; but in this matter I am weak. As it is written, "and I am hard of speech and heavy of tongue" (Exod. 4:10). Also, you should not hope for this in the future unless you merit to sanctify your physical body—the master of the tongue and the ears—that they should be as spiritual organs in actuality. But you are not able to understand this, as you do not deal with the hidden. But, as for me, all that I am permitted [to give] I do not withhold at all, God forbid, "as more than the calf wants to nurse, the cow wants to suckle."[19]

I will illustrate your relationship with me by way of a parable: A person is walking on the highway and sees a beautiful garden. He hears the voice of the King, who is in the garden, calling specifically to him. He is naturally very amazed, and in his amazement, he jumps into the garden with one bound. In his quickness, he does not sense that he is walking in front of the King and that the King is actually close to him and walking behind him. So he thanks and praises the King with all his might with the intention of preparing himself to receive the presence of the King. He does not sense at all that the King is actually close to him. Suddenly, he looks back and sees the King near him. At that moment, naturally, his joy is very great, and he begins to walk behind the King with praise and song as much as he can; for the King is before him and he is following the King.

So they continue to walk around until they come to the entrance. And the man goes out of the gate and back to his former place. But the King stays in the garden and locks the door. When the man looks, he sees that he has already separated from the King and that He is not with him. He starts to search for the door to the garden through which he left [so that he may re-enter the garden in such a way] that the King would precede him. But there is no such opening at all! The only way in is the first way, in which he precedes the King and the King is behind him without his sensing it.

So it needs to be now. But one needs to be a great man of faith for this.

Now understand and ponder this parable, for it is a true happening between us. When you were with me and I felt the coldness that had been born in you compared with your former state, then at least you should have hidden your face and not looked at me unashamedly as if I didn't know anything at all of what had happened to you and of what had been in your heart all the way until you arrived in my presence.

This is the matter of: "And the Children of Israel believed in God and in Moses, His servant" (Exod. 14:31).* For with the reward of: "And Moses hid his face because he was afraid to look on God" (Exod. 3:6)** "he merited to see the likeness of God" (Num. 12:8).[20] That is to say, if you would have believed in my prayer for you, and in my being with you, and that I had heard all the praise and song that you thought about me, then for sure you would have been very ashamed of the coldness that came in place of the warmth. And if you were ashamed and sorry, as is fitting, then you would have merited the mercy of God upon you. Then your enthusiasm would have returned to you, more or less, and you would have merited to unite with me, as is fitting, in a way that will never falter.

Yehudah Leib [21]

---

* At the parting of the Red Sea, when the Sages tell us that even the smallest handmaiden saw a great revelation of the light of God, nevertheless the people reacted with faith. "And the Children of Israel believed in God and in Moses His servant." This faith led to the Song of the Sea.

** On receiving the revelation of God in the burning bush, Moses straightaway hides his face rather than receive the revelation of God directly. For this, the sages tell us he merited to communicate with God, face to face.

The Letter Plus Commentary

London, *Parshat Pinchas* 5687 (14 July 1927)

Dear Rabbi Joshua, I am present here with these, my words, to reveal my heart to you openly. I feel shame that the companions are not longing for my forthcoming return home as they should.

The Shechinah speaks through the mouth of one who is a true Rabbi.[22] So all the modes of behavior that apply in our relationship with God also apply in our relationship with such a teacher. Just as one needs to yearn for the Creator, so one needs to yearn for one's true Rabbi.

I think about you, that at any rate, you are the best of them since you are not able to write to me and pour out your heart; therefore you need more of a welcome than the others. Because of the great difficulty that Rabbi Joshua had in writing explicitly on his desires, Rabbi Ashlag recognized that he was the greatest of the students because one who is greater has more difficulties.

Since this is so, I will think that you miss me more than the others do, and so I will talk and be refreshed. Because he felt that Rabbi Joshua really did miss him, but was having difficulty expressing his need, Rabbi Ashlag saw an opening to address him without waiting for a specific request from Rabbi Joshua.

On the other hand, let us discuss the gains that you have acquired in all your time with me. It is still not clear whose fault it is, but whatever the cause, your hope is weaker and needs strengthening. From my side, I cannot help you with this, I may only clarify for you that the blame is not in me at all, only in you alone. It is because of the lack of your dvekut or your weakness of faith, and such like. So all my prayers on your behalf cannot help you, because you have not yet understood how to bring forth your dvekut in actual practice. Therefore, I will give you a complete introduction and you should keep it and it will benefit you.

For when a person finds favor in the sight of God and God is calling to him to cling to Him, may the One be blessed—the call is felt within the person. When the person's thoughts and feelings are one with the exaltedness of God, love and longing for Him awaken within him. This is God calling him. This awakening does not come about by chance, but it is an action of God's.—**Then it is understood that the person is completely ready for this call with all his heart and all his being.** He has done all the requisite rectification of his intentions in both giving to God and in receiving from Him.

For if this were not the case, God would not have invited him to His banquet. The revelation of the light of God, the *Or d'Chochmah,* is designated as a banquet, in a metaphor of a meal of which one partakes with pleasure. For when God reveals Himself to a person, He is giving him the pleasure He desires to give, according to His purpose in creation.

And if the person's faith in his heart is like a stake that cannot be moved, then he understands the call and he recognizes his place for eternity. That is, he believes that every revelation of desire for God that arises within his heart actually originates from God's love for him, and therefore it arouses within him the desire of giving to God with greater strength.

The words "recognizes his place" mean that the person attains all aspects of his soul, Nefesh, Ruach, Neshamah, Chayah, and Yechidah.

So he acts and eats and receives the presence of the King, and is not concerned that he will lessen in his faith because of this, God forbid, since his connection with Him and his faith in Him are complete. "Receiving the presence of the King" means receiving the *Or d'Chochmah;* but this does not lessen his desire to serve God, neither does it diminish his faith in Him.

The sages of the Talmud said, "The Scripture: 'And fear the Lord your God' (Deut. 6:13) means to include oneself with the sages." To include oneself means to unite in true unity with a true sage. Happy are those who can tolerate this.—Happy is he who is able to receive this revelation of God's exaltedness yet still keep his *yirat HaShem* [reverence for God]. Furthermore, his *yirah* is not lessened by God revealing His highest light to him. The concern is that the person should not cause a defect in the glory of

God by attributing the revelation to his own work, which would cause his heart to become coarse within him.

You can see the truth of these words within yourself because when the time came and you were worthy for me to join with you, I did not miss the time by waiting until you could come to my house, but I was instantly with you, as an awakening from Above. **Even though you did not see my physical form, you felt my love and the exaltation of the holiness in the depths of your heart.** This was a gift from Rabbi Ashlag to his student. This gift from sage to student creates a tremendous longing in the heart of the student.

What was there more for you to do, but to hurry and come before me with love? That is, to merit this revelation. **And the desire does its own work. So you acted**—sending feelings of love, uplift of spirit, and joy to my ears, the whole way from your house to Givat Shaul, in true longing.

But once you came up to my house and saw me, the joy and the love started to diminish. That was due to your lack of faith in me. Consequently, there incurred a corresponding [lessening in the revealing] of my direct love for you because I reflected back to you as water reflects the face. At the time of the revelation of God's love and the corresponding uplift in the heart, there is a great danger that a person could infer that this awakening came as a consequence of his own efforts and not from God.[*] The correct way is for the student to believe that all that he feels is given to him by God and arises from God's great love for him. Here comes a testing point. Can he go in faith, above his rationale, or does he listen to his own logic? If he listens to his own logic, he immediately separates from the Creator. This separation comes about because, in every circumstance, whether at a time of spiritual descent or in a time of spiritual ascent, a person needs to believe in the love of the Higher One for him. Believing is an act of giving, and giving unconditionally joins a person with the

---

[*] Although the event happened between the student and Rabbi Ashlag, Rabbi Gottlieb interprets it as God acting through Rabbi Ashlag.

Creator; whereas the use of logic belongs to the consciousness of receiving and thus separates the person from the Giver.

This was the first defect between me and you: in your doubting the love between the Higher One* and the lower one, you immediately left that uplifted state and became distanced from me according to the precise measure of that doubt. For that is the nature of every spiritual entity: the matters are woven at tremendous speed so that pregnancy and birth occur in proximity. So once you entertained such a thought in your mind, immediately you gave birth to straw. You doubted both yourself and your pleasant and lofty thoughts of me and thought that they had been exaggerating my level; maybe I am not at this high level? Then that became so for you, God forbid, because feeling followed thought. Then, of necessity, I became separated from you. So I gathered together all my work and my toil in bringing this revelation of the love of God to you, as a deposit, to wait for a better time.

When that time occurred I came back to you as formerly. Again, Rabbi Ashlag inspired the student with the sense of the exaltedness of holiness, but you repeated your former actions, more or less. Sometimes you wanted to hear me speak on this explicitly, that is, on the love between the teacher and the student, and on the exalted level of the teacher, as one speaks to his fellow, no less; but in this matter I am weak. As it is written: "and I am hard of speech and heavy of tongue" (Exod. 4:10). Because these issues have to be left to the student's faith.

It is inconceivable that the Rabbi would reveal such matters to a student until the student's faith was complete. If the teacher were to reveal such matters directly, it would only add to the student's knowledge and would not help him with his faith. Also, you should not hope for this in the future, unless you merit to sanctify your physical body—the master of the tongue and the ears—that they should be as spiritual organs in actuality. Only

---

* Again, the "Higher One" could be the student's true teacher, of whom "the Shechinah speaks from his throat," or the term could apply to God.

if the student were to sanctify his will to receive completely so that it would be purified only to receive for the sake of giving benefit, could he then merit to experience such a revelation.

But you are not able to understand this, as you do not deal with the hidden, that is, you do not understand the importance of the issue of giving benefit. [Giving benefit is termed "hidden," since it has to do with the intentions of the soul], **but as for me, all that I am permitted I do not withhold at all, God forbid, "as more than the calf wants to suckle, the cow wants to nurse."** Rabbi Ashlag wants to give the feelings of the exaltedness of holiness to the student, but this depends on whether the student can direct such feelings only for the sake of giving benefit.

I will illustrate your relationship with me by way of a parable: A person is walking on the highway of the service of God **and sees a beautiful garden.** The garden represents the goodness and joy that the Creator, [represented in the parable by the King] has prepared for the created beings. **He hears the voice of the King, who is in the garden, calling specifically to him.** He feels an exaltation of holiness within him. For the voice of God is not something external to ourselves, but we hear it within us. Suddenly, he starts to contemplate the greatness of God and begins to feel His importance. These feelings are given to him by God Himself and this is the call of the King to him.

This is the first stage of connection between a person and the Creator, which forms the desire in the heart of the person to come to dvekut with Him. **He is naturally very amazed, and in his amazement, he jumps into the garden with one bound.** In one bound, he leaps over all materialism and receiving, and determines in his heart only to cleave to the Creator and have faith in Him. **In his quickness, he does not sense that he is walking in front of the King and that the King is actually close to him and walking behind him.** "The King is behind him" implies that God is concealed from him. He does not feel or imagine to himself that it is God who is actually giving him all these feelings; whereas, in fact, God is close to him.

So he thanks and praises the King with all his might, from the feeling of the exaltedness of God and his longing for Him, with the intention of preparing himself to receive the presence of the King for the sake of giving pleasure to Him. He does not sense at all that the King is actually close to him and that it was, in fact, He who brought him to this situation. Suddenly he looks back and sees the King near him. He receives a revelation of the light of God in actuality. This is designated as the *Or d'Chochmah*. At that moment, naturally, his joy is very great, and he begins to walk behind the King with praise and song as much as he can, as the King is before him and he is following the King. "Now the King is before him" implies he experiences God's light directly. We see that the call of God is initiated by God Himself and thus causes the person to long for Him. Then, the person forms the decision to do whatever he can to attain unity with God. Finally, God reveals His light to him in actuality.

So they continue to walk around until they come to the entrance. And the man goes out of the gate and back to his former place.

He goes out of the garden, back to the situation that he was in before the call of the King, that is, to complete concealment. But the King stays in the garden and locks the door so that there is no more possibility of his feeling the reality of God. When the man looks, and he sees he is already separated from Him, and the King is not with him, He starts to search for the door to the garden through which he left, [so that he may re-enter the garden in such a way] that the King would precede him. He wants to merit the revelation of the light of God as he did earlier, because of the great joy that he felt when God was revealed to him, but there is no such opening at all! The only way in is the first way, in which he precedes the King and the King is behind him without his sensing it.

A person should not long to experience the light of God directly because, in this state, there is no inner work of giving. Therefore, such a doorway does not exist. He needs to yearn for the first situation that he was in when he came into the garden in dvekut, but with the King behind him. That is, the state in which God's light is concealed and all of the person's work is carried out in faith: faith belonging to a paradigm of consciousness that is closer to God than is experience.

So it needs to be now. But one needs to be a great man of faith for this. That is, a person needs a great power of faith in order to fill the empty feeling he is left with, now that his direct experience of God's light is gone. That is to say that faith needs to become as important to him as is his actual experience.

Now understand and ponder this parable, for it is a true happening between us. **When you were with me and I felt your coldness that had been born in you compared with your former state, then at least you should have hidden your face and not looked at me unashamedly, as if I didn't know anything at all of what had happened to you, and of what had been in your heart all the way until you arrived in my presence.** The student needed to have faith and belief in the greatness of the Rabbi. Not only did the Sage know all that his student had experienced, but it was the Sage, himself, who had given him all these experiences.

We see that all the three stages mentioned in the parable occurred between the Sage and the student: (1) the calling out by the teacher, which created the longing for dvekut, (2) the receiving of the revelation of love from his teacher, (3) the student's rejection, because he was looking for proof rather than going with faith. These stages also happen in our relationship between ourselves and the Creator.

This is the matter of: **"And the Children of Israel believed in God and in Moses, His servant"** (Exod. 14:31), for with the reward of: **"And Moses hid his face because he was afraid to look toward God"** (Exod. 3:6)—that is, he preferred faith—**"he merited to see the likeness of God"** (Num. 12:8). Moses thus received a direct revelation of God for the sake of giving benefit. That is to say, **if you would have believed in my prayer for you when I was with you, and that I had heard all the praise and song that you thought about me**—if the student had believed in the exaltedness of his teacher in the paradigm of faith—**then for sure you would** have been very ashamed of the coldness that came in place of the warmth. He would have been ashamed of the way he related to the Sage, which stemmed from his unwillingness to rely on faith alone and the desire to receive confirmation of the Sage's love for him as knowledge. If you were ashamed and sorry, as is fitting, then you would have merited the mercy of God on you. Then your enthusiasm would have returned to you, more or less, and you would have merited to unite with me as is fitting, in a way that will never falter.

Yehudah Leib

Chapter Seven

Emphasis on the Inner

The poverty in Rabbi Ashlag's household was enormous. They simply didn't have two coins to rub together. The students would bring the necessities of life so that the children would have something to eat. However, the Sage knew that in order to fulfill his purpose, he needed to be totally dedicated to his work. He wrote in a letter (1927), "It is not for my honor or for my own need that I have composed this book, only for the sake of God." And so he wrote, "I have labored for God working for Him in whatever I find to do. There is no work in this world that I would not undertake for the glory of God. On the contrary, I always love and take pleasure in the greatest of labors that will give God satisfaction." (1928)

Once he said, "Materialism and spirituality are complete opposites. The whole world is chasing after the material; whoever doesn't have material goods feels distress. But when a person attains material fulfillment he is not satisfied but he feels empty. In spirituality, the matter is the opposite. No one in the world feels the lack of spirituality since a person can live without it. One needs, indeed, great labor in order to feel a lack in this matter. But whoever merits to attain even the tiniest contact with God merits exceeding happiness."

Inner and outer aspects exist within each one of us. These are well contrasted in Rabbi Ashlag's essay, the *Introduction to the Zohar*:

Now you must know that everything has an inner aspect and an outer aspect. In the world as a whole, Israel, the seed of Abraham, Isaac and Jacob, is considered to be the innermost aspect. The seventy nations are considered to be the outer aspect of the world. Within Israel itself, there is an inner aspect which consists of those people who are seriously committed to their spiritual work of serving God and there is an outer aspect consisting of those who are not involved in spirituality. Likewise, among the nations of the world, there is an inner aspect which consists of the saints of the world and an outer aspect which consists of those who are destructive and coarse.

Even among those of Israel who serve God, there is an inner aspect and an outer aspect. Those people who are privileged to understand the soul of the innermost aspects of Torah and its secrets comprise the innermost aspect of those who serve God; whereas the outer aspect is made up of people who deal with only the practical aspects of the Torah.

In a similar fashion, these two aspects may be comprehended within each individual person. Each individual has an innermost aspect, which is the aspect of "Israel" within him. This is the point of divine light within the heart. He also has an outer aspect that corresponds to the seventy nations of the world and which relates to the will to receive. These internal "nations of the world" have the capacity for transformation. When they do transform, they can then cleave to the innermost, divine part of the person's soul, and then these internal nations of the world become like righteous converts who join with the community of Israel within the person.

A person may reinforce and respect his innermost aspect, which is the aspect of Israel within him, over his external aspect, which is the aspect of the nations of the world within him. He then strives to put most of his energy and labor into increasing and enhancing his innermost aspect for the soul's sake. To those aspects of himself that correspond to his internal nations of the world, he gives only the minimum required. That is to say that he gives only the minimum to his wills to receive for himself, according to what is written in The Ethics of the Fathers, "Make your Torah your main occupation," and your work secondary to it. [1,2]

Rabbi Ashlag used a room close to the beit midrash where he prayed. His son Rabbi Baruch Shalom told us that when his father prayed alone, his prayer was very short.

Normally a person requires time and effort in order to direct his intention and his will toward God. But the Rabbi did not need to take time on this, as he was in continuous dvekut with God. This is like someone who is invited to meet a King: he makes many preparations and works out in advance what he will say and what he will not say. But one who is continually in the presence of the King does not require so much time to prepare.

On Shabbat eve and on the festivals, Rabbi Ashlag would join in the minyan and pray together with his students.

Rabbi Pinchas Brandwein:

I remember one Shabbat eve when our holy Sage had joined us in prayer. When he was saying the *Amidah* he stood for a very long time in total dvekut as if his entire being was being drawn upward. When he said the *Shema* he said it with total concentration, word for word, extremely slowly; and while he said it, he walked from side to side, from wall to wall, within the beit midrash.*

When we pray we need to be true to ourselves and to where we are in our spiritual life, fulfilling the mitzvot with sincerity.

Indeed, I must warn against a phenomenon that exists among people who delve into the innermost aspect of the Torah but don't relate to the practical aspects of the mitzvot and their fulfillment. This can happen for several reasons: because they are putting their emphasis on the intention and the feeling rather than on the action, or because they are unaware of the necessity of bringing their intentions into actual action in a balanced way according to the teachings of our sages. Many Jews nowadays approach Judaism from its more spiritual aspects, but it is incorrect to leave it at that. We must endeavor to ground the spiritual learning in actual deeds.

---

* The *Amidah* and the *Shema* are central elements in the Jewish liturgy. The *Amidah* is recited standing still and erect with the feet together, whereas in most communities the *Shema* is said sitting down. These positions have meanings in Kabbalah. However, chasidic communities have the custom of standing throughout prayer.

These are the words of Rabbi Chaim Vital, the great pupil of the Holy Ari:

> One should not say, "I will go and practice Kabbalah before I practice the Torah of the Mishnah and Talmud," for the rabbis have already taught that a person should not study Kabbalah if he has not already filled his belly with Mishnah and Talmud. This would be like a soul without a body, lacking any contact with this physical world. A person is not fully incarnate until he becomes involved at the physical level with the mitzvot of the Torah. But the opposite is also true. If someone studies Mishnah and Talmud without also spending time in studying the innermost aspects of Torah and its secrets, he is like a body sitting in darkness, lacking a human soul, which is the light of God that shines within. The body becomes dry because it is not taking from Torah, the source of life. [3]

Indeed, when Rabbi Zalman Lemburger, the son of Rabbi Moshe Baruch, was a young man, he asked if he could come into the lessons as a student. But the Sage refused, telling him he had not yet learned enough revealed Torah, that is to say, Talmud and halachah pertaining to the practical fulfillment of the mitzvot. Only when he had learned sufficiently in this area could he come and learn the innermost aspect of the Torah.

There are some who mistakenly think that whoever studies the Zohar and the writings of the Ari or who knows the gematrias (numerical values) of holy names is a Kabbalist and therefore must be on a high spiritual level. But these matters are only outer covers for the inner meanings of the Torah and are not the secrets of the Torah themselves. In fact, there is not necessarily a connection between the study of the Zohar or that of the Ari and the innermost aspects of the Torah. For the innermost aspects of the Torah are a guideline for our intentions in our behavior and should not be used simply as a source of information.

Like Jacob and his ladder, Rabbi Ashlag reached up to the heavens, but his conduct was firmly based on the ground, complete in the practical fulfillment of the mitzvot. Likewise, we, too, need to grasp the innermost aspects of the Torah with both hands and practice the Torah and mitzvot according to the halachah, as our sages throughout the generations have taught us.

However, the words of Rabbi Chaim Vital, brought above, also apply to those religiously observant who fulfill the practical aspect of the mitzvot but without paying attention to the required intention. Indeed, in our particular generation, we live in a world so involved with externals, drowning in the mire of animal appetites and self-interest, that even seemingly spiritual pursuits may lose their divinity. I found the following excerpt in the book *Meir Einai haGolah* by Rabbi Avraham Yissachar Binyamin Eliahu Alter that tells of the life and works of the Rabbi of Gur, in which the holy chasid Rabbi Bunam of Lublin related the following episode:

> Once, I was walking with our holy Rabbi of Gur in the courtyard of the beit midrash. It was then the month of *Elul*. My teacher asked if the shofar had been sounded that day in the beit midrash. After that, he added, in these very words, "When a person becomes the leader of the generation then all the trappings required for leadership come into place. The need arises for a study-house with rooms, tables, and benches: one person is appointed to be the treasurer, another, the organizer, and so forth. But then the ego comes and snatches the innermost spark, leaving the rest revolving around as previously. One needs to fear this; the time may come when everything will run exactly as it does now, but the innermost spark will be missing." Then he cried out in a loud voice, "May God help us!"[4]

The concern of the Rabbi of Gur has come true before our very eyes. We see a generation, impoverished and orphaned, a generation that has everything—except the true spark of a real connection with our Creator.

Indeed, among certain of the religiously observant there is a tendency to immerse themselves in the details of the practice of the mitzvot without paying due attention to their inner intention—the question of why they are doing what they are doing. Neither have they been given proper guidance by their rabbis and teachers on how to carry out the mitzvot with genuine feeling. When such religious people wish to increase their service of the Creator they do so by adding yet another aspect to the practical side of the mitzvot alone, when in fact their real lack consists of a deficiency in turning their hearts to the Creator. So they continue to add more and more stringencies, becoming more and more extreme.

This lack of connection with the soul is also an indirect cause for the increasing secularization of society. For as people see the inner emptiness of the religious they reject their path. The holy Baal Shem Tov already warned, "Do not be over-punctilious," [5] because over-involvement with too many strictures causes the innermost spark of Torah and mitzvot—the Creator—to be forgotten.

The lack of a dynamic connection with the Creator leads both young and old to feel a great dryness in their practice of the Torah, until finally it becomes an external ritual, undertaken without happiness or pleasure, out of social obligation only, or from habits engendered by education. Then the next generation tends to reject it. Such practice is termed by the sages, "commandments of people carried out by rote." This phrase is taken from the scriptural text, "And the Lord said, 'Because these people draw near to Me with their mouth and their lips to honor Me, but they have removed their heart far from Me; their fear of Me is that of a commandment of people learned by rote. Therefore, behold, I will proceed to do a marvelous work and a wonder: for the wisdom of their sages shall perish, and the prudence of those who have understanding shall be hidden" (Isa. 29:13–14).

When we fulfill the mitzvot with attention to their inner intentions, which we learn through studying the innermost aspect of the Torah, the Kabbalah, our soul awakens and reconnects us with the living essence of the Torah. This is because the innermost aspect of the Torah (sodot haTorah) is itself a revelation of God. Indeed, the Zohar states: "The name 'Torah' means it teaches and reveals that which is obscure and unknown." [6] The Torah is the garment for the essence of God, for it is He who is hidden in the Torah. Indeed, as one of the earliest chasidic sages, Rabbi Meshulam Feibish Heller, taught, every letter of the Torah hints at how we can come closer to God. [7]

Rabbi Baruch Shalom used to tell a parable on this:

If a person is walking down the street and he sees two men talking with each other, it doesn't interest him. But if he knows they are talking about him, their conversation arouses his curiosity, for it becomes like a secret for him.

Likewise, if a person is learning the Torah but he doesn't know that the Torah is talking about him as an individual, that it is teaching him personally how he can get closer to God, and is showing him the way to cling to the Source of all life, he does not feel either curiosity or interest to know what is written in it. Then the person looks at the Torah as a series of historical events that happened to his fathers and mothers, Abraham and Sarah, Isaac and Rivkah and so forth. This external view is potentially disastrous; it destroys the best of the souls of Israel, for then the stories of our forefathers and foremothers take on the aspect of historical chronicles, and the person doesn't understand the relevance of these matters to himself at all and loses every interest in its words.

But if a person would believe our holy sages, that every crown of every letter of the Torah has the specific purpose of pointing the way for his own soul, directing it how to cleave to the eternity of God and to complete happiness, then he would be interested in the Torah and investigate every letter with all his soul and might, researching even every crown of its letters in order to uncover its secret.

Prayer

Bestow upon us *De'ah* [connection with You], *Binah* [understanding] and *Haskel* [wisdom].

Blessed are You, O Lord, who has bestowed upon us the consciousness of Your holiness.

Bestow upon us forgiveness and atonement for all our sins, our rebelliousness, and our lowly acts.

Blessed are You, O Lord, who has forgiven our sins.

Bestow upon us simple, pure, and certain faith, until we may be sure of ourselves that we will not return to our foolishness any longer.

Blessed are You, O Lord, who has fixed Your faith within us for eternity.

Guard us that we should not pollute ourselves with any pleasures of the body and do not let us have material pleasures more than those required by the soul. And purify our heart completely that we should not desire such things at all, and we should not want for anything more than is required to give satisfaction to You.

Blessed are You, O Lord, who has purified our heart until we do not want anything other than to give satisfaction to You.

Bestow upon us Your great blessing on all the works of our hands, as it is written, "In every place that I cause my name to be mentioned, I will come to you and bless you" (Exod. 20: 21).

Blessed are You, O Lord, who has bestowed upon us all the blessings that You have prepared for Your created beings.

Redeem us with a complete redemption from the seventy nations that oppress us and cause us to sin.

Blessed are You, O Lord, who has redeemed us.

Grant us great favor in Your eyes.

Blessed are You, O Lord, that we have found favor in Your eyes.

Bring us, O Lord, into Your innermost rooms, where You share love with Your created beings.

Blessed are You, O Lord, who has brought me into Your rooms.

Reveal to us all Your secrets and don't hide anything from us that you have revealed to all Your prophets and sages who know Your name.

Blessed are You, O Lord, who has revealed to us the inner meanings of the Torah and the reasons for the mitzvot.

Give us the merit that we may come to complete teshuvah from reverence of You and from love of You. And gather together all the arrogant acts and lowly acts that we have ever perpetrated with which we have acted rebelliously against You. Transform them into merits for the revelation of the light of Your countenance in accordance with Your omnipotence.

Blessed are You, O Lord, who has gathered together all our sins and transformed them into merits.

Give us the merit to say before You at least one word or even one letter in perfect clarity during the days of our life.

Blessed are You, O Lord, who has fulfilled all our requests.

Reveal in our heart wondrous love for You, no less than the love a man feels for a woman.

Blessed are You, O Lord, who has chosen us in everlasting and natural love.

Plant the love of You in our heart in such a way that even when I walk in the marketplaces, and in the streets, and in my business, I don't turn your Godliness from my heart, even for a minute, but I meditate on You day and night.

Blessed are You, O Lord, who has connected all my limbs and my sinews with Your love.

Grant your servant merit to serve You with great works that give You satisfaction, and I am prepared to labor to the utmost of my strength, as an ox to the yoke and as a donkey to the burden, in order to magnify Your name in the world.

Blessed are You, O Lord, who has given me the merit of laboring for You without ceasing.

Yehudah Leib Ashlag

Chapter Eight

Kabbalah and Redemption

Rabbi Ashlag taught that the time in which the footsteps of the Messiah can be heard is the time in which the innermost aspects of the Torah will be revealed.

Here are the words of Rabbi Chaim Vital, the main disciple of the Ari:

So writes the young man, in humility, from the city of renowned men, of whom I am the least, Chaim Vital, the son of Rabbi Joseph Vital of blessed memory:

When I was thirty years old my strength failed me. I sat as if paralyzed, and my thoughts were confounded, for the time of the harvest has gone, the summer has ended, and we have not been saved. No healing has come to our sickness, there is no medicine for our flesh and no salvation for our wound—the destruction of the Temple, which was destroyed one thousand five hundred and four years ago.

Woe is us because the day is ending. One day for God is equivalent to one thousand of our years, and we are already five hundred and four years into the second day. The evening shadows fall. All hope is lost and still, the son of David [the Messiah] does not come. And we know from what the sages of the Talmud have told us: "A generation in which the Temple is not built is regarded as if it was destroyed in its day." [1]

So I turned my attention to inquire and know: Why are we in this situation? And why is the end of our tikkun and our exile so prolonged? Why does the son of Jesse not come?

Filled with grief and sorrow and faint at heart, I bring an article from the *Tikkunei haZohar:**

> The second pathway: **"And the spirit of God hovers over the face of the waters" (Gen. 1:2): What do the words "the spirit" mean?**
>
> **Since the holy Shechinah went down into exile, this spirit hovers over those who occupy themselves with Torah, for the holy Shechinah is to be found among them.**
>
> **This spirit becomes a voice that says, "You who sleep! You, who have sleep in your eyes, whose hearts are closed, come and wake up for the sake of the holy Shechinah! For your heart is empty and you lack the understanding to know and attain Her, even though She is in your midst."**
>
> The inner meaning of the Scripture, **"A voice says, 'Call out!'"** (Isa. 40:6) is that a voice is knocking in the heart of each and every one of Israel to encounter and to pray for the raising up of the holy Shechinah, which encompasses the souls of all Israel. The Zohar brings a proof that "calling out" means prayer, as in the book of Job: "Call out now! Is there any that will answer you? And to which of the holy ones will you turn?" (Job 5:1)
>
> The Shechinah herself says, **"'But what shall I call out?'** (Isa. 40:6) I have no strength to raise myself from the dust because **'all flesh is as grass'** (ibid). Everyone is behaving like animals eating grass and clover. That is to say, they carry out the mitzvot without any inner connection as if they were beasts. **'All their loving-kindness is as the flower of the field'** (ibid). Even all the kindness that they do, they really do

---

* The words from the *Tikkunei haZohar* are in bold, and are interspersed with the commentary by Rabbi Ashlag, taken from his *Hakdamah l'Sefer haZohar* (Introduction to the Zohar), paragraph 69.

primarily for their own benefit. They don't have the intention of carrying out the mitzvot in order to give pleasure to their Creator, but the mitzvot they do perform are carried out only to further their own self-interest. **Even those who strive in Torah carry out all their deeds of loving-kindness for their own selves.** Even the best of them, who give of their time to the study of Torah, only do this to serve their wills to receive for themselves alone and without a true intention of giving pleasure to God."

The psalmist said about such a generation (Ps. 78:39): "**Then God remembered that they are flesh; a spirit that goes and does not return**" to the world. This is the spirit of the Messiah, who is needed to redeem Israel from all their sufferings and bring them to the final redemption, when the Scripture, "The world will be filled with the knowledge of God, as the water covers the sea" (Isa. 11:9) will be fulfilled. It is this spirit that departs from the world and does not give light to the world.

Woe to those people who cause the spirit of the Messiah to depart and leave the world, unable to return to it. They make the Torah a dry desert without any moisture of inner understanding and knowledge. They confine themselves to the practical aspects of Torah **and do not make any effort to understand the wisdom of Kabbalah.** They will not contemplate the innermost principles of the Torah and the deeper reasons for the mitzvot.

Woe to them! These people cause the flow of the light of wisdom to depart. By their actions, they cause poverty, war, violence, pillage, killings, and destructions to occur in the world.

And this spirit, which is the spirit of Messiah, departs, as we have already said. And that is the holy spirit, which is the spirit of good counsel and strength, the spirit of knowledge and of reverence for the Lord (Isa. 11:2). [2]

Rabbi Ashlag elaborates on these words of the *Tikkunei haZohar* in the closing paragraphs of his essay, *Hakdamah l'Sefer haZohar* (Introduction to the Zohar):

> These words concern those people who study the Torah, but disparage both their own inner selves [the soul] and the intimate part of the Torah, [the Kabbalah] leaving them aside. They treat them as if they are something unnecessary in the world, and they don't set aside the required time for them.
>
> In relation to their own innermost aspects, they are like the blind groping along a wall. They strengthen the outermost aspects of themselves, that is, their will to receive for themselves alone. They act similarly with regard to the Torah, emphasizing the outermost aspect of Torah over the innermost aspect of Torah.
>
> Thus they cause by their deeds that all the outer aspects of the world are strengthened over the innermost aspects of the world, each aspect according to its essence. In this case, the outer aspects of Israel prevail and neutralize the innermost aspects of the community, who are the great Masters of the Torah. Likewise, the outermost aspects of the nations of the world, who are the warlords among them, prevail and hold sway over the innermost aspects, who are the saints and pious ones of the nations of the world. Then the external aspect of the whole world, which is the nations of the world, prevails over and negates the Children of Israel, who are the innermost aspect of the world.
>
> In a generation such as this, all the warlords of the nations of the world raise up their heads and want primarily to destroy and kill the people of Israel. As it is written in the Talmud, "Sufferings come to the world only on account of Israel."[3] This is exactly what we see written in the above passage in the Zohar. This is what causes poverty, violence, robbery, killing, and destruction in the whole world.
>
> To our great sorrow, we ourselves have born witness to everything that has been said in the above passage. The finest of us were destroyed in the Holocaust. As the Talmud tells us, "The righteous are the first to suffer."[4] All that remains of the community of

Israel that was destroyed in Europe is a remnant in the Holy Land, and it is incumbent upon us, the remnant, to heal this grave error.

Every one of us, from now on, should take upon himself or herself, with all our soul and strength, the work of enhancing the innermost aspect of Torah—to give it its true place as being more important than the Torah's outward aspect. In this way, each of us will strengthen our own innermost aspect, which is the aspect of Israel within us. This is the need of our soul, as opposed to our external aspects, which are our wills to receive for ourselves alone.

This power will then touch all the community of Israel, until the other nations, which are aspects within us, will recognize the value of the sages of Israel and will then want to listen to them and obey them. Likewise, the innermost aspects of the nations of the world—the righteous ones among them—will prevail and subdue the outer aspect of the nations of the world—the violent and destructive elements.

Then the innermost aspect of the world, Israel, will fulfill its true function with respect to the other nations, who will recognize, appreciate it, and value it. Then will the prophecies of Isaiah be fulfilled, "And the people shall take them and bring them to their place and Israel will settle in the Land of the Lord" (Isa. 14:2).

This is why the Zohar states: "Through this book of yours, Rabbi Shimon Bar Yochai, which is the Book of the Zohar, the redemption of the world will come about in love."[5]

Amen, may this be God's will.[6]

The Relationship Between the Individual's Inner State and the State of the World

In the above passages, we see that there is an intimate connection between how we value and relate to our inner selves and the way the world values and relates to its own inner aspects. Rabbi Ashlag enlarges on this connection:

An individual's deeds affect both the inner aspect and the external aspect of the world as a whole. When a person enhances his own innermost aspect, he causes the spiritual level of Israel to go up and then the nations of the world, which comprise the external aspect of humanity, recognize and value Israel.

But if God forbid, the opposite occurs, that an individual of Israel reinforces and values his outer aspects—the aspects of the nations of the world within him, over and above his inner aspect of Israel, then, according to the prophecy of Deuteronomy, Chapter 28, "The stranger that is within you," which refers to the external aspects of the person, "will ascend over you higher and higher, and you,"—as you are in yourself, in your innermost aspect, in your aspect of Israel within you—"will go down further and further" (Deut. 28:43). Then the person causes, by his deeds, that the externality of the world, which is the nations of the world, ascends higher and higher and has power over Israel and humiliates it to the dust, and they, that are the innermost aspect of the world, go down further and further, God forbid.

Do not be surprised by the fact that an individual person, through his or her deeds, can cause an elevation or degradation of the whole world. There is an unalterable law that the macrocosm [the totality] and the microcosm [the individual] are as like to each other as two drops of water. The same procedures that occur with respect to the macrocosm occur with regard to the individual and vice versa. Furthermore, it is the individual components themselves that make up the macrocosm, and, thus, the macrocosm is revealed only through the manifestation of its individual components according to their measure and their quality. So certainly, the act of a single person, according to his or her capacity, may lower or elevate humanity as a whole.

This is how we can understand what the sages stated in the Zohar: that it is through the study of the Zohar and the practice of the true wisdom that we may bring about an end to our state of exile and come to a complete redemption.

We could ask what studying the Zohar has to do with redeeming Israel from among the nations.

From what we have already seen, it is easy to understand that the Torah, like the world itself, has an inner and an outer aspect. Likewise, whoever occupies himself with Torah has these two levels. So to the degree that a person, when practicing Torah, strengthens and focuses on the innermost aspects of Torah and its secrets, he or she gives strength in this measure to the innermost aspect of the world, which is Israel. Then Israel begins to fulfill its true function with respect to the nations, who then value Israel's role among them.

Then shall the words of the prophet be fulfilled: "And the people shall take them and bring them to their place. And the House of Israel will settle in the Land of the Lord" (Isa. 14:2). Similarly, "Thus says the Lord God, 'Behold, I will lift up My hand to the nations and set up My standard to the peoples. And they shall bring your sons in their arms and your daughters shall be carried on their shoulders. And kings shall be your foster fathers and their queens, your nursing mothers'" (Isa. 49:22). [In other words, Israel, that is to say, the will to receive only in order to serve God and each other, will triumph over the will to receive for oneself alone, which will then act as a support to the will to receive in order to give.]

... Therefore, we can see that the redemption of Israel and all the worth of Israel are dependent on the learning of the Zohar and the innermost aspect of the Torah. The opposite is true also. All the afflictions and degradations that have come upon the Children of Israel are on account of their neglecting the most intimate part of Torah and not having valued it, but having related to it as something superfluous, God forbid.

From the words of the Sage, we see here clearly that our first obligation with regard to the tikkun of the world is to deal with our own tikkun, as it is through our own tikkun that the tikkun of the world will be carried out.

Prophetic Vision of Service

The following piece of writing, which tells of a personal vision of prophecy and of the service to which Rabbi Ashlag was called, was found among Rabbi Ashlag's manuscripts. It dates from around 1917.

It came to pass in the years of the war—during the days of the appalling massacre—that I was consumed with prayer, and I cried and wept all night. And it came to pass, as the morning dawned, I saw, in my inner vision, men of the whole world as if gathered together in one assembly. One man was hovering among them at their head, holding a sword over their heads, and he swept with his blade at their heads. And their heads flew up on high, and their bodies fell into a very great valley and became a sea of bones.

Then a voice came to me: "I am *El Shaddai*, who conducts the world with great mercy. Stretch out your hand and take hold of the sword, for now I give to you strength and power." And I became clothed in the spirit of the Lord and I took hold of the sword. Immediately, the man disappeared. I looked well to his place, but he was not. Yet the sword was in my possession for my own.

Then God said to me, "Take up your journey, leave your birthplace, and go to the pleasant land, the land of the holy fathers. There I will make of you a great and mighty sage, and through you all the wise men of the earth will be blessed. For I have chosen you to be the tzaddik and the sage for all this generation, in order that you may repair the breach of humanity with a salvation that will endure.

"Now, take this sword in your hand and guard it with your soul and with all your might. For it is the sign between Me and you that all these good things will be upheld through you. For until now, I had no other person as faithful as you to whom I can hand this sword. Therefore the destroyers have done what they have done. From now on, every destroyer who sees My sword in your hand will instantly disappear and be removed from the earth."

I hid my face for I feared to look at the One who spoke to me. But the sword that I had seen in my inner vision as a simple sword of iron, like a dreadful destructive weapon, behold! when I had it in my possession, it changed into sparkling letters of the holy name, *El Shaddai*, whose shining brilliance was filled with light, contentment, ease, and safety for the entire world. I said in my heart: If only I could give all the inhabitants of the world a pure drop from this sword, then all would know that the pleasantness of God is in the land.

And I lifted up my eyes — and behold! God was before me and said to me, "I am God, the God of your fathers. Lift up your eyes from the place where you are standing before Me and see the entire reality that I brought into existence as creation: the higher ones and the lower ones together, from the beginning of their coming forth to the revelation of existence and throughout all time, in the arrangements of their development until they will come to the fulfillment of their work as is fitting to the work of My hand to be glorified." So I saw, and I rejoiced exceedingly over the wondrous creation, and over all it contains, and in the joy and the good that all the inhabitants of the world are delighting in. And I gave thanks to God.

Then I said to God, "Before You, we shall serve in fear of being separated from You and with awe, and we will give thanks to Your name continually, for from You the evil will not go forth with the Good. Indeed, a chain of pleasantness is laid out before us, from the beginning of creation to the end, and happy are those who tread in Your world that You have prepared for them for pleasantness and delight and all good. There is nothing crooked or twisted in all the works of Your hands, neither in the higher ones nor in the lower ones." And I became filled with tremendous wisdom, and above all, the utter wisdom of the Divine Providence. So I went and added wisdom day by day, for many days: one hundred and eighty days.

In those days, it came to my heart to pray to God, saying, "Yes, I have become filled with wisdom to a greater measure than all those who came before me, and it seems as if there is nothing in the world too wondrous for me. However, I do not understand the words of the prophets and of the sages of God at all; also the holy names of God, for the most part, I do not understand." And I pondered: Yes, God has promised me wisdom and knowledge until I will become a wonder among wise men and among all created beings, yet I still do not understand their discourse.

Before I even called out, behold! God's presence inspired me, and He said, "Yes, you will see your wisdom and your comprehension go higher and higher over all the wise men that were on the earth until now, so what do you ask of Me that I have not given you? Why do you grieve your spirit in that you do not understand the words of prophecy? You should not doubt that their words were said at a lesser level than you have already grasped. Do you want Me to lower you down from your level so you could understand all their words as they did?" So I was silent and I rejoiced in ample glorification and I did not answer anything.

After that, I asked God, "But until now I have not heard anything regarding my bodily existence; all the goodness and the destiny have come to me through spirituality alone, and to spirituality it is all destined. But what will happen if through some illness or defect of the body, my intelligence becomes confused and I will sin before You? Will you cast me away from Your presence and all this goodness will be lost, or will You punish me? Then God swore to me—since you have already come to your purpose, and I have forgiven all your sins—by His great and awesome Name and by His eternal Throne, that His kindness will not leave me forever. Whether I sin or not, He will not remove His loving-kindness and His holiness from me for eternity. And I heard and I rejoiced exceedingly.

In the fullness of these days, I paid great attention to all the destinies and promises that I was destined for from God, but I did not find in them a provision and a language with which I could talk to the peoples of the world to bring them to the purpose that God wants, as He had made known to me. I could not refrain from walking among people who are empty of all, who speak wickedness about God and His creation, while I was satisfied and full of praise and rejoicing. And it seemed as if I were laughing at these unfortunates, and the matter touched me to my heart.

Then I decided in my heart that no matter what the consequences, even if it meant that I would descend from my high level, I must pour out feverish prayer to God that He should give me attainment and knowledge in the words of prophecy and wisdom and a language that will be of use to the unfortunate peoples of the world to raise them up to the level of wisdom and pleasantness like myself. Even though I already knew that it was forbidden for me to grieve my spirit, nevertheless I did not hold back, but I poured out my concern and prayer very warmly.

It came to pass in the morning, I lifted up my eyes and I saw God laughing at me and at my words, and He said to me, "What do you see?" I said, "I see two men wrestling with each other. One is wise and complete with every strength, the other is small and stupid like a little child just born. Yet the second one, who is uncoordinated, small, and weak, fells the great and perfect warrior." And God said to me, "This little one, he will be great." And the little one opened his mouth and said to me some verses that I did not understand sufficiently. Nevertheless, I felt within them all the treasures of the wisdom and the prophecy that were practiced among all the true prophets, until I knew that God had answered me and given me access to all the prophets and the sages of God. Then God said to me, "Arise on your feet and look to the east." So I lifted up my eyes and I saw this little child, in one moment, rise up and become equal to the stature of the great one. But he was still uncoordinated and lacking intelligence as before, and I marveled greatly.

After that, the word of God came to me, in a vision, saying, "Lie down on your right side." And I lay on the ground, and He said to me, "What do you see?" And I said, "I see nations and many peoples lifted up and destroyed, and their appearance is corrupted of human form." Then God said to me, "If you can give a form to all these nations and breathe into them the spirit of life then I will bring you to the land that I swore to your fathers to give to you and all My purposes will be accomplished through you." (*Manuscript in Rabbi Ashlag's own writing, found among his papers.*)

Whoever contemplates this piece of writing can see that not many years ago a great soul came to our world and lived among us. The world needs such a soul to enlighten the generations, for we, in our spiritual poverty, are like the blind feeling along a wall because of the domination of the material in our lives. Indeed, as the holy sage of Gur, Rabbi Yitzchak Meir Alter, taught:

> When the sage Rabbi Menachem Mendel of Kotsk lay dying, the chasid Rabbi Hirsch Leib of Warsaw heard the Rabbi of Gur say, "As the generations unfold, we are given, from Heaven, a greater leader, because as the generations grow sicker, they require a greater guide to lift them up. This is similar to the adage, 'the sicker the patient, the greater the need for a specialist doctor.'"[7]

Thus the Creator gave the soul of Rabbi Yehudah Leib Ashlag a unique clarity in understanding the pathways of serving God that is suitable for our generation. Such a shining soul comes to the world once in ten generations to teach those who search for the way to truly serve God. Rabbi Ashlag's teaching burns with a flame of truth.

Before the Coming of the Messiah the Darkness Increases

Rabbi Ashlag:

> Let not the heart of the reader pound when he sees elevated knowledge in my books that has never before been exposed to the light of day and until now was spoken of only behind closed doors that were locked with a thousand seals. All our predecessors, may their memories be for a blessing, prepared this, our generation, so that we should not be amazed at the revelation of the light of God as it will shine in our generation, before the manifestation of the redemption. As it is written, "and your sons and daughters will prophesy" (Joel 3:1), and as it is written in the Zohar, "and this work will be revealed at the end of days."[8]
>
> The Scripture states: "A time to act for the Lord, for they have broken your law" (Ps. 119:126). For I see that a cloud of darkness has begun to spread out in the world that will push away, as if

with both hands, all those who want to come closer to the service of God in order to cling to Him.

Through the mercy of God on this poor generation, we have been given permission to reveal the most awesome secrets to those who would understand, so that they may know the righteousness of God, that He did not withhold His providence from us. On the contrary! It is the nature of all *tikkunim* [rectifications] that before the rising of the dawn, the darkness deepens profoundly; yet the light is perceived as greater when it emerges from the dark.

We are now nearing the end of this work of creation, that is to say, we are near the end of the tikkun—the full realization of the purpose of the entire creation that is before us, which is the purification of the souls that they may become refined and cleave to His light forever. Consequently, all the powers of holiness, which hitherto were sufficient for the previous generations to enable them to cling to God in Torah and mitzvot, have been removed from this generation, and it seems to us as a sudden destruction of the forces of holiness that our fathers and mothers had bequeathed to us.

This generation does not display dissension, except in the wave of the denial of God, which has swept the world in the most extraordinary and sudden measure. This wrath has occurred in order to enable the revelation of the innermost secrets of the wisdom of God. For now there is no fear that the wicked will know how to serve their Lord [which was the reason these secrets were hidden] because such wicked, who wanted to serve God for their own self-gain, have already passed away in our time, as they are prevented from taking even the first step on the path of holiness because the power of atheism pounds them in the mortar of despicable bodily appetites without mercy.

As for the remnants, who have already been purified sufficiently to despise such bodily appetites, they are fit to know the ways of the King.[9]

Preparation for the Redemption Through Loving our Fellow

At first, the main part of our work is carried out between ourselves and our fellow. However, we find it hard to love our fellow really unconditionally because of our own innate will to receive pleasure, which constitutes the essence of our selfish love.

But there is a light that shines out from the study and application of the innermost aspect of the Torah, the Kabbalah. It is a light that illuminates our souls and directs us toward unconditional love for our fellow and for God. It gives us the motivation to do our work of letting go of our innate selfishness so that we may serve God and give to our fellow wholeheartedly, according to His will. Such work is a necessary prerequisite for the coming of the Messiah and the redemption, as the Sage of Gur (known as the *Beth Yisrael*) taught:

> The Scripture states: "He [Moses] went out on the second day, and behold, two Hebrew men were quarreling, and he said to the wicked one, 'Why do you strike your friend?'" (Exod. 2:13)
>
> The inner meaning of Moses' question was, Why don't you pay heed to the injunction, "Love your neighbor as yourself," seeing that the main cause of the exile was the lack of peace among the sons of Jacob?
>
> Furthermore, it is written: "And he [Moses] went out to his brothers and he saw their burden" (Exod. 2:11). This verse teaches us that Moses suffered along with his fellows. In so doing, he acted kindly to his fellow and increased love, which is the opposite of causeless hatred.
>
> This is what Moses our teacher began to do, and by this means, he brought the redemption of the Children of Israel closer.
>
> Likewise, in the future, when there will be love of friends and the precept of "Love your neighbor as yourself" will be upheld, then the true redemption will come. [10]

The Clear Light

The clear light! From the heavens it shines its radiance;
There, from within the curtain of the *Masach*.
There, the innermost aspect of the tzaddikim is clarified,
And they will illumine, together, the light and the darkness.

It is exceedingly good to search out His works,
But to Him, take care not to stretch out your hand.
Then you will hear Him, and so you will meet Him,
The unique Name,
In the tower of returned light.

Then a true matter will become pleasant to you.
You will be able to speak a word with no untoward influence.
And all that you will envision,
Your eyes will see,
With no intrusion from the other side.

Yehudah Leib Ashlag
Cheshvan 4, 5697 (1936)

Chapter Nine

Writing the Books

In 1927, Rabbi Ashlag journeyed to London where he was to stay for a period of two years. Although the reasons for his journey are not entirely clear, it appears that a wealthy Jew, named Margolies, had invited him as a guest, offering to supply him with all his needs, and thus providing the Sage with an opportunity to devote all his time and energy to the writing of his first major work. However, as the Sage wrote to his son, Rabbi Baruch Shalom, from Antwerp, a major reason for his journey was a desire to visit the extensive collection of Hebrew manuscripts housed at the Bodleian Library, Oxford, which the Sage wished to consult in connection with his work.

In London he would sit in his room, writing without pause for eighteen hours a day or more, completely divorced from all worldly cares. Here, Rabbi Ashlag composed the *Panim Meirot uMasbirot* (Illuminating and Welcoming Revelations). This is a commentary on the teachings of the great sixteenth century Kabbalist, Rabbi Yitzchak Luria, known as the Holy Ari. The Ari, who taught in the city of Safed, in the Galilee, did not write anything himself but taught orally. All his teachings were written down by his student, Rabbi Chaim Vital, in the book *Etz Chaim* and other works.

This first book of Rabbi Ashlag's was completely revolutionary. It not only explained the ideas of the Ari in detail, but also arranged the Ari's teachings into a logical order.

The *Panim Meirot uMasbirot* consists of two commentaries that complement each other. In the *Panim Meirot*, Rabbi Ashlag defines and explains the meanings of individual terms and phrases as they appear in the *Etz Chaim*; in the *Panim Masbirot*, Rabbi Ashlag gives broad explanations of the ideas expounded by the Ari in each section.

As each chapter was completed, Rabbi Ashlag would send it off to his students in Jerusalem, where the book was to be published. The first part of his commentary on the *Etz Chaim* reached the students on *Adar* 21, the yahrzeit of the great chasidic sage Rabbi Elimelech of Lizensk. This gave the students great joy and they resolved to hold a holy meal of thanksgiving. The only place they could find to host it was in the home of Rabbi Moshe Baruch Lemburger, consisting of the kitchen and one other room, where they all crowded in together, filled with the joy of the mitzvah. "Never did a person say the place is too crowded for me in Jerusalem" (*Pirkei Avot* 5)!

It was in this period that Rabbi Ashlag wrote to the students, urging them, again and again, to increase their efforts of establishing ever-stronger bonds of brotherly love among them. This led Rabbi Moshe Baruch Lemburger to write to the Sage, asking if it were possible for the students to make a written pledge among themselves in which they would promise to be faithful to each other and to support each other to the utmost. Rabbi Ashlag assented, writing, "I received your letter of *Tishrei* 14, and I gained much pleasure from it. Your actions are praiseworthy in your efforts to increase the love among the companions. May God bless you that you may also receive a perfect intention."

Before leaving Jerusalem, Rabbi Ashlag had requested the students to write to him of any new insights they gained in their Torah learning; for insights in Torah reveal a person's spiritual state. It was from this period that many of the letters that Rabbi Ashlag wrote to the students originate. Some of these were addressed to the individual in response to a question the student had raised; others were letters addressed to the group as a whole. Today these letters form a priceless trove of spiritual guidance on how to serve God in practice. (See The Letters on page 74.)

In a letter written to the students dated *Parashat Masai* (July 1927), in which we read the *parashah* that tells of the journeys of the Children of Israel in the wilderness, Rabbi Ashlag writes:

And what shall I tell you, natives of the land? Do you think that I am outside Israel, God forbid, and you are in the Land of Israel? I call the holy Torah as my witness! Moses, our teacher, transmits the word of God, commanding us, "The Lord spoke to Moses, saying, 'Command the Children of Israel and say to them, "When you arrive in the Land of Canaan, this is the land that shall fall to you as an inheritance, the Land of Canaan according to its borders: Your southernmost corner shall be from the desert of Zin along Edom, and the southern border shall be from the edge of the Dead Sea to the east. ..." (Num. 34:1-12) In these verses, Moses, our teacher, sets out and defines the borders of the land, with an explanation so complete that everyone who comes to the Land of Israel can have no doubt about them at all.

At this point, the Sage begins to expound the spiritual roots of the above borders of the Land of Israel. He concludes:

... Here I give you horses. If only you can set riders on them! Then you will arrive to dwell in the good and ample Land of Israel forever. Until that time, don't say that it is I who journeyed from the Land of Israel, God forbid, but it is you who are negligent in this and are not yearning, as is fitting, to dwell together with me in the Land.[1]

In the language of Kabbalah, "the Land of Israel" refers to the high level of spiritual consciousness, wherein all the person's actions, both of giving and receiving, are conducted only for the sake of giving benefit and the person is constantly in dvekut with the Creator. From this letter we see that even though Rabbi Ashlag was physically in London, in his consciousness he was one with the spiritual level designated "the Land of Israel."

Rabbi Moshe Baruch Lemburger and Rabbi David Mintzberg began the work of publishing the *Panim Meirot uMasbirot* while Rabbi Ashlag was still in London. But they managed to print only a portion of the book because they lacked the money. So they wrote on the book's frontispiece, "We would like to announce to all who are of good heart and who have the means that we have received explanations on the entire *Etz Chaim*, consisting of about two hundred articles, from the renowned author. But due to lack of means, we have been able to bring only this portion to press. We ask that you come to our aid to publish this work in its entirety."

Later on, having experienced the difficulties incurred in printing the *Panim Meirot uMasbirot*, Rabbi Yehudah Tzvi Brandwein borrowed money and, with great difficulty, opened his own printing house, "Yehudah and Jerusalem," whose purpose was to print the rest of the commentary on the *Etz Chaim* as well as to publish Rabbi Ashlag's other writings.

Rabbi Baruch Shalom:

My father asked Rabbi Lemburger and Rabbi Mintzberg to formulate the title page of the *Etz Chaim* with the commentary, *Panim Meirot uMasbirot*. Each wrote his own version, but my father rejected them, and himself wrote: "The work of the Sage, the Holy Man of God, the Living Ari."

There are many who mistakenly think that a humble person is one who lies about himself: Even though he may be aware of his own good qualities, he says of himself that he is unworthy. But this is not true humility. All the great sages knew clearly what spiritual level they had attained, in accordance with the teaching of the Talmud: "And Raba said, 'A man should know in his soul if he is a complete tzaddik or not.'" [2] That is to say, every person has an obligation to know his own spiritual level.

Those who walk the path of serving God truly see that they cannot make any movement at all without His help, but all the created beings are "as clay in the hand of the potter. With His will, He lengthens, and with His will, He shortens" (*Piyut on the night of Kol Nidrei*). Certainly, a person should not think, "It was my hand and my power that did all this" (Deut. 8:17), but he needs to come to the recognition that the human being, in himself, is puny. It is God who is gracious and gives holiness and good virtues to the human. So we see that a person should certainly be cognizant of his virtues, so that he may give thanks for all that God has given him because he is aware that all he has comes from Him. This is true humility.

Copies of the manuscript of the *Panim Meirot uMasbirot* were sent to Poland. Somehow one fell into the hands of one Hillel Tzeitlin, a Jew, who, originally from a chasidic background, had renounced his upbringing and become involved in the ideas of western philosophy. Tzeitlin published an article in the Yiddish newspaper, *Der Moment*, praising the innovative work of the holy Sage. But when Rabbi Ashlag heard that his work had fallen into the hands of Tzeitlin he was deeply shocked. Praise from such a man would only arouse opposition to his work in the orthodox circles of Warsaw. He wrote to his father:

Erev Shabbat Parshat Shelach 5687 (1927) London
To my honored father and teacher, Rabbi Simchah Halevi,

After asking after your welfare as is fitting, I must let you know that I just received a letter that pains my soul greatly, in which I learned that certain persons have handed over my holy writing to those who don't have faith in God, to make play with as they wish. And now you understand me and my oft-repeated warning to keep my work secret. This is why I did not send out my work before now, for I was afraid of this. Indeed, I had wanted to send you the articles first. Now what I feared has come to pass. Empty-heads have acted wrongly against me, doing that which I have not asked for, even after I had warned sternly against revealing my work to anyone, whoever he may be. Now they have sullied my reputation in the eyes of this generation and have placed an obstacle in my elevated service of giving satisfaction to my Creator. Who can forgive them this?

But let Heaven be my witness that I labor with all my strength to bring the holiness of the Blessed One to this generation. However, the *sitra achra* [the framework of evil] always finds men willing to do its bidding, placing obstacles in my path at every turn, obstructing my endeavor to benefit others. Nevertheless, "there are more with us than are with them" (Kings II 6:16), and the Holy Blessed One does not withhold my reward, so I am gradually making progress and clearing a pathway, sometimes more, sometimes less, but always advancing with the help of God, until

I will merit to depose those who hate the Creator, with the help of His great and awesome name.

Now don't be afraid of those who speak evil of me: my little finger is thicker than the loins of my detractors. This is what God has desired, and this is how He has acted with me. Who can tell the Blessed One what to do and how to act? The merit of my Torah is greater than the merit of their fathers.

Likewise, for Amos the prophet: the people of his generation mocked him, saying, "Didn't the Holy Blessed One have anyone else on whom to inspire the Divine Presence except on this stutterer?"[3] But it is written, "A true tongue will be established forever, whereas a lying tongue, just for a moment" (Prov. 12:19). In the end, the men of truth will have the victory. Amos is alive and endures eternally, while who has even heard of his opponents?

Such is the case here: lying tongues can only hurt their own kind. Indeed, the storm will start on the heads of the wicked. The truth is living and enduring, not weakened by the different lies, but strengthened by them, as a sown field is strengthened by the compost thrown on it. So these difficulties will actually give rise to the blessing of fruitfulness, with the help of God.

As yet, I do not feel the damage that will come to me through those who distributed my Torah, so as yet I do not know what steps to take that I may provide an appropriate vessel for its light, and save the Torah from their wickedness. But certainly, if I do perceive damage, I will take issue with them according to the rule of the Torah, and I will measure my strength against them, and whatever is in my power and my ability to do, I will do, for I fear *Elohim* and there is no other power than His.

In general, you should know for yourself that I did not write this book for my glory or for my own need, only for the sake of the Blessed and Exalted One alone. For I saw a tremendous confusion in the writings of the Ari. This has come about because the Ari did not write or arrange his own work himself, as would have been fitting for the depth of this exalted wisdom, but it was written down by Rabbi Chaim Vital, who, at the time when he heard and wrote down the teachings, had not yet attained the complete spiritual levels necessary to understand them to their root, for he was then still young of age.

Rabbi Chaim Vital was only twenty-nine years old when he first stood before the Ari. It is told in the *Sha'ar haGilgulim* [4] that in the year 5331 [1570] the Ari, who was then residing in Egypt, received the message to go to Safed in order to teach Rabbi Chaim Vital. However, the Ari's sojourn in Safed lasted only seventeen months. The Ari became ill in the year 5332 on *Rosh Chodesh Av* [the first of the month] and died at the age of thirty-eight on the 5th of *Av* that year. So we see that at the time of the Ari's passing, Rabbi Chaim Vital was only thirty years old.

It is further written in the *Sha'ar haGilgulim* that when the Ari passed from this world, Rabbi Chaim Vital was not present. This is what Rabbi Chaim Vital recorded:

Rabbi Yitzchak HaCohen told me what occurred when my teacher, may his memory be for a blessing, was dying. As I left his presence, Rabbi Yitzchak HaCohen came in. He cried before him, saying, "But this is our hope for which we all yearned; that in your lifetime, we would see good, and Torah, and great wisdom in the world." And the Ari answered him, saying, "If I had found even one complete tzaddik among you, I would not have departed this world before my time."

We still spoke on this, and then the Ari asked me, "Where did Chaim go? At such a time as this, he leaves me?" and he was very grieved. Rabbi Yitzchak HaCohen understood from the Ari's words that he wanted to pass on some inner teaching. Then Rabbi Yitzchak HaCohen said to him, "What should we do from now on?" And he said, "You shall tell the students, in my name, that from today on they should not occupy them- selves at all with this wisdom that I have taught, for they have not understood it as is fitting; however, Rabbi Chaim Vital alone may study it in a whisper in secret." And then Rabbi Yitzchak HaCohen said, "So, God forbid, there is no more hope?" And he said, "If you merit it, I will come to you and teach you." And Rabbi Yitzchak HaCohen said, "How will you come and teach us if you have already left this world?" And he said to him, "You do not need to know the mysteries of how I will come to you."

Immediately, the Ari left this world for the life of the world to come.[5]

I have copied out these words from the *Sha'ar haGilgulim* of Rabbi Chaim Vital so that you can see that the Holy Ari forbade Rabbi Chaim Vital to teach his Torah to others because, at that time, Rabbi Chaim had not completely understood the Ari's teachings with the necessary clarity. This is why Rabbi Chaim Vital did not want even to organize the notes he had made of the lessons he had heard from his Rabbi.

Those who organized these records were of the third generation; that is, Rabbi Ya'acov Tzemach, Rabbi Meir Farparsh and Rabbi Shmuel Vital, none of whom had a complete set of the teachings of the Ari. Indeed, six hundred pages of the writings were stolen in Rabbi Chaim Vital's lifetime.

Rabbi Tzemach organized most of the *Etz Chaim* and other articles from the manuscripts. But Rabbi Chaim Vital had decreed that some of the manuscripts were to be buried [placed in a *genizah*], and this had been done. The third part, he left as an inheritance for his son, Rabbi Shmuel Vital, who organized the *Shmoneh She'arim* [The Eight Gates] that are known. After a long while, Rabbi Ya'acov Tzemach, together with other students, took the third part of the writings out of the *genizah* and organized them into the first and second part of the *Etz Chaim*, the *Olat Tamid*, and other writings.

So you see that at no time did any of the collators have more than one-third of the material. But this material really needs to be considered as a whole; it is one entity, one structure. May God grant that it should suffice! Since each of the collators had only a small portion of the manuscripts, they could not understand the wisdom to its depth. Thus they confused the subject matters as they did not know how to arrange them.

You should know for sure that since the time of the Ari until this day, there was no one who understood the system of the Ari to its root. For it would have been easier to have attained a consciousness twice as great and holy as that of the Ari himself than to have attained understanding in this system, on which so many different people, from the first scribe till the last, had laid their hands, when none of them had attained the matters in their highest root. Thus each one transposed and confused the materials.

Now by the Highest Grace, may the One be blessed, I have merited to receive the soul of the Ari within me. Not because of my good deeds, but because of the Highest Will—which is hidden also from me as to why I should have been chosen to receive this wonderful soul that no man has merited to receive since the passing of the Ari until this day. I cannot talk further on this subject, as it is not my way to speak of miracles. But I find myself obliged, because of the honor due to you as my father to tell you of this, so you may be calm against the flood of strong water that comes from slaves,..., who burst out against their masters and who haven't yet understood how to separate their animal soul from their spiritual soul. For you should know, it is forbidden to have fear of these forces, which spring forth only in order to wash away everything that is holy, God forbid. May the Holy Blessed One preserve us from their hand.

I think you will believe me, for it has never been my way to lie, exaggerate, or pursue honor or fame among such stupid people. Until this day I have borne with them, as I did not have even the will to fight with them.

To give greater force to what I have said, so that you should not be confused by these soldiers of the *sitra achra*, I will tell you of a clear sign that we received from the Ari, may his memory be for a blessing, by which we may know who is a true tzaddik, or who is a tzaddik who is not true, but only has the potential to be a tzaddik and towards whom one also has to give honor.

As is known among the chasidim, signs and wonders don't prove anything, so do you think we need to draw lots in order to know who serves God and who doesn't serve Him? Perish the very thought!

You should know that Rabbi Chaim Vital asked this very same question of the Ari, and this is explained in the seventh of the Eight Gates of the Ari, *Sha'ar Ruach haKodesh*. These are his words, letter for letter:

> The sign that my Teacher of blessed memory gave me: if we can see that the tzaddik substantiates all his words, and all his words are directed only for the sake of Heaven and not even one letter of his words is nullified, and if he knows how to explain the inner meanings of the Torah and its secrets, then we may certainly trust him.

Rabbi Chaim Vital himself concluded this with these words, "And according to his words we can know and recognize his greatness and his eminence according to his connection with the Holy Blessed One." The explanation of this, is, as he wrote earlier, that when a tzaddik is truly righteous and pious, occupied in Torah and praying with due intention, then his words create holy angels and spirits, in the inner meaning of, "He who does one mitzvah acquires an angel-advocate" (*Pirkei Avot* 4:11) and the breath that comes forth from his mouth becomes a vehicle for the souls of the first tzaddikim, allowing them to descend and learn Torah with such a person. Look there carefully. He further says there, that if the mitzvot that the person does are not complete, then the angels and holy spirits that are formed from them are similarly not complete. These are called "*maggidim*."

Thus the Ari gave us a sign, that if the person's practice of the Torah and the mitzvot is complete, then he merits to a complete spiritual attainment and knows how to explain all the inner meanings of the Torah. But if he is lacking in this, in that he only knows how to explain some of these inner meanings, then certainly his deeds are not perfect. Look well there.

Now all those who would become my opponents, oppose me because they do not even understand my discourse. How is it then possible to regard them as true sages? And I have given you a clear sign.

I have already written to you that my book does not need any endorsement since I have not added to the words of the Ari, not even one word. On the contrary, I have already made references for every argument, citing their place in his writings. The Ari, may his memory be for a blessing, certainly does not require any endorsement from anyone of our generation!

I have thus acted purposefully, with intention, since I perceived the evil against me from the beginning. My own work is hardly perceptible as additional [to that of the Ari] throughout these two explanations of the Ari's writings. That being the case, on what grounds can anyone take a stand and wage a battle against this book? If such people have a complaint concerning what I have learned, well, I am more fluent in the work of the Ari than they are. If they hadn't wasted their time on nonsense they could have used this time studying the writings of the Ari. But since they were idle, now they eat their flesh (after Eccles. 4:5).

I hope you are well and my mother also and my brother Shmuel

. . . .

I await your answer to this letter. Please let me know all the details of this matter, for I need to know the details in order to take up a shield, for this is not a small matter, but it is God's work.

Yehudah Leib [6]

The Granting of Permission

Rabbi Binyamin Sinkovsky:

What was the purpose for which my teacher came into this world, and what did he innovate?

The importance of our intentions concerning how we receive and the necessity of giving unconditionally were matters already known from the writings of the Ari, but Rabbi Ashlag brought them out of silence and gave them a living expression.

Thus, in Rabbi Ashlag's work we find great prominence given to the matter of the Second *Tzimzum* [the union of Compassion with strict Judgement] and its rectification, which my Sage and teacher brought out from the hidden; clothing them with a living, useful language as a single continuum until the end of the tikkun. This is the Torah to which the Sage gave a new voice, in the inner meaning of: "The eye has not yet seen it, O God, besides You" (Isa. 64:3). For until the Ari appeared on the scene there was no knowledge of the Second *Tzimzum* and its role. Even those of the Ari's students who were closest to him did not attain what this additional *tzimzum* was about until our teacher came and opened that which the Ari had left closed.

Rabbi Ashlag revealed to me in a private conversation, not long before he departed this world, that many tzaddikim, as, for example, Isaiah the prophet and others, had reached the spiritual stage that the Ari used at the time of his teaching of the *Etz Chaim*, but they were not given permission to reveal these matters. The Ari was given permission to reveal more, and full permission was given to our Sage. He also told me that if Rabbi Chaim Vital had been present when the Ari was departing this world, then he, Rabbi Ashlag, would not have had any new Torah to add, for Rabbi Chaim Vital would have already revealed all these matters.[7]

Rabbi Ashlag:

I am happy that I was created in a generation such as this, for now it is permitted to publish the true wisdom. If you were to ask me how do I know it is permitted, I will answer you. It is because I have been given permission to reveal. That is to say, until now, those ways in which it is possible to occupy oneself in this wisdom openly, before the whole community, explaining every word according to its usage, were not revealed to any sage. For I, too, swore an oath to my Rabbi—as did all the other students before me—that I would not reveal. But this oath, this prohibition, applies only to those ways that are handed down, mouth to mouth, from generation to generation, even from before the time of the prophets. For these ways, if they were to be revealed to the common people, would cause great loss, for reasons that are hidden but known to us.

However, the way which I practice in my books is a permitted way. Indeed! I was commanded by my Rabbi to enlarge on it as much as I possibly could. This method is called by us "the clothing of matters." Look in the *Sha'ar Ma'amarei Rashbi** on the way that is called "the granting of permission." This is the way that the Holy Blessed One has granted me in a full measure. It is accepted by us that this method does not depend on any genius on the part of the sage, but solely on the state of the generation. This is in accordance with what the sages of the Talmud have taught [*Masechet Sanhedrin* 11a, see below]. It is in this vein that I have said that any merit that I have in the way of revealing this wisdom is not mine, but is due to my generation. [8]

Sha'ar Ma'amarei Rashbi:
Zohar
The son of Yochai, (Rabbi Shimon bar Yochai) knew to guard his ways, and if he entered into the deep sea, (the Malchut) he watched carefully before he entered, considering how to pass it at one time and swim in the sea. [9]

Ari
Know that the souls of the tzaddikim vary. Some have the aspect of *Or Makif* (surrounding light), some have the aspect of *Or Pnimi* (inner light). All those who have the aspect of *Or Makif* have the power to speak on the hidden and secret aspects of the Torah with great concealment in order that only those who are fit to do so will understand them. Rabbi Shimon Bar Yochai's soul was from the aspect of *Or Makif*; consequently, he had the power to clothe the matters and explain them in such a way that even if one would explain them to many people, only those who are fit to do so would understand them. Thus, he was given permission to write the book of the Zohar. Such permission was withheld

---

* *Sha'ar Ma'amarei Rashbi* is one of the *Shmoneh Sha'arim* of the Ari and consists of teachings of the Ari on the Zohar as recorded by Rabbi Chaim Vital.

from his teachers, the sages who preceded him, even though they certainly knew this wisdom even to a greater extent than he did, but they did not have the power of clothing the matters as he did. Now you can understand the great concealment that exists in the book of the Zohar that Rabbi Shimon Bar Yochai wrote. Not every mind can understand his words.

Masechet Sanhedrin 11a
The sages taught: When the last of the prophets—Chaggai, Zechariah, and Malachi—died, the holy spirit departed from Israel. However, there still issued a heavenly voice (*bat kol*). One time, the sages were sitting in an attic in Beit Guriah in Jericho, and a heavenly voice came from heaven, saying, "There is one here on whom it is fitting that the Shechinah should rest, as it rested on Moses our teacher, but the generation is not meritorious for this."

Music of the Soul

During his stay in London, Rabbi Ashlag composed melodies expressing his love for God and his longing to serve God. He picked out the notes on a piano, even though he had never formally learned to play any musical instrument. When he returned to Jerusalem, he taught the melodies to his students.

> The chasidic *niggun* [melody without words] reflects the spiritual state of its composer. The *niggun* is a certain experience expressed through melody, and the *niggun* itself creates the experience.
> *Rabbi Yosef-Yitzchak Schneersohn (the sixth Rebbe of Lubavitch)*

The Zohar teaches us the tradition of song and melody with which we express our delight when God's light—the *Or d'Chochmah*—is clothed with our unconditional giving—the *Or d'Chassadim*:

Zohar
All of them lined up in rows, in arrays, these opposing these, to sing and praise the Lord. These are the maidens of song.

Perush haSulam

Song and tune belong to the spiritual stages that are drawn from the revelation of the light of God, the *Or d'Chochmah*. But this illumination of the *Or d'Chochmah* cannot shine without the garment of the light that comes through loving-kindness (*Or d'Chassadim*).

Thus song is conducted when the light that comes through acts of loving-kindness—the *Or d'Chassadim*—is included together with the illumination of the *Or d'Chochmah*, the revelation of the light of God. [10]

In the Torah we find song expressing great thanksgiving for the overt miracles given to our forebears, as, for example, in the song that Moses and the Children of Israel sang when they witnessed their deliverance at the parting of the Red Sea. Then a great revelation of the *Or d'Chochmah* was revealed to all; furthermore it was clothed by the light that comes from giving unconditionally, the *Or d'Chassadim*. We can see this clearly from the description in the Torah: "And Israel saw the great hand that God had wrought against the Egyptians" (*Or d'Chochmah*), "and the people had reverence for the Lord and believed in the Lord and in Moses, His servant" (*Or d'Chassadim*). This is immediately followed by: "Then Moses and the Children of Israel sang this song to the Lord... ." (Ex. 14:31–15:1) Such a song is thus a vessel for the revelation of God's light when it is clothed in the light of giving, as explained in the Zohar above.

The psalms sung by David are, likewise, a celebration of the revelation of the light of God as he rejoiced in the holy spirit that descended on him. "Sing to the Lord a new song" (Ps. 96:1). The words of the psalms are spiritual vessels for the light of God. Later, the singing of the Levites in the Temple formed the foundation of the melodies of prayer.

After the destruction of the Temple, the expression of joy through song in Jewish life became restricted to times when the revelation of God's light is more manifest, such as on the Sabbath, the festivals, and celebratory occasions such as weddings.

It was the Baal Shem Tov, the founder of the Chasidic movement, who innovated the *niggun*, which is a melody sung with or without words. The *niggun* is sung to express the yearning of the soul for connection with the Holy Blessed One through the opportunity of serving Him. A *niggun* may therefore be sung at any time as there is no need to wait until God's light is actively revealed, for giving is right at any time.

The soul's yearning to give to the Creator finds expression in two opposite feelings, both of which are given a voice in the *niggun*. First, the soul feels its separation from God and longs to come closer to Him. This is felt as exile, a feeling of sorrow, which leads to prayer that wells up from the depths of the heart, piercing the firmaments. These feelings of separation form the vessel for the light of God. The second feeling arises when subsequently a person merits to come close to God. He no longer takes this closeness for granted, but feels the delight and preciousness of the merit he has been given. At these moments a person is able to feel the importance of spirituality in his life. Feelings of joy and gratitude well up when he realizes that the Creator has granted him the merit of serving Him.

Thus we find that some *niggunim* express our longing for God and our sorrow at our separation from Him, while others express gratitude and thankfulness that God has brought us near to Him, giving us the privilege of serving Him, yet others move, within the same melody, from one state of consciousness to the other. Thus the chasidic *niggun* does not replace the song of the traditional prayer service or the *zemirot* (table hymns) of Shabbat, which are sung when the light of God is revealed, but adds a new dimension.

Many chasidic masters composed *niggunim*. For the master it is an expression of his joy of being allowed to serve God and his longing for unity with the Creator; for the disciple who sings, the *niggun* connects him with the heart and soul of the sage and imbues him with the same desires and joys.

The *niggunim* of Rabbi Ashlag uniquely express both his clear vision of the spiritual worlds—his vision of a higher consciousness—and his longing to give to the Creator. The melodies and songs of the Baal HaSulam are sung and played today in ever-widening circles.

Chamol al Ma'asecha

חמול על מעשיך

ר' יהודה ליב הלוי אשלג זצוק"ל

חֲמוֹל עַל מַעֲשֶׂיךָ

words: *Rosh HaShanah* liturgy
music: Rabbi Yehudah Leib Ashlag

Chamol al ma'asecha	חֲמוֹל עַל מַעֲשֶׂיךָ
V'tismach b'ma'asecha	וְתִשְׂמַח בְּמַעֲשֶׂיךָ
Vyomru lecha chosecha	וְיֹאמְרוּ לְךָ חוֹסֶיךָ
Btzadekcha amusecha	בְּצַדֶּקְךָ עֲמוּסֶיךָ
Tukdash adon al kol ma'asecha	תֻּקְדַּשׁ אָדוֹן עַל כָּל מַעֲשֶׂיךָ
Ki makdishecha bikdushatecha kidashta	כִּי מַקְדִּישֶׁיךָ בִּקְדֻשָּׁתְךָ קִדַּשְׁתָּ
Naeh l'kadosh pe'er mikdoshim.	נָאֶה לְקָדוֹשׁ פְּאֵר מִקְּדוֹשִׁים

Chamol al Ma'asecha — Have Pity on Your Works

Have pity on Your works
And rejoice in Your works.
Let those who shelter with You say
They take up Your burdens according to Your righteousness.
Be sanctified, O Lord, over all Your works,
For You have sanctified with Your holiness those who proclaim Your holiness.
It is fitting for the Holy One to receive glory from those who are holy.

Return to Israel

In September 1928, the Sage wanted to return to Israel, but he didn't have the money, so his wife sent him a ticket so he could return. In the event, he did not return to Givat Shaul. Instead, the family moved to the area called Batei Warsaw, next to Meah Shearim, where they lived nearby the home of Rabbi David Mintzberg.

In 1932, Rabbi Ashlag moved to the Naveh Shalom district of Tel Aviv, close to Jaffa. The family joined him as soon as he had found permanent lodging. Usually, the Sage chose an apartment that had one large room for the purpose of holding prayers and studying. But it appears that this time, there was no possibility of finding such a place, so the students and the families built a beit midrash adjoining the apartment outside. Everyone helped. Even the women and children carried buckets of cement and sand and hoisted the wooden planks.

Batsheva Reichbard, his daughter, relates:

> My father's students built the building with their own hands. I remember that my brother, Rabbi Baruch Shalom, and his friend Rabbi Yehudah Tzvi Brandwein, would get up to learn at one o'clock in the morning. Straight after morning prayers, they would start work on the building. Rabbi Brandwein had also moved apartment in order to help with the building, after which he moved back to Jerusalem. However, even after he had returned to Jerusalem, he and the other Jerusalem students would journey regularly to the Sage.

In 1936, when Rabbi Ashlag moved to Bnei Brak, he established his beit midrash on Ben Petachiah Street.

Reaching Out: *Matan Torah*

Rabbi Ashlag's vision extended far beyond the province of the religious world. As we will see in chapter sixteen, he sought contact with the socialist leaders of the Jewish Yishuv in Palestine. At this time, he began to write a set of articles specifically for the secular Jew—articles in which he sets out the philosophy underlying the Jewish religion.

This is the philosophy of unconditional giving. Rabbi Ashlag also demonstrates the specific role the Jewish people has in giving this philosophy of altruism a practical expression for themselves and in bringing it to the rest of the world.

In some of these articles, it is clear from their language that Rabbi Ashlag was well-read in the different schools of modern Western philosophy. He knew the work of Descartes, Kant, John Stuart Mill, and others, which he seems to have read in their original languages.

Rabbi Ashlag's interest in and use of philosophy does not imply that the philosophers were in any way the source of his ideas. All his ideas are clearly traceable to the works of the Ari and the Zohar, which provided the well-spring of his inspiration. But his knowledge of modern western philosophy enabled Rabbi Ashlag to consider how the teachings of Kabbalah, fitted with or contended with the prevailing thought governing contemporary secular society, and to address these issues appropriately. Furthermore, it enabled him to couch the teachings of Kabbalah in terms that were familiar to secular society. This was, and still is, important, as the language of Kabbalah is not one easily acquired, and thus the ability to express its main ideas in a familiar language is of great value.

These articles were originally published individually as small pamphlets, but the mandatory British authorities, who were the controlling government at the time, forbade Rabbi Ashlag to continue with their publication on the grounds that the articles constituted a newspaper; and they issued licenses for newspapers only to those who could prove they had a secular education of a certain literary standard. At first, Rabbi Ashlag tried to get around the British by putting out the articles under a different name, but when he saw that the British persisted in their efforts to stop him he desisted. In 1933 the published articles were first gathered together under the title *Matan Torah* (Gift of the Torah).

For many years, this book was composed of the twelve articles that were known.* But recently the organization, Or HaSulam, has managed to discover many that Rabbi Ashlag wrote, but had been unable to publish. Although Rabbi Ashlag wrote these essays specifically for

---

* For a list of articles, see *Matan Torah (The Gift of the Torah)* on page 344.

the secular Jew of his day, their appeal has widened and they now have much to say to people of all streams and backgrounds.

Talmud Eser haSephirot (The Study of the Ten Sephirot)

While living in Tel Aviv, Rabbi Ashlag commenced writing his major work, the *Talmud Eser haSephirot*, a work that encompasses most of the Ari's teachings. As in his previous work on the writings of the Ari, the *Panim Meirot uMasbirot*, Rabbi Ashlag re-arranged the teachings of the Ari into a logical order, describing the development of the spiritual levels as they give rise, one to another.

On his reasons for this additional work he wrote:

> There is one strict condition to the study of this wisdom, which is to not make any materializations concerning either imaginary or physical terms. If a person is not careful with this, he may infringe the commandment, "You should not make any idol or graven image for yourself." The person would then be damaged rather than helped by this material. It was for this reason that the sages warned that this material should only be studied by someone over the age of forty or directly from a master, as a precautionary measure, so that no one would fall into the above-mentioned trap.
>
> I have prepared, with God's help, my explanations of the *Etz Chaim* with just this purpose in mind, to ensure that the reader does not err regarding his understanding of terms that are borrowed from the physical world, but which refer to purely spiritual realities.
>
> However, after the first four volumes of this explanation [*Panim Meirot uMasbirot*] were printed and distributed, I saw that I had not fulfilled my obligation in explaining this material as well as I had thought. All the tremendous effort that I had put into explaining and expanding on this material—so that it would be readily understandable—was almost completely wasted. This was because those who studied the material did not feel the great necessity of being absolutely clear about the meaning of every single word used and the need to go over each word many

times. It is important to remember the precise meaning of each word in every place where it occurs throughout the book. By forgetting the precise meaning of even one word, the matters under discussion become confused. Due to the sensitivity of the material, a misunderstanding of one word is enough to undermine one's whole understanding.

In order to rectify this, I began to write an explanation of essential terms, arranged according to the alphabet. I included all the words that require an explanation that are to be found in the books of Kabbalah. In this dictionary, I put the Ari's explanations together with those of earlier Kabbalists, listing everything they had to say about the word in question. I also included a summary of all these explanations and I gave my own definition of the term. This material is quite sufficient for anyone interested in understanding the meaning of a word, whenever he or she should come across it in any true book of Kabbalah, written by either the early or the later Kabbalists. I continued with all the frequently used words in Kabbalah. I have already published, with God's help, the words beginning with the letter *Aleph* and some of the words that begin with the letter *Bet*. This material already runs to almost a thousand pages.

However, due to lack of funds, I had to cease this work in its early stages. It has been almost a year during which I have been unable to continue with this most important work. Only God knows what will be its fate, for it is very costly, and at present, I have no one to help me.

Therefore I have taken another course, on the basis of the Talmudic maxim: "A vast goal is difficult to achieve, whereas a limited goal is very achievable," [11] and so I have written the book *The Talmud Eser haSephirot* [The Study of the Ten Sephirot].

In this book I have collated all the principal articles from the writings of the Ari that are relevant to the explanation of the ten Sephirot. I have placed the words of the Ari at the top of each page, and I have written a comprehensive commentary on the specific words the Holy Ari uses. I have called this commentary *Or Pnimi* [Inner Light].

I have also composed an additional commentary for each chapter that explains the concepts that the Ari teaches, at every spiritual stage. I have called this commentary, *Histaclut Pnimit* [Inner View]. These two commentaries together explain every word and concept to be found in the words of the Ari, as set out at the top of the page, as simply and as clearly as I can.

I have divided the book into sixteen chapters, and a particular aspect of the ten Sephirot is addressed in each chapter. The *Or Pnimi* primarily explains the words of the Ari found in that chapter and the *Histaclut Pnimit* explains the general issues that are discussed.

I have also set out a table of questions and answers concerning the words and the concepts discussed in each chapter. After the reader has completed each chapter, he should try to answer all the questions by himself. Then he should compare his answers with those provided. Even if he remembers the answers very clearly, he should go over the questions many times until he is utterly familiar with the concepts. Then he will remember the meaning of every word when he needs it, or, at the very least, he will remember where to look up its definition, and God will help him to succeed.[12]

This great work thus organizes the work of the Ari into a logical and progressive sequence, starting from the level of the Ein Sof (the Infinite) and describing the spiritual levels through which the soul passes in the framework of holiness before it comes into the body. The processes of the soul that we find described in the works of the Ari and in the Zohar are all descriptions from the perspective of the "created beings." The term "created being" refers to the human being who exists at all conscious levels, from one who is completely separate from God in his consciousness to one who is a tzaddik in complete dvekut with the Creator. Of all created beings, it is only the human being who can feel himself to be separate from God.

When we first encounter this work and others that Rabbi Ashlag wrote on the Torah of the Ari, they appear to us to be discourses of technical information regarding spiritual processes. But if we ponder them slowly, we begin to see that they actually consist of precise and detailed descriptions of processes that pertain to ourselves. Their study opens us to an awareness of ourselves and our processes in great precision and honesty, and also leads us to appreciate the deep benevolence of the Divine Providence. For an in-depth appreciation of the scope of this great work, see *The Talmud Eser haSephirot* (The Study of the Ten Sephirot) on page 336–342.

Batsheva Reichbard:

> My holy father would work on his book, the *Talmud Eser haSephirot*, every night. He wrote it in very long columns, in a very small handwriting, in which the words were written close together. Every morning, he would give me the work of the night before to type on the typewriter, following which, a stencil was made of the pages for the purpose of printing them.

The Introductions and Essays

Some of the introductions that the Sage wrote to his works, namely, the *Hakdamah l'Panim Meirot uMasbirot* (the Introduction to the Illuminating and Welcoming Revelations), the *Hakdamah l'Talmud Eser HaSephirot* (The Introduction to the Study of the Ten Sephirot), and *Mavo l'Zohar* (The Prologue to the Zohar), are not introductions in the usual sense of the word. The main works which they preface are all volumes of deep complexity dealing with the dynamics of light and vessel. The introductions, however, are written in a totally different style, containing philosophical dissertations on the nature of creation, and our role in it. They cover such diverse ideas as the essence of the human being; our purpose in our incarnation; the paradoxical association of ego and soul; the true nature of Torah, its path and its destination; the nature of our relationship with the Creator; the language of Kabbalah and many others. (See Rabbi Ashlag's Works, The Introductions and Essays on page 343 .)

Rabbi Baruch Shalom said, "My father told me that he wrote the introductions in such a way so they would appear simple on the surface. This was intentional so that only one who is fitting would be able to see the true depths in them." Indeed, although these essays are often the first material the student learns, they contain profound ideas that are not apparent on first reading.

Rabbi Ashlag's Shofar

It burned within him. The memory of his vision of humanity lost and wandering never left him, neither did he forget the charge laid on him to help and succor. He wrote and wrote until his dying day. In this moving piece, Rabbi Ashlag likens his writings to the sounding of a shofar, calling out to we, who are lost, to come to the oasis of the inner wisdom and drink.

Our society is analogous to a band of travelers who, starving and thirsty, are wandering in a desert. Suddenly, one of them finds a settlement wherein there is all good. He remembers his unfortunate brothers, but he has wandered far away from them and doesn't know where they are. What can he do? He begins to shout in a loud voice and sound the shofar [ram's horn]; maybe his starving and wretched companions will hear the sound and draw near to him, and then they also can come to the settlement filled with good.

So is the matter before us: we, together with the rest of humanity, have been wandering in the dreadful desert of the lack of knowledge of God. But now we have found a great treasure, filled with all good—the books of Kabbalah. This is the treasure that satisfies the yearning of our souls and fills us with contentment and ease. So we eat our fill and even have some left over.

But the memory of our companions, who are still lost in the dreadful wilderness, is engraved on our hearts. Even though the distance between us is great and we cannot communicate with them, nevertheless, we have organized this shofar with which we call out. Maybe our brothers will hear, come close to us, and be happy like ourselves?

Know, my dear brothers, my own flesh, that the main thrust of the wisdom of Kabbalah is the knowledge of how the world devolves from the perfection of the heavenly heights all the way down to our lowliness.

The end of an action is contained in its original thought. The fulfillment of thought when it pertains to the Creator is instantaneous. Unlike ourselves, the Creator does not require any vehicle in order to implement thought. Therefore, in accordance with His Thought of Creation, we emerged directly in our complete perfection in the Ein Sof,* and then we devolved down to this world. It follows that it is very easy for us to find all the required *tikkunim* [rectifications] that we have yet to do from the knowledge of the processes of the spiritual worlds that preceded us, and from them, we may know how to correct our ways from now on.

The human being has an advantage over the beast, whose spirit descends. That is to say, it cannot see further than itself. It has no intelligence or understanding to know what it went through in the past in order to correct its future. Humankind has an advantage in that the spirit of the human ascends to the past [that is, to the higher worlds from which we emerged in our spiritual past]. A person may look into the past—since the world devolves from the perfect to the imperfect—as one looks into a mirror; thus he may see how to correct his defects. So a person who is intelligent looks into his past—as described in the wisdom of the Kabbalah—and consequently rectifies his needs from then on. **

By contrast, there is no spiritual development for the animals. They still stand at the same level of consciousness at which they were created, because they do not have a mirror through which

---

* The Ein Sof is the spiritual level at which the Thought of Creation is manifest.

** The Holy Ari described the dynamic processes of light and vessels that pertain to each of the spiritual worlds as they devolve down to this world. Since the work of the human being is to ascend this spiritual ladder, he may learn how to progress up through understanding the processes involved in the descent of the worlds. See the discussion Rabbi Ashlag's Works, The Talmud Eser haSephirot (The Study of the Ten Sephirot) on page 336.

they can understand how to correct their ways, and through which they could gradually develop, as the human has.

Humankind gradually develops, day by day, until its worth is certain and felt. All this is true regarding our dealings with natural, external ways, that is, in our dealing with the nature of the physical reality surrounding us: our food, and our external affairs, for which our natural intelligence is certainly sufficient. However, regarding our inner selves and our essence, our natural intelligence is not sufficient. We do develop a little, but our development and improvement occur by being pushed from behind, through suffering and the spilling of blood. This is because we have no [natural] tactic through which we may attain a mirror that will enable us to see the innermost aspects of those who lived in generations gone by. This is even more the case with regard to the innermost workings of the souls and of the worlds, [we need such a mirror] so we may learn how they developed, and how we came to this dreadful destruction to which we bear witness today; such a great destruction, that we will have no surety of our lives, and we are about to be slaughtered through strange deaths within the next few years, and all acknowledge that we have no counsel how to prevent this.

Just imagine for yourselves: If, for example, today, you were to find a book that describes the generations that will come to be in another ten thousand years—a book that describes both the wisdom of the nations and the ways of the individual, then our leaders would be searching in it for every remedy by which we may organize our life here and now, until we come to the state in which, "there is no scream in our streets" (Ps. 144:14), when all the slaughters and the dreadful suffering will be nullified and everything will come to its correct consciousness in peace.

And now my friends, here, in this cabinet, you have arranged and laid before you, the book in which all the wisdom of the nations, and all the ways of the individual and of the community that will actually come about at the end of days, is written and explained. This is the book of the Kabbalah, in which are laid out the rectified worlds that came forth in perfection, since, from God, perfection comes forth first. Accordingly, we may correct our ways and come to the same perfection that already exists and is manifest in the highest world of the Ein Sof, in the original Thought of Creation, according to the principle that the completion of an action depends on its original conception.

From the Perfect, the imperfect can emerge only through a gradual process, stage by stage. In the realm of spirituality, nothing is lost, every stage exists and is described in all its likeness and character, both in its general aspect and in detail, in the wisdom of the Kabbalah.

Open these books and you will see the correct order of the good that will become manifest at the end of days. From them you will obtain a good doctrine on how to organize matters today, even regarding the needs of this world. We can learn from the history of what has passed and thus correct the history yet to come.

And all this I have placed on my heart until I can no longer refrain. I received approval from God to reveal something of what I perceive and of what I have found written in these books of Kabbalah concerning the ways of the *tikkun* [rectification] of our certain future. I will go forth to the children of the world with this shofar, which, in my opinion and evaluation, will suffice to gather all those who have merit, that they should start to learn and meditate in the books and thus tilt themselves, and all the world, to the side of merit. [13]

Chapter Ten

Why Should We Study Kabbalah?

As we saw from the letter that Rabbi Ashlag wrote to his father, he anticipated the furor the publication of his work was going to cause. The whole question of whether an ordinary person is even permitted to study Kabbalah was a burning one. For generations, the study of Kabbalah had been hidden from the general populace. Now that Rabbi Ashlag was opening up this intimate part of the Torah for everyone, it became necessary for him to address the concerns of ordinary people regarding the permissibility and even the value of such study. This is how Rabbi Ashlag opens the *Hakdamah l'Talmud Eser haSephirot* (Introduction to the Ten Sephirot):

> At the beginning of this discourse, I discover a great need within myself to shatter an iron curtain that separates us from the wisdom of Kabbalah since the time of the destruction of the Temple right up to our own generation. This barrier has burdened us to a serious degree and awakens the fear that Kabbalah might even be forgotten in Israel, God forbid.
>
> When I begin to advise people concerning the study of this subject, their first question always is, "But why do I need to know how many angels there are in heaven and what their names are? Surely I can keep the whole of the Torah in all its fullest details without this type of knowledge."
>
> Secondly, they ask, "Didn't the sages already decide that before studying Kabbalah, a person must first 'fill his belly' with Talmud

and Jewish Law? And who could possibly fool himself into think-ing that he has already completed the entire revealed Torah and all that he lacks is the concealed Torah [Kabbalah]?"

Thirdly, some people are afraid that they may go off the path as a consequence of this study. There have been cases in the past where people strayed from the way of Torah as a consequence of studying Kabbalah. Therefore people ask, "Why should I risk it? Why should I be so foolish as to place myself in danger for no good reason?"

Fourthly, even those who love this learning permit it only to very righteous people who serve God; and not everyone who wants to take it up may do so.

But the fifth objection that people raise is the main one. There is a halachic principle that where there is a case of doubt we look at the common practice. A person tells me, "When I look at the people who practice Torah in this generation, I see that they have unanimously abandoned the study of this hidden wisdom. They even counsel those who ask them that, without any doubt, it is better to spend one's time studying a page of Talmud than to occupy oneself with Kabbalah."

These are questions that Rabbi Ashlag was faced with then, and many of us still ask them now. He answered:

However, if we consider only one very famous question, I am sure that all these questions and doubts will vanish over the horizon and disappear as if they had never been. The burning question asked of all the inhabitants of this world is, What is the point of our lives? Why do we live these number of years, which cost us so dearly? We go through so much pain and suffering in order to complete them till their end. Who can really say that he enjoys his life? Or, even more pointedly, is there anyone who benefits from my life? The truth is that the philosophers have left off pondering this question, and it is certainly the case that in our generation no one even wants to consider it.

Nevertheless, the essence of this question still stands in all its force and bitterness. Sometimes it comes upon us unawares and bores into our brains, casting us down to the very dust until we hit upon the well-known strategy of allowing ourselves to be swept up thoughtlessly into the stream of life, just as we did yesterday.

Scripture gives the solution to this obdurate riddle in the phrase, "Taste and see that God is Good" (Ps. 34:9). Those people who fulfill Torah and mitzvot in the correct way are those who taste the true taste of life. They see and bear witness to the fact that God is good. The sages have taught us that God created the worlds in order to benefit us and all created beings. It is in the nature of the Good to do good. But it is certainly the case that one who has not yet tasted the life of fulfillment in Torah and mitzvot can neither understand nor experience that God is good in the way that the sages taught: that God's whole intention in creating the human being was only to give benefit to all. Therefore the best recommendation for us is to begin to practice Torah and mitzvot in the correct way. [1]

What constitutes the correct way to practice the Torah and mitzvot? Rabbi Ashlag discusses this issue:

> There is a general opinion among the populace that the main purpose of the Torah and the religion is solely to provide practical training. This would imply that their purpose may be achieved through the fulfillment of practical mitzvot without any additional accompaniment; without anything further coming from the mitzvah beyond its actual performance. If this were the case, then those who say that it is enough for us to learn only the revealed Torah—which deals solely with practical issues—would be correct.
>
> But this, in fact, is not the case, as the sages have already taught:
>
>> "What does God care if we slaughter the animal from this side of the neck or the other? The mitzvot were given only to purify human beings from their selfishness and to bring them into affinity of form with the Creator." [2]

So we see, there is yet another purpose that springs from our fulfillment of the practical mitzvot: that our practical fulfillment of the mitzvot prepares us to purify our ego. It is obvious that if the mitzvot aren't being carried out in a way that fulfills the purpose for which they were specifically designed, it as if they aren't being fulfilled at all! Indeed, the Zohar states: "A mitzvah without intention is like a body without a soul." So obviously, it is necessary that the correct intention should accompany the practical performance of the mitzvot.

Furthermore, it is clear that the intention needs to be a true one that befits the action. The sages of the Talmud taught that the Scripture: "'And you shall be holy to Me, for I the Lord am holy, and I have set you apart from the peoples that you should be Mine' (Lev. 20:26) means that a person should not say, 'I don't like pig meat, therefore, I will not eat it,' but he should say, 'I like it, but what can I do since God has decreed otherwise?'"[3]

If the person refrains from eating pig because it disgusts him or for health reasons, then his restraint cannot be considered a mitzvah. But if he were to accompany his restraint with a fitting and unique intention of fulfilling the commandment solely because the Torah has specifically forbidden the eating of pig meat, then his action is counted as a mitzvah.

Such considerations hold true for every single mitzvah. Combining intention with action through the practical fulfillment of the mitzvot according to the intended purpose of each mitzvah, allows a person's ego to gradually refine. This is the ultimate aim.

Therefore, for us to confine our learning to the practical aspects of the mitzvot is not sufficient. We also need to study matters that will bring us to desire the correct intentions so that we will be able to fulfill every mitzvah through faith in the Torah and faith in the Giver of the Torah.

Certainly, to acquire faith in the Torah and to acquire a true understanding of the consequences of our actions, whether favorable—bringing us into affinity of form with the Creator, or, God forbid, separating us from Him, requires much study of suitable books. Even prior to performing the mitzvot, we need studies that will purify the ego and accustom it to having faith in God, in His

Torah, and in His Divine Providence. As the sages of the Talmud have said, "I created the *yetzer hara* [evil inclination], I created the **Torah** to be its healing." [4] The sages did *not* say, "I created the *yetzer hara*, I created the mitzvot to be its healing," because "the guarantor would need a guarantor itself"! [5] Indeed, the *yetzer hara* delights in throwing off any yoke and will not allow us to fulfill the mitzvot with the proper intention unless we gain the requisite inspiration and motivation from the Torah. [6]

The light that is in the Torah helps us recognize the propensity for evil that is within us that separates us from the Creator and also gives us the strength to prevail over this evil. Therefore, a person who sincerely wants the truth should, after a certain period of time, ask himself the question, "Has my study of the Torah helped me in my purpose of dealing with my selfish love?" In many of his writings, Rabbi Ashlag demonstrates that it is easier for many people to achieve this aim from the study of Kabbalah. Kabbalah is the inner aspect of the Torah and does not hide the essence of God, whereas, in the revealed Torah, the light in Torah is more hidden.

Indeed, Rabbi Chaim Vital, the great student of the Ari, wrote in his introduction to the *Etz Chaim*:

> But if the student finds that the study of Talmud is burdensome and hard for him, it is best that he leave it and turn to the practice and study of the true wisdom, which is Kabbalah. This is what is meant by the passage in the Talmud, "If a student of Torah does not see a sign of blessing in his studies after five years, then he never will." [7]

The question is: What do the sages mean by "success in study"?
Rabbi Ashlag answers:

> By the term, "not succeeding," Rabbi Chaim Vital does not intend intellectual understanding or expertise, but rather, he means that the person finds that his egoism is still active within him in all its force and has not softened at all.... .

> If this should be the case, Rabbi Chaim Vital advises the person to turn to the study of Kabbalah because it is easier through the

practice and effort of the study of Kabbalah to draw to oneself the illumination inherent in Torah, than it is through labor in the revealed Torah.

The reason for this is very simple. The wisdom of the revealed Torah [the Talmud] is clothed in external physical garments: it deals with issues such as stealing, robbery, damages, and the like. Therefore, it is very difficult for anyone to keep focused on God and to draw to himself the light of Torah while learning this material. This is even more so for one who finds the study itself difficult. How is he meant to remember the Creator during his study when the subject matter pertains to the physical world? How can he possibly keep his intention directed toward the Holy Blessed One when dealing with material matters?

Therefore, Rabbi Chaim Vital counsels such a student to occupy himself with the wisdom of Kabbalah because this wisdom is entirely clothed in the names of God. Then, naturally, the student will be able to direct his mind and heart toward God during his study without effort, even though the subject matter is extremely difficult since this wisdom and God are one. [8]

Rabbi Baruch Shalom taught at the *Rosh Chodesh* gathering *Tammuz,* 5744 (1984):

> Cleaving to true books influences a person and brings him to the desires and powers of the authors of such books. The purpose of the study is not the knowledge *per se*, but the knowledge is the means that brings the desire for holiness—the will to give benefit unconditionally—to the heart. "At the end of the matter, everything is understood: 'Revere God and keep His commandments, for this is the whole purpose of Man'" (Ecc. 12:13). And this is the measure of his stature as a human being.

Rabbi Baruch Shalom (A lesson from 1989):

> The sage Rabbi Chaim of Sanz said, "When a person comes to me and asks if he can learn Kabbalah before the age of forty, I answer, 'It depends why you want to learn. If you want to learn in order to increase your knowledge of the Torah, then it is forbidden. But if

you want to learn in order to attain *yirat shamayim* [reverence of God] it is permitted.'"

Likewise, Rabbi Baruch Shalom quoted Rabbi Avraham Isaac Kook as saying:

If a person wants to learn the wisdom of Kabbalah in order to fulfill the commandment of learning Torah—that is, just as he wants to complete his learning in the Torah that pertains to halachah so he wants to complete his study in the hidden part of the Torah—then he needs to wait until he is forty years old. Only when he has already filled himself sufficiently in the revealed Torah is he permitted to turn to this wisdom. But if someone wants to learn Kabbalah because he feels empty and unsatisfied, he feels he lacks faith and *yirat shamayim*, he is full of questions and doubts, then there is no limit at all whatsoever.

Rabbi Ashlag writes at the end of the *Hakdamah l'Talmud Eser haSephirot* (Introduction to the Study of the Ten Sephirot):

We can ask why the Kabbalists said that it is important for everybody to study Kabbalah?

In this lies an important matter, which should be stated publicly. Studying Kabbalah is of inestimable value in a person's spiritual progress. Even though a person may not understand what he is studying, through his great desire and strong will to understand, he awakens the lights that surround his soul.

Everyone is destined to arrive at this wondrous level of consciousness that God intends to bestow on all creatures according to the Purpose of Creation. If a person does not reach this level in this incarnation, he will certainly reach it in a subsequent one until he becomes worthy of fulfilling the specific purpose that God has planned for him. Until a person reaches his perfection, the lights that are destined for him in the future remain as surrounding lights. This means that these lights are ready and prepared for him, but are waiting until he merits the attainment of suitable vessels for these lights, and then the lights will be clothed within the transformed vessels.

Therefore, even at a time when the person lacks such vessels, but is occupying himself in the study of this wisdom, whenever he mentions the names of the lights and the vessels with which his particular soul has a connection, they immediately shine upon him to a certain degree.

However, they shine without being clothed in the innermost part of the soul as the person still lacks the transformed vessels to receive the lights. Nevertheless, the illumination that the person receives, time after time, whenever he studies Kabbalah, brings down upon that person favor from the higher worlds, and the higher worlds bestow upon him an abundance of holiness and purity, which bring a person very close indeed so that he may come to his perfection. [9]

However, one must not fall into the opposite trap of studying Kabbalah without the revealed Torah and mitzvot; both need each other, as Rabbi Chaim Vital writes:

"A person should not say, 'I will go and practice Kabbalah before I practice the Torah of the Mishnah and Talmud,' for the Rabbis have already said, 'No one should study Kabbalah if they have not already filled their belly with Mishnah and Talmud. This would be like a soul without a body, lacking any contact with this physical world. A person is not fully incarnate until he becomes involved at the physical level with the mitzvot of the Torah.'

But the opposite is also true: If one studies Mishnah and Talmud without also spending time in studying the innermost aspects of Torah and its secrets, he is like a body sitting in darkness, lacking a human soul, which is the light of God that shines within. The body becomes dry because it is not taking from Torah, the source of life. Therefore a student who wishes to practice Torah for its own sake needs to start by occupying himself with Bible, Mishnah, and Talmud, absorbing as much as his intellect can gather. Afterward, he should turn to the practice of Kabbalah and come to know his Creator through it, in the way that King David commanded his son Solomon, "Know the God of your father and serve Him" (Chron. 1 28:9). [10]

The Necessity of Establishing Schools
Where the Innermost Aspect of the Torah is Learned

Rabbi Ashlag:

Why is it written in the Zohar, "that it is this composition that will deliver the Children of Israel from exile"? [11] Likewise, it is written in other places in the holy books that only when the wisdom of Kabbalah is widely known among the people will we merit the full redemption.

Our sages have said, "The light that is in the Torah will bring a person back to the good way." [12] They made this statement with great precision and intention, informing us that it is only the illumination that is in the innermost aspects of the Torah that can bring a person back to the good way. This is analogous to the orange in the proverb, "A word fitly spoken is like an orange on a silver-plated tray" (Prov. 25:11); the peel is thrown away and all its goodness is contained in its innermost aspect. It is this innermost aspect that has the virtue of bringing a person back to the good way.

Neither an individual nor a nation can accomplish the purpose for which they were created except through the attainment of the innermost aspect of the Torah and its inner meanings. Even though the complete perfection of knowledge will come to us only with the advent of the Messiah, nevertheless it is written, "[God] grants wisdom to the wise and knowledge to those who know understanding" (Dan. 2:21) and "in the heart of every wise person I have given wisdom" (Exod. 31:6). Therefore, as a requirement prior to the coming of the Messiah, we need the widespread propagation of the innermost wisdom of the Torah throughout the community so that we will be fit to receive the benefits that the Messiah, our righteous one, will bring us. Thus we see that the widespread dissemination of the wisdom and the coming of the Messiah are dependent on each other. Understand this deeply.

Since this is the case, we must establish houses of study and write books in order to hasten the promulgation of this wisdom among all people. Such houses of study were not established in former times because of the fear of having students who were not worthy. However, the lack of such study is the reason the exile has continued, through our many sins, to this day.

The sages of the Talmud have said, "The Messiah, the son of David, will come only in a generation that is entirely worthy or in one that is entirely wicked."[13] What is a worthy generation? One in which everyone abstains from chasing after their own honor and desires. Then it will be possible to establish houses of study for all people to enable them to prepare for the coming of the Messiah, the son of David.

Or, as the Talmud continues, the Messiah may come in a generation that is entirely wicked, that is, in a generation like ours, "in which the face of the generation is as the face of a dog and which rejects those who fear sin and for whom the wisdom of the scribes stinks."[14] Then, equally, it will be possible to remove the excessive watchfulness that kept Kabbalah closed and hidden from the general community. In this circumstance, the remnant of the House of Jacob, whose heart yearns to attain this wisdom and to fulfill the purpose for which they were created, will also be able to come and learn. There will not be then any fear or suspicion that a student will falter in his ethical standards, who would still want to go and sell this wisdom in the marketplace for his own purposes, for there will be no buyers among the entire populace, the wisdom being despised in their eyes. So the seller will not get anything for it: neither fulfill his desire nor gain honor.

Of this remnant of the House of Jacob, the Scripture states: "And it shall come to pass that every survivor shall be in Zion, and everyone who is left in Jerusalem, 'holy' shall be said of him, everyone who is inscribed for life in Jerusalem" (Isa. 4:3). Therefore, whoever wants to enter into this wisdom may come and enter. And many will wander, but the knowledge will increase for all those who are worthy of it, and through this, we may soon merit the coming of the Messiah, the redeemer of our souls, speedily, in our days, Amen. [15]

Chapter Eleven

Connections with the Great Sages of Israel

Rabbi Ashlag was greatly esteemed among the true sages of his generation. These came from diverse streams in Judaism including, Lithuanian, Chasidic, and Sephardi. In general, his work was not valued by those of lesser stature who, not understanding it or estimating its importance, tended to oppose it. But the generation in which Rav Ashlag lived was most blessed in that there were sages of great caliber who welcomed his teaching.

Rabbi Yisrael Alter — the Beit Yisrael — the Sage of Gur

The Beit Yisrael, Rabbi Yisrael Alter, remained deeply connected with Rabbi Ashlag throughout his life. Together with his saintly father, Rabbi Avraham Mordecai Alter, he had miraculously escaped Poland during the war, but many thousands of Gur chasidim perished in the destruction of Polish Jewry. Rabbi Yisrael Alter's life work was to rehabilitate the orthodox tradition in Israel in general and that of the chasidic tradition of Gur in particular with the remnants who survived.

Rabbi Alter held Rabbi Ashlag in great esteem, journeying several times a year to be with him and to be nourished from his Torah. Once, when Rabbi Ashlag wanted to return the visit, Rabbi Alter was genuinely surprised and sent a messenger to Rabbi Ashlag begging him not to take such pains and expressing his astonishment at the very idea that such a holy man of God should trouble himself for him!

When the students of Rabbi Ashlag came to Rabbi Yisrael Alter to request an endorsement for the books, he asked, "Why should Rabbi Ashlag need an endorsement from anyone?" They answered that their real reason was their lack of funds to publish the books and that such endorsements would help to obtain financial support.

Following the passing of Rabbi Ashlag, Rabbi Baruch Shalom continued the connection with Rabbi Yisrael Alter and would meet with him twice a year, on *Chol haMoed* Succot and on *Chol haMoed* Pesach. At these meetings, the two sages would discuss the inner meanings of the Torah and the service of God. When they parted, it was with great love and respect. Rabbi Baruch Shalom said, more than once, that Rabbi Alter had a very strong attribute of truth.

Rabbi Avraham Yeshaya Karelitz—the Chazon Ish

The Chazon Ish belonged to the Lithuanian tradition and was the son of the Rav of Kosova. His mentor was Rabbi Chaim Ozer Grodzinski. He left Vilna for the Holy Land in 1933 making his home in Bnei Brak. Although he lived a secluded life dedicated to Torah studies, he was widely read in astronomy, mathematics, anatomy, and botany. He became a formative influence on the chareidi community in Israel.

In 1936, when Rabbi Ashlag moved to Bnei Brak, he established his beit midrash on Ben Petachiah Street. The Chazon Ish lived opposite and a great friendship sprang up between the two rabbis. On *erev* Pesach, the Chazon Ish came to bake his matzot in Rabbi Ashlag's oven.

The Gaon, Rabbi Shmuel Auerbach, tells that one day Rabbi Ashlag came to visit the Chazon Ish and they spoke together for a long time before they parted. For the rest of that day, the Chazon Ish repeatedly exclaimed that he had learned from the Sage that a person needs to give of his utmost, and indeed, sacrifice all that is dear to him, for this is the inner meaning of the Scripture: "and all of its fat he shall offer up as a sacrifice from it" (Lev. 7:3) —that is to say, from himself.

Rabbi Avraham Ashkenazi:

The Chazon Ish would correspond regularly with Rabbi Ashlag. In those letters he would ask many questions on Kabbalah to which my teacher would write answers. I was the messenger who passed the letters between them.

Rabbi Azriel Lemburger:

Once, Rabbi Ashlag taught one of the Chazon Ish's students: The Scripture states, regarding the tribe of Issachar: "Issachar is a large-boned donkey lying down between the sheep-folds. He saw a resting place that was good and the land that was pleasant, but he bent his shoulder to bear [burdens] and became an indentured laborer" (Gen. 49:15).

Issachar found that of all things that which he most prized was rest; nevertheless, he gave up his rest and "bent his shoulder to bear [burdens] and became an indentured laborer." This teaches us that the Holy Blessed One wants us to give up to Him that which we most value; that which we feel has the most importance for us. Issachar gave up that which he most prized—his rest—for the sake of God.

When the student told this to the Chazon Ish, his enthusiasm knew no bounds. The Chazon Ish was known for his extreme diligence in his labor in Torah and would not cease until he was really unable to continue.

Rabbi Avraham Yitzchak HaCohen Kook

Rabbi Avraham Yitzchak Kook (1865–1935) was the first Ashkenazi chief rabbi of British Mandatory Palestine. He advocated the combination of Zionism with the orthodox practice of Judaism and founded Mercaz HaRav, the foremost religious Zionist yeshivah. Known for his great piety and deep concern for his fellow Jew, he was a renowned Torah scholar, combining an extraordinary proficiency in both Halachah and Kabbalah. Like Rabbi Ashlag, Rav Kook knew that the time in which Kabbalah needs to be opened to the general community had come.

In a letter written in May 1927, Rav Kook wrote:

The light of salvation and source of blessing for the last generation will shine forth in the revelation of the inner secrets of the true Torah. Many will roam its paths, the knowledge of it will increase, as will the discussion of its wisdom; and the glory of the Torah, through its innermost secrets, will be known throughout all the borders of Israel. May the name of the Master of all wonders be magnified and sanctified. May He speedily bring us the light of salvation.

Great souls, such as Rav Kook and Rabbi Ashlag, are rare, and when they occur in the same generation they take delight in each other. Indeed the two sages formed strong bonds of friendship and mutual regard.

When Rabbi Ashlag was in London, he specifically asked Rabbi Yehudah Tzvi Brandwein to take copies of his manuscript, *Panim Meirot uMasbirot*, to Rav Kook. On reading the work, Rav Kook wrote:

Tevet 9, 5690 (January 9, 1930)

I come with these words bearing good tidings for all those who seek God and who yearn and thirst for the words of the living God, the Torah of truth, which is stored up, hidden by His might.

Regarding the words of the holy Zohar and its sages: The foremost of all the holy vessels in which the holy and hidden lights are sealed with chains and concealed is the Torah of the most holy sage, the Ari z"l. This was organized in the holy and awesome book the *Etz Chaim* by his disciple Rabbi Chaim Vital, for whom the light of the East shone.

And now has come the godly sage, master of understandings, the holy treasure, the honorable sage in awesome holiness, our rabbi and teacher Rabbi Yehudah Leib Ashlag of Givat Shaul, on whom the spirit of the Lord has rested to compose this holy work—the *Panim Meirot* as a condensed explanation; and the *Panim Masbirot* as a contemplative stroll through the *Pardes* of Torah—in sweetness of thought and in amplitude, explaining every hidden aspect in well-sourced introductions. It is the truth of Torah in authentic foundations. [Rabbi Ashlag] has enlarged on the wisdom, penetrating it deeply and has brought up holy pearls from its depths. Every palate that tastes of it will say, "This enjoyment suffices me!" Blessed is she who bore him.

Words go forth from this Elder who has acquired wisdom and holy knowledge and who walks the path of holiness and purity. He is fit to serve the crown of the Torah of truth that was hidden away in the highest service of God.

Sometimes Rabbi Ashlag would sit in on Rav Kook's shiurim listening intently to his teachings. One of Rav Kook's pupils, Rabbi Zusman, reported that he noticed Rabbi Ashlag sitting quietly at the side during the shiur. He did not draw any attention to himself neither did he say who he was. When Rabbi Ashlag's work began to be published, Rabbi Zusman felt tremendous surprise that this quiet man was a sage of great stature. Rabbi Moshe Yair Weinstock and Rabbi Yehudah Tzvi Brandwein would also attend shiurim of Rav Kook's; whereas, one of Rav Kook's foremost students, Rabbi Ya'acov Moshe Harlap, often joined with the students of Rabbi Ashlag.

Following the passing of Rav Kook, Rabbi Ya'acov Moshe Harlap was appointed the head of Mercaz HaRav Yeshivah. He wrote:

1937
My heart is greatly sorrowed over the humiliation of the Torah, in particular with regard to the learning of Kabbalah. For despite the fact that in recent generations the holy obligation to occupy ourselves with the Torah of the Kabbalah has been clearly publicized and it is through its study that we are spared from the evil inclination and our entire hope of salvation depends on this holy learning, nevertheless, it has been completely abandoned. Without a doubt it is true that through this neglect our spiritual and physical sorrows and troubles multiply in all our communities.

My heart truly rejoices when I see the awakening brought through my friend, the great Kabbalist and teacher, Rabbi Yehudah Leib Ashlag, who has taken such pains to publicize the importance of this holy Torah and has established a beit midrash for learning the wisdom of Kabbalah. I beg to strengthen his hands and request all those who know me to strengthen those who are learning in this school, so we will all merit to taste from the Tree of Life.

May we speedily see that God redeems His people. May the light of His true Torah and the revelation of His glorious and sovereign name be blessed and revealed speedily and in our time. Then all flesh will see together, for the mouth of the Lord has spoken.

Waiting for the near salvation,

Ya'acov Moshe Harlap

Sages from all streams of Judaism, including even some of those who opposed the views of Rav Kook, notably Rabbi Yosef Chaim Sonnenfeld and Rabbi Doek, venerated Rabbi Ashlag greatly and studied his works. Prominent among them were Rav Eliahu Dessler and Rav Eliahu Lopian, who were great sages of the Mussar movement.

Yet for the most part, Rabbi Ashlag remained hidden, concentrating on his life's work. This can be seen from the following excerpt of a letter that Rabbi Leib Tzaddik, author of the work *Tzidkat haTzaddik*, wrote after Rabbi Ashlag's death:

> You asked me to write to you about the Kabbalist, Rabbi Ashlag. I don't know what to write to you. He hid himself, not wanting the world to know of him. But I can tell you that since the days of the Holy Ari there was none like him who revealed new Torah in the learning of Kabbalah. He mostly wanted—and in this he succeeded—to give explanations to the students so that they would know what they are learning, even organizing an index of questions in his book, the *Talmud Eser haSephirot*, so that they could check for themselves what they had learned and understood. From Heaven he was sent to us, to enlighten the eyes of the generation so we will not deceive ourselves.
>
> This much is clear, that before the coming of the Messiah this wisdom will be revealed. And this will be through the hands of Rabbi Ashlag, may his memory be for a blessing.

Chapter Twelve

The Synagogue in the Bukharian Neighborhood

In 1937, Rabbi Ashlag returned to Jerusalem. The family moved several times within the city before settling in a house on Mayesof Street in the Bukharian Quarter. Rabbi Ashlag was given free use of this building by a Bukharian Jew, whose only request in exchange was that Rabbi Ashlag should bless him with the traditional blessing given at the reading of the Torah each Shabbat.

Batsheva Reichbard:

> My father hardly ever left the doorway of the house. Indeed, wherever we lived, a room was always set aside so he did not need to go out. He did all his writing at home where he would pace the roof of the house, deep in thought and in connection with his Creator.
>
> I was educated at home as at that time there were no suitable schools for girls. My father arranged for a woman to come and teach my sisters and me to read the prayer book and the Bible. But when I was older, I complained, "Father, I am already grown, but I don't know anything." He answered, "If you can get up at five in the morning, I will teach you." So thereafter followed a period in which I rose at five, and my father dedicated some of his precious time to me and taught me Torah and some mathematics.

Rabbi Azriel Chaim Lemburger:

> The Rabbi wrote the *Mavo l'Zohar* [Prologue to the Zohar] in one night, but on the following morning, he suffered a heart attack. The family called Rabbi David Mintzberg and my father, Rabbi Moshe Baruch, who arrived at nine in the morning. I remember my father telling me, "The Sage has already finished his work in this world with regard to the tikkun of his soul. However, each time he searches for another way with which to serve God and then another way. Because he had finished the work of the *Mavo l'Zohar*, he was in a state of completion, and thus he suffered a heart attack. The truth is that for himself, he no longer has any need to be in this world."
>
> I remember that our holy Sage sat at the table. He had no strength to do anything. On the table were some candlesticks. Without intending to, he touched one. He became alarmed. He said he felt as if it was the Shabbat now. My father explained that since the Sage was not writing, it seemed to him as if the Shabbat had come [when it is forbidden even to touch the candlesticks].
>
> The family doctor visited the Sage and told him that in order for his nerves to rest, he must not concentrate deeply on his study. He suggested that, instead, it would be beneficial for the Sage to recite psalms. But Rabbi Ashlag replied, "But how can one say psalms without pondering deeply on them?"
>
> Following this episode, Rabbi Ashlag required a long period of rest until he recovered sufficiently to return to his writing.

Rabbi Binyamin Sinkovsky

It was at this time that a new pupil, Rabbi Binyamin Sinkovsky, arrived.

Rabbi Binyamin was born in Kovno, Lithuania, and was connected to the great Rabbi Chaim Soleveitchik of Brisk. Not long after his arrival in Israel, he met with Rabbi Ashlag in Tel Aviv, and from then on, he remained devoted to the Sage with all his heart and soul. Rabbi Binyamin exuded goodwill and a strong desire to get closer to God. When in prayer, he would pace from wall to wall, full of love and enthusiasm.

Rabbi Azriel Chaim Lemburger:

> My father, Rabbi Moshe Baruch, said that Rabbi Binyamin's joy
> gives testimony, equal to that of a thousand witnesses, that he is
> not a simple person.

An ordinary person, not involved with the service of God, is happy and
joyful when his life is flowing for him, but sad when the reverses of life
afflict him. The chasidim, however, place great emphasis on maintaining one's joy in every circumstance, both positive and negative. If we are
sad, it is as if we are telling the Creator, "The way You run the world is
not a good way!" Rabbi Ashlag taught that sadness is even considered
as *lashon hara* (slander) against the Master of the universe. As Rabbi
Nachman of Bretslav taught, "It is a great mitzvah to be happy!" Rabbi
Binyamin's ability to maintain his happiness in all situations and in
every circumstance testified that he was a man of great spiritual stature.

Rabbi Ashlag dearly loved Rabbi Binyamin and held many private
talks with him especially toward the end of his life. Rabbi Binyamin
carefully noted down all his encounters with the Sage: teachings that
he received as well as conversations, many of which he recorded verba-
tim in Yiddish. In his notes, which have been collected as *Yad Binyamin*,
we thus have a precious record of *yechidut*, the one-on-one, sage-to-
pupil encounter, which, in just a few moments, may change a person's
life entirely.[1]

Yechidut: Entering the Sage's Presence

Rabbi Azriel Chaim Lemburger:

> When I was seventeen, I came into Rabbi Ashlag's presence with
> a list of requests. Before I entered the Sage's room, my father
> crossed something off the list and then the Rabbanit let me in,
> telling the Sage, "He is already a man in his own right." (Until then,
> they had all related to me as a young boy.) The holy Sage stretched
> out his hand and I felt a tremendous feeling of joy. After that, he
> blessed me, actually, on the very thing that my father had crossed
> out! As he read the note, he made no discernible movements, but

his face turned color, from red to white, then from white to pale, then back to red. All this, while he read the note. It was a most amazing thing to see.

When I left his presence and went out into the street, I felt as if the passersby were absolutely mad. Who would leave eternal life and busy themselves with things of no moment? It seemed completely crazy! The feeling I took with me from the few moments I was in the Sage's presence stayed with me for about ten days and then gradually disappeared. Much later, I asked him, "Why did this wonderful feeling disappear?" He answered me, "A child, while he is yet small, needs to be led by his hand. Only after that, does he learn to walk on his own."

When I was a young man, the holy Sage said to me, "Be devoted to the books of the Baal Shem Tov and his students."

Even a simple sentence when said by a man of God takes on enormous significance.

The Festivals

Just as the festivals are special days in the life of the Jewish people so they were in the lives of Rabbi Ashlag and the students.

Rabbi Ashlag writes in his commentary on the Zohar:

The twelve months of the year, from beginning to end, constitute the tikkun of the souls, which, collectively, comprise the tikkun of the Malchut [the Shechinah]. Only at the *gmar hatikkun* [the perfected state of creation] will this tikkun be complete. Until then, we need to return each year and rectify Her. [2]

The year is divided into months, weeks, and days, according to the Scripture, "And God said, 'Let there be lights in the firmament of the heaven to divide the day from the night; and let them be for signs, and for seasons, and for days, and for years'" (Gen. 1:14).

Each day is distinguished by its place in the week; each week is distinguished by its place in the cycle of the year—designated by the weekly Torah portion; and each month is distinguished by *Rosh Chodesh*, its first day, and by the festivals unique to it.

Thus every single day has its own specific tikkun. Every prayer, even though it uses the same words as yesterday, is a completely new prayer. Likewise for the festivals—even though we celebrated the festival last year, this year is an entirely new festival, for its particular light has never been in the world before. Therefore, we need to prepare for it with a fresh and unique energy, as the sages teach in the Talmud:

> A man is required to give joy to his children and his household on the festivals, as it is said, "And you shall rejoice on your festivals" (Deut. 16:14). With what should he give them joy? With wine.
>
> Rabbi Yehudah says, for men, with what is fitting for them, and for women, with what is fitting for them. For men, what is fitting is wine, but what is fitting for women? Rabbi Yosef taught, in Babylon, colored clothes are fitting; in the Land of Israel, linen clothes that are ironed. [3]

If we examine this paragraph from the Talmud using the language of the Kabbalah as a key to its meaning, we can see that the sages of the Talmud are actually holding a discussion determining what is the essence of a festival, and what are the appropriate means with which to receive that essence.

In the language of Kabbalah, "male" relates to the mode of giving unconditionally; "female" relates to receiving for the sake of giving; "wine" refers to the *Or d'Chochmah*—the light that comes directly from the Creator; and "clothes" refer to the specific vessels, that is to say, the desires with which we may receive the light of the festivals.

So the sages of the Talmud are teaching us that the essential essence of a festival is a unique time of revelation of the divine light, the *Or d'Chochmah*, "the wine." In order to receive this light, we need to prepare specific vessels for it. These, the sages refer to as "clothes." Through our preparations for each festival, both physical and spiritual, and through the festival's specific mitzvot and customs, we create the appropriate vessels within ourselves with which we may receive the great light of the festival. Indeed, the joy of the festival is felt both in the preparations and on the festival itself in giving and receiving unconditionally.

Preparations

Succot

Already, from *Rosh Chodesh Elul,* a full six weeks in advance, the students would be on the watch for a beautiful etrog for the Sage's use on Succot.

Batsheva Reichbard:

> My holy father did not usually spend his time in dealing with physical matters, but when it came to Succot, he would draw different designs for beautifying the succah. He would pass these on to my brothers, Rabbi Baruch Shalom and Rabbi Shlomoh, who would engrave them in wood. We also used to hire Persian carpets from the carpet factory which we would lay down in the succah. All this meant that we had to amass a considerable sum of money in preparation for the festival.

Rabbi Azriel Chaim Lemburger:

> Once, the Sage sent me to the shop to buy some specific building material for the succah. But when I brought it to him, he told me to change it, and then he sent me back again and again! My own nature is such that if I buy something from a shop and I later see that it isn't exactly what I want, I don't go to change it because I feel embarrassed. I manage with what I have. But when I went on these errands for the Rabbi, I didn't feel such embarrassment. Even when I had to go back and change the merchandise, I would do so very willingly. I didn't feel any inconvenience either to myself or to the seller. I know the Rabbi sent me specifically to teach me that it is in accordance with our appreciation of the greatness of the Creator that we are blessed with new powers and are able to dedicate ourselves to His service.

Building the succah took a long time, with Rabbi Ashlag taking the utmost care with its construction and beauty. The students helped—first building the succah of the Sage and then turning to build their own.

Pesach

The preparations for Pesach were immense: All Jews spend the month between Purim and Pesach preparing the house by ridding it of *chametz* (leaven) and procuring the necessary foods for the festival. But the Rabbi kept many additional customs according to the chasidic traditions of his own teachers. To our limited understanding, some of these customs may seem irrational, but the students kept them willingly, through faith in the wisdom of the sages. These strictures meant that Rabbi Ashlag did not rely on factory-produced food during Pesach. He would eat only matzot baked on the eve of Pesach after midday from flour that had been stone-ground by hand.

Since all the students drank the coffee, 15 kilograms of coffee beans were purchased on *Rosh Chodesh Nisan*, two weeks before the festival. These needed to be sorted through, roasted, and ground by hand. This was a huge job that took much time.

"Kosher for Pesach" sugar was bought before the festival, cooked with water, and the liquid sieved. This syrup served as sweetener throughout the festival. For salt, the students would drive to the Dead Sea where they dug from the big salt rocks, which they would then crush in a grinder kept specially for this use.

Several months before Pesach, the families and the students would buy some of the little hot red peppers called "shata" and lay them out to dry. This would be used for flavor on the festival.

Wine was bought from a trustworthy, religious Jew who made the wine himself and who did not add any other substances to the wine; not even sugar.

All the meat and fish, fruit and vegetables were purchased before the festival, and the eggs boiled beforehand. Rabbi Ashlag ate only those fruits and vegetables that are possible to peel. The surfaces of the kitchen were covered with tin or stainless steel as the Rabbi did not use any vessels made of plastic or nylon. All utensils were glass or metal.

Festival Customs

Usually the Sage prayed in his room, close to the beit midrash, even on festivals. However, on Rosh HaShanah, he would join the minyan to hear the sounds of the shofar; his whole being aflame with holiness. He would call out the notes for Rabbi Ya'acov Mordecai Brandwein who blew the shofar.

At dawn, on the eve of Yom Kippur, Rabbi Ashlag would fulfill the custom of *kapparot* (atonement ritual) according to the teachings of the Holy Ari. The shochet would come and the Sage would check his knife for the *shechitah* (ritual slaughter of the chicken used in this ritual). Only those specifically trained are qualified to check the shechitah knife, which needs to be checked for minute defects, with great patience, twelve times. Only when the Sage had approved the kashrut of the knife would he allow the shochet to do his work. In fact, whenever they ate meat, the Rabbi would check the knife himself.

Batsheva Reichbard:

> My father was extremely strict concerning the fast of Yom Kippur, even with regard to pregnant women. This was in contrast to the fast of Tisha b'Av for which he took a more lenient approach.

On Simchat Torah, the Sage would dance with the Sefer Torah on every *hakafah*.* His dance was very unique; an upward yearning of connection with the Creator.

Rabbi Zalman Lemburger:

> On Purim, our holy teacher would arrange his table as a *tisch*, lasting twelve or even fourteen hours! In all that time, he would drink an enormous quantity of wine, but this was not at all noticeable. He would discourse on the innermost meanings of Purim over many hours. Between every talk, the students danced with all their might. Even the most serious of the students would dress up, no one taking any account of their prestige.

---

* On Simchat Torah, the Torah scrolls are taken out of the ark, and with much joy, the men encircle the *Bimah*, dancing with the scrolls. Each *hakafah*, encircling, represents a Sephirah.

Rabbi Baruch Shalom:

My holy father always used to say that the most beautiful verse in the *megilah*, the book of Esther, is: "And Mordecai went forth from the presence of the King in royal apparel of blue and white, and with a great crown of gold, and with a robe of fine linen and purple; and the city of Shushan shouted and was glad" (Esther 8:15).

Rabbi Avraham Brandwein:

On Purim, the students would usually stage a play based on their study. Once, my father and Rabbi Baruch Shalom dressed up as two chasidic sages; one as the "Sage of Nemenov" [*nemen* means "to receive" in Yiddish] and one as the "Sage of Giterov" [the sage of giving].

The Great Light of the Festival Shines Out

Usually, Rabbi Ashlag hid his spiritual attainment, but on the festivals, his intimate connection with the higher worlds became more obvious. Rabbi Zalman Lemburger:

> On the first day of Succot, when our holy teacher entered the succah for the first time, his face would change color with a deep excitement, his feet treading heavily on the floor. All of us could feel him burning with a huge energy, an energy not possible to express in words.

For all the students, the high point of every festival was the *tisch*, at which the students would gather, sitting for hours, as the Sage—his whole being aflame in unity with the light of God—expounded on the innermost meanings and teachings of the festival, its specific light of revelation, and the vessels we must rectify in order to receive this light. These discourses form an entire web of wondrous instruction in the service of our Creator and in the inner meanings of each festival. When the festival was over, Rabbi Baruch Shalom would transcribe from memory all he had heard his father say. Rabbi Baruch Shalom's notes have been gathered together and form part of the collection entitled *Shamati*. Through Rabbi Baruch Shalom's untiring efforts, we have been privileged to receive these unique teachings with which Rabbi Ashlag opens a doorway for us to connect with the light of each festival, a light that comes to us from the higher worlds.

The Second World War

Rabbi Zalman Lemburger:

> During the Second World War, airplanes bombed Tel Aviv and many people fled the city. At that time, Rabbi Ashlag was living in Jerusalem. However, he called to my father and the Rabbanit and asked them to rent a flat for him in Tel Aviv.
>
> They traveled to the city and on finding a suitable flat, approached the owner to sign a contract with him, but he was an honest man and told them about the bombing and the flight of the people. So they returned to Jerusalem. When they told the Sage what had happened, he told them to go back and rent the flat, as it was precisely because of the bombs that he wished to move to Tel Aviv. Indeed, three days after the Sage moved to Tel Aviv, the bombing stopped completely, and after a fortnight, he returned to Jerusalem.
>
> The students asked him why he did not travel to Europe and protect it from the Nazis in a similar way. But Rabbi Ashlag said that his presence was able to help only within his immediate surroundings.

Rabbi Ashlag's chevruta and friend of his heart, Rabbi Mordecai Moshe Shultz, did not survive the inferno. Rabbi Ashlag also lost his brother, Rabbi Shmuel, in the Holocaust. May their memories be for a blessing.

Rabbi Yehudah Leib Ashlag — The Baal HaSulam

"I will go forth to the children of the world with this *shofar*... ."

"And you shall teach them diligently to your children and speak of them,"
(Deuteronomy 4:7)

A hand-written page of Rabbi Ashlag's commentary
on the *Etz Chaim*, the *Panim Meirot uMasbirot*

ספר הקדוש

עץ החיים

מהאר"י ז"ל

עם שני המאורות הגדולים מסביב לו מאירים ומסבירים דרך

עץ החיים ה"ה

פנים מסבירות	פנים מאירות
ביאור רחב המסביר טיב עומק החכמה כראוי	ביאור קצר ומספיק, לפרש דברי המחבר
למתחילים: בתוכן עשר הספירות, והעולמות,	זלה"ה בתכונתם הרוחני, למעלה מהמקום
והפרצופין, ותכונת השתלשלותם זה מזה,	ולמעלה מהזמן: ומפנה כל מקשה
ודיוק מקומות הלבשתם זה את זה, ואשר כל	מהדרך. בהגלותו אדני החכמה בעומק
אלה מתחיבים בדרך קודם ונמשך, מנקודת	תחת, ובעומק רום:

הצמצום עד לעה"ז ועד לגמה"ת, ונותן דרכי התבונה בכללות בכתבי האר"י ז"ל, בכדי
לראות לאורותיהם. גם בדברי הזהר והתיקונים, אשר עליהם סובבים הקדמותיו ז"ל.

מפעלות אדומו"ר איש אלקים קדוש האר"י החי' יהודה הלוי אשלג שליט"א הרב
ודמו"ץ בגבעת שאול פרור ירושלים עיה"ק תובב"א.

חלק א'

ואנו מודיעים לאנשי לבב ולבעלי חיכולת שהשיגנו מכ"ק אדומו"ר המחבר שליט"א הפירושים הנ"ל על כל
העץ החיים כמאתיס קונטרסים אשר מחזור אמצעים לא עלה בידינו להדפים זולת ב' חלקים ואנו מבקשים
שתבואו לעזרתינו להוציא כל החיבור לאור.

המו"ל דוד מינצבערג משה ברוך למבערגער

נכאים דבית החסדים המסתופפים בצל קדושת המחבר שליט"א.

נדפס

בעיה"ק ירושלים תובב"א

שנת תר"ץ לפ"ק

בדפוס "יהודה וירושלים" מול בתי אורנשטיין

Rabbi Moshe Baruch Lemburger—
Unending devotion to his Rav

L to R: Rabbi Karelitz, Rabbi Baruch Horovitz, Rabbi Baruch Shalom Ashlag,
Rabbi Joshua Sender Horovitz
"Behold! How good and pleasant it is for brothers to sit together."
(Psalms 133:1)

Rabbi Baruch Shalom Ashlag *(left)* with
Rabbi Menachem Simchah Edelstein—
He radiated joy to all who came into contact with him.

Rabbi Baruch Shalom Ashlag *(left)* with
Rabbi Avraham Ashkenazi—
He was wholehearted in his service of God.

L to R: Baal HaSulam's grandson at his wedding; Rabbi Azriel Chaim Lemburger (*standing*); Rabbi Yehudah Leib Ashlag; Rabbi Shlomoh Binyamin Ashlag (*brother*); Rabbi Yehudah Tzvi Brandwein.

Signing the *Ketubah*

Rabbi Baruch Shalom HaLevi Ashlag,
Baal HaSulam's first-born son and devoted student.
Later on, sage, following his father.

Chapter Thirteen

The *Perush HaSulam* on the Zohar

In 1942, Rabbi Ashlag began his great work, his commentary on the Zohar, the central text of Kabbalah. He called his commentary *Perush HaSulam* meaning "The Ladder," and he became known as "Baal HaSulam," "The Master of the Ladder."

He wrote:

> The depth of the wisdom that is in the holy Zohar is closed with a thousand locks, such that our human language is woefully inadequate to fully explain even one word in this book. The commentary that I have written is only a ladder to help anyone, who is so moved, ascend to the heights of the matters, and be able to look and investigate the words of the book itself. [1]

Rabbi Ashlag put his whole self into writing this work. Even though he was suffering terribly from rheumatism, he would sit and write for eighteen hours a day. On many occasions his hands would swell from the strain of the writing. His granddaughter, Rachel Levi, told us how the members of the household would put cushions under his arms to try to lessen the pain. But he continued to write in a state of complete dvekut with the Creator. Nothing deterred him, for he knew that this was the will of God. He paid no attention to anything that could distract him. In addition to his writing, he also continued his shiurim for the students, who would arrive from all over the country.

A Jew named Chaim Naeh, who lived in a nearby neighborhood testified:

> The Sage would have the holy Zohar open in front of him together with the pages of his commentary. He would meditate deeply on the Zohar, write a few pages, and then go out into the courtyard where he would pace back and forth. Then returning, he would write again, and again go out to the courtyard. And so he did, night after night.

Typesetting and Printing

The material simply flowed. Anyone who looks at the amount of written work the Baal HaSulam produced is amazed. His ideas did not need revision or editing; they flowed directly from his attainment in the higher spiritual worlds onto the paper in front of him. In this way, thousands of pages came from his pen. As he wrote, he organized the pages into the final form they were to take, such that each page was ready for printing. The words of the Zohar were written right across the page, and underneath, Rabbi Ashlag wrote the *Perush haSulam* in two parallel columns.

Rabbi Baruch Shalom took overall charge of the printing of the *Perush haSulam*. Once, his father came to the printing shop, and as he sat there, he began to say out loud a completion to a certain page. So on the spot, Rabbi Baruch Shalom set up the metal type letters on the printing press as his father spoke.

It was extremely difficult to raise the money to pay for the printing of the books. The Sage and the pupils all lived in dire poverty. Furthermore, at that time, the price of paper and ink was prohibitively expensive. In many instances, the Baal HaSulam wrote that he had cut his explanations short because of the cost.

To finance the printing of the Zohar, the students decided that whoever came to the Sage's weekly shiur, which was held on Wednesday evenings between seven and eight, would pay four lira. In those days, this was a huge sum of money, equivalent to several thousand shekels today. The students decided to collect the money together, and each week a different student would go to the lesson. When the shiur was over the student would give over what he had learned to the others.

One Wednesday night, it happened that the students collected a large sum of money, one hundred and eighty lira! But they were delayed and managed to get to the shiur only at ten minutes to eight. They thought that when the Rabbi saw how much money they had managed to collect and the efforts they had made, he would continue the shiur beyond the fixed time. But to their surprise, at eight o'clock precisely, the holy Rabbi closed his book and left the beit midrash.

All the students took part in this endeavor, but it was Rabbi Moshe Baruch Lemburger who dedicated his whole life to the publication of the Baal HaSulam's books. He sold his share in the bus company that he had started during the Givat Shaul period and donated the money to the printing of the books. Every spare penny he had, went for this purpose. Indeed, he sold the contents of his own home many times over in order to finance both the books and the household of the Sage.

On the festivals, the students followed the custom of auctioning the *aliyot* to the Torah. All the sums of money collected were dedicated to pay for the cost of printing. Rabbi Pinchas Brandwein remembers that one Simchat Torah, they sold the *"Chatan Torah"* (the honor of finishing the yearly reading of the Torah) for the enormous sum of six hundred and thirteen lira! Of course, the buyer was none other than Rabbi Moshe Baruch Lemburger. In order to give the reader an idea of how large this sum was, the salary of a teacher in those days was only four lira a month. Indeed, it was Rabbi Moshe Baruch Lemburger who always bought the most expensive *aliyot*. In order to pay for these, he would borrow money, as he himself lived in great poverty, and then he would spend his days paying off the loans.

The students further decided that whoever suggested *any* sum in the auction for the *aliyot* would pay it, even if the *aliyah* subsequently went to someone else. All the money so collected was dedicated to the printing of the Zohar.

Rabbi Avraham Brandwein:

My father had a student named Baruch Horonchek, who understood the importance for our generation of printing the Zohar with the *Perush haSulam*, so he dedicated all his salary from his work in the ironwork factory for this purpose.

It is astonishing to us, who live in a world where material values have taken such a prominent role, to think of these students who reduced themselves and their families to the bare minimum in order to contribute to a task they considered of paramount importance.

In the year 1946, the Baal HaSulam moved to Tel Aviv, where he continued writing the *Perush haSulam*. He worked unceasingly, saying that he wanted to complete the *Perush haSulam* no matter what. However, in the winter of that year, he again suffered heart attacks. One came when he was writing the commentary on the beginning of the *Parashah va Yechi*, the last of the book of Genesis, which tells of the sojourn of Ya'acov in Egypt. The second, more severe attack, occurred when he was writing on the passage of the Zohar that deals with the end of the *parashah*. This passage holds great prophecies relating to the end of days. Eight lines before the end of the commentary, he was forced to stop writing.

He was too weak to leave his bed, and this state of weakness continued for several months. The doctors informed the family that there was a great problem with the Sage; his body was not able to function properly, but his mind was working without ceasing. The doctors maintained that as long as he did not rest fully he would not be able to recover. This kind of rest was extremely hard for him, so his recovery was prolonged. During this period, Rabbi Benjamin Sinkovsky came into the Sage's presence and asked him, "What will happen to the *Perush haSulam*? The world needs it!" The Rabbi replied, "Don't worry, I will not leave work in the middle." Then Rabbi Moshe Baruch said, "The Rabbi does not live for himself, for he has already corrected himself completely. All his life force comes through the flow of light from the Creator, brought into the world through the writing of the *Perush haSulam*. So we may be sure that HaShem will help him finish it."

Once he had recovered, the Sage sat up in order to carry on his holy work and finish the last eight lines of *Parashah va Yechi*, but again he felt pain in his heart. He called his assistant, Rabbi Zalman Lemburger, and told him that whenever he tried to continue writing, he felt pain in his heart. Rabbi Zalman suggested that they call Rabbi Baruch Shalom, who would act as secretary. But even when the Sage tried to say the words, he immediately felt pain and was forced to stop. At that point, he said it seemed the world was not yet ready for this learning, and it was from Above that he was prevented from continuing. Despite this, after a further few days, he managed to finish the section on his own and subsequently continued the writing until the very end.

Following this heart attack, the doctors commanded the Sage to rest for at least ten hours out of the twenty-four. The Baal HaSulam divided this rest period into portions, going to sleep at nine in the evening, arising at one in the morning and then going back to bed to rest again until about five in the morning. The lessons he gave the students were changed from daily to weekly, and the frequency with which he held a *tisch* with the students was greatly reduced as he lacked the strength for the intense inner work involved. Nevertheless, every time he completed writing the commentary on a volume of the Zohar, he held a joyous festive meal of thanksgiving together with his students.

The Significance of the Commentary

Prior to the spread of the writings of the Baal HaSulam, the Zohar had been closed to the Jewish world in general, as was indeed the learning of Kabbalah as a whole. In the Sephardi communities, some connection with the Zohar had remained, since they recite portions of the Zohar in the daily and sabbath prayers. But these portions had been omitted in the Ashkenazi tradition, leading to the community of Ashkenazi Jews losing all connection with the Zohar. In both communities, the Zohar had remained a book closed to understanding and comprehension except for those of great spiritual caliber who were able to understand it through their own spiritual perception.

But the time for its revelation, so critical for the redemption, had come.

On the Authorship of the Zohar

The Baal HaSulam wrote:

All serious students who have studied the holy Zohar—that is, those who understand its contents—universally agree that its author is the holy sage Rabbi Shimon Bar Yochai. Only those who are far from a true understanding of this wisdom have doubts about its authorship. On the basis of external evidence, they claim that its author was the noted Kabbalist, Rabbi Moshe De Leon or one of his period.

As for myself, from the day that I merited, through the light of God, to understand a little in this holy book, it never occurred to me to question its authorship, for the simple reason that from the content of the book there came to my heart a sense of the holiness of the *Tanna* Rabbi Shimon Bar Yochai, which was immeasurably greater than that of the other holy *Tannaim*. If it were completely clear to me that the author was someone else, such as Rabbi Moshe De Leon, then I would think of him as having attained a level far beyond that of the *Tannaim* and even greater than that of Rabbi Shimon Bar Yochai. Actually, the book reaches such a depth of wisdom that if it turned out that its author was one of the ancient prophets of the Bible, I would find that even more reasonable than ascribing its authorship to one of the *Tannaim*. Even were it to be proved that Moses, our Teacher, received it straight from God at Mount Sinai, I would have no difficulty accepting this fact, so deep is the wisdom I see in it.

Therefore, since I have been privileged to write an explanation of this book in such a way that anyone who is interested can understand something of it, I feel myself discharged from the need to research the identity of its author. When the reader begins to appreciate the depth of this work, he will feel satisfied that it must have been written by someone who has attained, at the very least, the spiritual level of the holy Rabbi Shimon Bar Yochai. [2]

The Nature of the *Sulam* Commentary

We saw in the letter that Rabbi Ashlag wrote to his father (page 124) that he testified that the soul of the Ari had incarnated within him. He demonstrated an intimate attainment in the work of the Ari impossible to understand or describe. It was this that came to his aid in explaining the inner meanings of the Zohar.

The Baal HaSulam:

> I have explained and clearly demonstrated the spiritual analog that exists for every entity, stripped of any material image, not connected to space and time. Those who are interested can see this for themselves. I have made it possible for everyone in the House of Israel to study the holy Zohar and warm themselves by its holy light. I have called my commentary, *"HaSulam,"* meaning "The Ladder," to illustrate the fact that the purpose of my explanation is the same as that of any other ladder. If you have an attic full of bounty, all you need is a ladder to go up, and then all the good of the world is within your reach.
>
> However, the ladder is not a goal in itself. If you were to rest on the steps of the ladder and not enter the attic, then you would not have fulfilled your intention.
>
> So it is with my explanation of the Zohar. The Zohar's words are of unfathomable depth. The means by which to express its depth have yet to be created. However, my explanation, at any rate, constitutes a path and an introduction, which any person can use to ascend and to look deeply into the book of the Zohar itself. Only then, would my intention in writing this explanation be fulfilled. [3]

The first three volumes of the *Perush haSulam* on the Zohar consist of extremely detailed commentary. In these three volumes, Rabbi Ashlag explains every single word, laying the foundations for understanding the Zohar in depth. However, in later volumes he wrote detailed explanations only in certain places and left some of the Zohar unexplained, accompanied only by simple translation from the original Aramaic of the Zohar—which most people nowadays don't understand—to Hebrew. When asked why he had done this, Rabbi Ashlag answered that many people will be inspired by the simple stories of the Zohar that give us motivation to work for God, whereas if he were to explain everything according to the Sephirot and the various spiritual levels, many people would not feel any connection with the Zohar.

The Language of the Zohar

The Zohar, when looked at directly, without the *Perush haSulam* to guide us, appears to be filled with images drawn from the physical world. In reality, however, the language of the Zohar is a language of desire—the desire of the human to connect with the Creator and the desire of the Creator to enable such a connection. The various manifestations of desire for the goodness of God are termed in the language of Kabbalah, "vessels," and the fulfillment of these desires is called "lights."

The Baal HaSulam:

> The language of Kabbalah is an actual language in the fullest sense of the word. It is extremely accurate, both with respect to **root and branch**, and with respect to **cause and effect**. This language has a particular virtue because, through it, **it is possible to refer to and discuss individual or particular elements without limit**. Through this language, **it is also possible to get straight to the element under consideration, without the need to connect it with what precedes it or what follows it**. [4]

If we consider the above paragraph carefully, we can see that Rabbi Ashlag considers the language of Kabbalah with respect to four main characteristics which we will discuss below. These characteristics derive from the nature of reality itself, and each is worthy of a chapter on its own. But here we will briefly consider these characteristics of reality as they are represented in the Zohar. For people who wish to go into these concepts more deeply, please refer to the translator's introduction on the language of Kabbalah (page xix). Later on in this chapter, we will see these characteristics in play through learning an actual piece of Zohar with Rabbi Ashlag's commentary.

The four characteristics of the language of the Zohar that Rabbi Ashlag points to are:

(1) **Root and Branch:** The content of the Zohar is based on the intimate connections that exist between the worlds. Every element of a lower world—the branch—has its equivalent in the corresponding higher spiritual world—the root; each branch receiving its light from its root. The sages of the Zohar rely on these connections, which they can clearly perceive. So in their discussions in the Zohar, they employ everyday words derived from elements of this physical world—the branches, when actually, they are referring to the branches' spiritual roots. Thus the language of the Zohar is designated the "language of the branches."

(2) **Cause and effect:** The sages of the Zohar discuss the way in which the vessels develop, one from another, as well as how our actions as humans influence the flow of light through the worlds.

(3) **It is possible to speak of individual elements without limit:** The sages of the Zohar take specific verses or individual words from the Tanach and discuss the most subtle details of their inner meanings.

(4) **It is also possible to get straight to the element under consideration, without the need to connect it with what precedes it or what follows it:** In their discussions, the sages of the Zohar get directly to the detail under review. This phenomenon is prevalent in the Zohar. For the most part, the Zohar records the details of a particular spiritual stage without making note of which spiritual stage is being discussed. Furthermore, there is no continuity of organization of the subject matter in the Zohar. The discussions of the sages of the Zohar are nominally based on the weekly scriptural portions, but in practice, every discussion stands on its own.

However, these elements and processes of the Zohar are hidden from a reader who has yet to attain a substantial spiritual level. Without being able to determine the spiritual stage under discussion, without being able to discern the issues of root and branch and of cause and effect, such a reader is unable to understand even one word of this wisdom correctly.

Our understanding of the Zohar depends more on our spiritual purity than on our intellectual ability: The innermost aspect of the Torah and the essence of the soul are one, in the inner meaning of the phrase, "the Holy Blessed One, the soul, and the Torah are one." [5] Therefore, the revelation of the light of the Zohar and the attainment of its wisdom depends on the work that we do in correcting our vessel of receiving. Only by leaving off our natural egoism—our receiving for ourselves alone—and through giving unconditionally, will we be in affinity of form with the Zohar's great light, and only thus can we receive it and comprehend it.

It was the great Kabbalist, the Holy Ari, who, through his deep contemplation of the Zohar, was able to discern the order and processes of the spiritual stages concealed within its pages. These he taught as the dynamics of light and vessel as they develop through the spiritual worlds. His teachings were mainly recorded by his student, Rabbi Chaim Vital.

The Ari, however, died at an early age, and for the most part did not teach how to apply the principles of the dynamics of light and vessel (that he, himself, had extracted from the Zohar) to the specific discussions of the sages of the Zohar. He left a short work, *Ma'amarei Rashbi*, which, in some ways, is a forerunner of the *Perush haSulam* of Rabbi Ashlag, but its scope is limited. The Ari taught only in response to his students' questions, and they were all men of vast spiritual attainment.

It was left to the Baal HaSulam to apply the teachings of the Ari to the Zohar in a systematic and complete way. This he did in the *Sulam* commentary on the Zohar. In each portion of the Zohar for which he wrote a detailed commentary, he reveals the spiritual stage under discussion, to which Sephirot the sages of the Zohar were relating, and the dynamic processes of the vessels involved. Thus the *Perush haSulam* is made up of:

(1) **Translation from Aramaic to Hebrew:** On occasion, the Baal HaSulam points to the source of his translation as being taken from the *Targum*, the Aramaic translation of the Tanach, or from the Talmud.

(2) **Explanation of the words of the Zohar using the processes of light and vessel according to the work of the Ari,** which Rabbi Ashlag does in the following ways:

Firstly, Rabbi Ashlag identifies for us which spiritual stage each of the elements under discussion belongs. An element may be a personality in the Torah, or it may be an action that someone performs in the Torah. It may be a particular word or phrase used in the Torah, or it may be an object mentioned in the Torah. Equally, it may be a mitzvah from the Torah. In each case, Rabbi Ashlag identifies for us which spiritual world we are dealing with and which of the Sephirot are involved. This enables the reader who has some background in the method of the Ari to orient himself within the spiritual cosmos. Thus, the reader will be able to follow the discussion in the Zohar according to the dynamics of light and vessel.

As we described earlier, the Zohar is written in the language of the branches. Rabbi Ashlag translates from the language of the branches to our spoken language. This translation enables a true understanding of the discussion in the Zohar and prevents false interpretations based on literal readings of the text.

As part of his commentary, Rabbi Ashlag shows how the metaphors brought by the sages of the Zohar are actually teaching us how to serve the Creator. The Zohar deals with the content of higher worlds only in regard to their relevance to the *tikkunim* and processes of the human soul. Thus, the Zohar provides a key for understanding ourselves, enabling our own tikkun and showing us ways to ascend in holiness.

When we study the Zohar with the *Perush haSulam*, we thus merit a treasure of the wisdom of divine revelation, truly without compare. Learning the Zohar illuminates the innermost aspect of the Torah. The Zohar teaches us the intentions in the words of God, as well as the intentions of our forefathers and foremothers in their deeds, in their words, and in the events of their lives. The Zohar also teaches us the intentions hidden within the mitzvot.

Through this learning, each of us may begin to understand the inner intentions and desires of our own souls. This is because, as the Zohar states, "the Holy Blessed One, the soul, and the Torah are one."[5] It follows that this wisdom illuminates, in equal measure, the ways of the Creator, our souls, and the innermost aspects of the Torah. Through studying the *Perush haSulam* we learn about our most subtle thoughts and feelings—aspects of ourselves that are hard to express in words. We learn the ways that we can align to different levels of consciousness that we call "spiritual worlds." We learn the dynamics between light and vessel and how these operate within ourselves, within the souls of the Jewish people, and within the souls of humanity.

The Zohar brings the revealed Torah to life, shining its light on the deeds of our forefathers and foremothers. We discover that all the events of their lives, their words, and their deeds were vessels for the divine light. Similarly, the Zohar sheds its light on the oral Law, illuminating the discussions of the sages of the Talmud, and teaching us the inner reasons for the mitzvot so that the light contained within them shines out for us.

An Article from the *Perush haSulam:* Oraita v'Tzaluta (Torah and Prayer)[6]

Before we turn to study the Zohar itself, it is always useful to look at the biblical verse that the sages of the Zohar are discussing. Here is the relevant piece from Isaiah:

> In those days Hezekiah was sick unto death. Then Isaiah the prophet, the son of Amotz, came to him and said to him: "Thus says the Lord, 'Set your house in order; for you shall die and not live.'"
>
> Then Hezekiah turned his face to the wall and prayed to the Lord, and said, "Please, O Lord, please remember that I have walked before You in truth and with a whole heart, and I have done that which is good in Your sight." And Hezekiah wept greatly.
>
> And the word of the Lord came to Isaiah saying, "Go and tell Hezekiah, 'Thus says the Lord, the God of David, your father: I have heard your prayer; I have seen your tears. Behold! I am adding fifteen years to your life.'" (Isa. 38:1-5)

Now we turn to look at the Zohar itself.*

Zohar

(180) Rabbi Shimon opened his discourse on the Scripture: "And Hezekiah turned his face to the wall and prayed to the Lord..." (Isa. 38:2)

Come and see. How strong is the power of Torah, how elevated it is above all! Whoever occupies himself with Torah is neither afraid of the higher beings nor of the lower beings. Neither is he afraid of evil sicknesses that are in the world, because he is holding onto the Tree of Life and learns from it all day.

(181) For the Torah teaches a person how to walk in a true way. It teaches him counsel on how to repent before his Master to annul a [negative] decree. For, even if it is decreed against him that the decree will not be annulled, it is annulled immediately and passes from him and doesn't rest on him in this world. Therefore, a person needs to occupy himself with the practice of Torah, day and night, and not remove himself from the Torah, as it is written: "And you shall meditate on it day and night" (Josh. 1:8). But if he turns away from the Torah, or is separated from the Torah, it is as if he has separated from the Tree of Life.

Perush haSulam

Explanation of the Zohar's words: We see that Rabbi Shimon Bar Yochai opens his discourse with a verse from the Scripture that concerns prayer: **"And Hezekiah turned his face to the wall and prayed to the Lord... ,"** but he explains this verse by referring only to the Torah. [Why?]

Rabbi Shimon's reason is explained in another place in the Zohar, in *Parashah vaEtchanan:*[7] "Hezekiah's prayer was accepted because there was nothing that was acting as a barrier between himself and the holy Shechinah." Rabbi Shimon Bar Yochai is pointing out that Hezekiah's prayer worked only because of the

---

* The paragraph numbers refer to those used in the *Perush haSulam*. The quotes from the Zohar that Rabbi Ashlag refers to in his commentary are in bold typeface.

power of Torah. It was through the Torah that he attained such a complete repentance that there was no barrier between himself and the holy Shechinah. Thus, the decree that Hezekiah was to die was annulled.

Rabbi Shimon concludes that we see that the power of Torah is so great it can even nullify the decree of death. It follows that **a person should occupy himself with the Torah day and night and not turn from it.**

["Death," according to the language of Kabbalah, the language of the branches, means separation from God rather than physical death. So Rabbi Shimon is telling us that when we feel separated from God, the power of the Torah can bring us back. Furthermore, he is advising us to occupy ourselves with Torah, both in the "day," when God's goodness is manifest to us, and in the "night," when His goodness is concealed from us.]

Zohar

(182) Come and see. Here is counsel for a person: when he goes to bed at night he needs to accept upon himself the higher Malchut (the governance of the Shechinah) with a whole heart, first proffering to it a security for his soul. Immediately, he is saved from all evil sicknesses and from all evil spirits, which then have no rule over him.

Perush haSulam

Explanation of the Zohar's words: "For God called the light 'day'..." (Gen. 1:5). This is the light of dvekut and of holiness that we attain from the Creator, may the One be blessed. This is the governance of the day.

"... the darkness, He called 'night.'" "The night" refers to the forces of separation that separate us from His light, may the One be blessed. This is the governance of the night. Therefore, we sleep at night. Sleep is one-sixtieth of death—spiritual death being the governance of the *sitra achra* [the framework of evil]. Because these two frameworks of governance—that of holiness and that of the *sitra achra*—rule us, we are unable to maintain our dvekut with God on a permanent basis. We cease our dvekut with Him because of the governance of night [that separates us from the Creator] that repeatedly comes upon us and interrupts us from our service of the Holy Blessed One.

To rectify this, Rabbi Shimon is giving us counsel that every night before we go to sleep ["sleep" refers to times when we are not aligned with the consciousness of giving, so the light of God cannot shine as there is a lack of affinity of form. Nevertheless,] we **should accept upon ourselves the governance of the higher** Malchut [**the Shechinah**] **with a full heart.** For when the aspect of night [the separation from God] will be rectified, in accordance with the fulfillment of creation, as it is written in the Scripture, "and it was evening and it was morning, one day" (Gen. 1:5), then night and day [separation and dvekut] will be unified into one body and one day. At this point, the governance of the night will be designated "the governance of the Malchut" and no *klipot* [the lights that sustain the evil] will be able to interfere with Her.

Therefore, we need to accept upon ourselves this higher Malchut with a full heart without any barrier coming between ourselves and the Malchut [the Shechinah]. We need to accept upon ourselves the *Malchut Shamayim* [the rule of the Shechinah], whether for life [connection with the Creator] or, God forbid, for death [separation from the Creator], such that nothing in the world is able to move us or distance us from the higher Malchut even by a fraction, as in the inner meaning of the Scripture, "And you shall love the Lord Your God, with all your heart, and with all your soul, and with all your might" (Deut. 6:5).

If we were to take this on ourselves with a whole heart, then we may be sure of ourselves that no further barrier between ourselves and the Creator, may He be blessed, may be fashioned. This is what Rabbi Shimon means when he says that we have first given **a security for our soul,** for we first give our soul into the hand of the Holy Blessed One. This means we are ready to fulfill God's commandments completely, even to the point of self-sacrifice.

When, in this state, we sleep, and even though our spirit leaves, we no longer taste one-sixtieth part of death—which is the power of the *sitra achra*—but we taste only the aspect of giving of ourselves to the Creator in the way of the mitzvah. For now, the power of death does not rule over us, as we have brought ourselves into the energy of the self-sacrifice of the mitzvah. Then the governance of the night cannot hurt us again by interrupting us from the pleasantness of our service of God, as now, for us, the night and the day have become as one day and the night is only a part of the day in all actuality.

Therefore, the Zohar says: **Immediately a person is saved from all evil sicknesses and from all evil spirits, which then have no rule over him.** For his night has already left the domain of the *sitra achra*. Nothing may now form a barrier between himself and the holy Shechinah as the power of the *sitra achra* and the judgment that follows it no longer rule over him.

Zohar

(183) And in the morning, when he arises from his bed, he needs to bless his Master and enter into His house and bow down before His temple in great *yirah* (reverence).

And after that, he prays his prayer. And he takes counsel from the holy fathers, as it is written, "And as for me, in the abundance of Your loving-kindness, I will come to Your house, and I will bow down toward Your holy temple, in *yirah* [reverence] of You" (Ps. 5:8).

Perush haSulam

And he takes counsel from the holy fathers: For the prayer that we pray is for the tikkun of the holy Shechinah, to draw light to Her and to replenish all Her lacks. Therefore, all our requests are worded in the plural, as, for example, we say in the prayers, "Be gracious to **us** and grant **us** Chochmah, Binah, and Da'at." Also, "Bring **us** back, our Father, to Your Torah," and so forth.[8] For, we pray for the whole community of Israel. Everything that is in the holy Shechinah is in the community of Israel, and whatever is lacking in Her is lacking in the community of Israel. It transpires that when we pray for the whole community of Israel, we are praying for the needs of the holy Shechinah, for they are the same. We find that before we pray we need to look and see what She lacks so that we may know what we need to rectify in Her in order to replenish Her.

Since all the generations of the community of Israel as a whole are included in the holy Shechinah, we don't need to work on the *tikkunim* that She has already received through the work of previous generations. But we need to complete the *tikkunim* that are still lacking.

The holy fathers constitute the generality of the whole community of Israel, for they are the three roots of all six hundred thousand souls of Israel of all generations [that have come, and will come into being,] until the end of the tikkun.

All the lights that the community of Israel draws on and receives throughout the generations are first received by the holy fathers. It is from the holy fathers that the light reaches the general community of Israel of any particular generation who are drawing on a specific light.

For this is the way that spirituality is ordered: A branch can only receive light through its root. The main aspect of the illumination remains in the root, and only part of the illumination comes to the branch. Therefore, all the *tikkunim* that have already been rectified in the holy Shechinah are valid and enduring within the souls of our holy fathers.

This is what the sages of the Zohar meant when they said, "**A person should not enter the Beit Knesset** [house of prayer], **unless he first obtains permission from Avraham, Yitzchak, and Ya'acov.**" * For the purpose of our prayer is to complete that which is still lacking in the Shechinah after the *tikkunim* that have already been accomplished for Her.

Therefore, we first need to know and draw to ourselves those *tikkunim* in the holy Shechinah that have already been rectified, and then we will know what we need to add to them. This is what Rabbi Shimon means when he says that before a person enters the Beit Knesset, he should first consult the holy fathers. For we need

---

* See paragraph 184, below

to take counsel with them in order to know what we need further to correct. And this is possible, only after we have already drawn into the holy Shechinah all that the holy fathers have already rectified within Her. Then we can see what there is yet lacking in Her.

The tikkun of the holy Shechinah is the prayer established by the holy fathers: the tikkun of Avraham is the morning prayer; that of Yitzchak, the afternoon prayer; and that of Ya'acov, the evening prayer. Since this is so, we first need to draw on the entire measure of the tikkun that they have already established in prayer. Then we will know what to pray for, to rectify what is lacking in Her.

Zohar

(184) They established it thus: A person should not enter the Beit Knesset unless he first obtains permission from Avraham, Yitzchak, and Ya'acov, because they rectified the prayer before the Holy Blessed One.

This is a requirement based on the above verse from Psalms. The phrase, "As for me, in the abundance of Your loving-kindness, I will enter Your house," refers to Avraham, who is Chesed. "I will bow down to the palace of Your holiness," refers to Yitzchak, for whom the Malchut is designated as a palace. "In your *yirah*," refers to Ya'acov, who embodies the Sephirah Tiferet, which is designated as *yirah* [reverence for God].

A person first needs to include himself with the fathers, and then he can enter the Beit Knesset and pray his prayer. And then the Scripture: "And He said to me, 'You are My servant, Israel, in whom I glory,'" (Isa. 49:3) is upheld.

Perush haSulam

Now Rabbi Shimon goes on to explain the three general *tikkunim* that the fathers established for the holy Shechinah: Avraham rectified the Shechinah as a **house**. This implies that he rectified the Shechinah in the aspect of a fixed dwelling, such that a person can cling to Her continually as his permanent dwelling.

Yitzchak added a tikkun that rectified the Shechinah as **a holy palace,** which means that the King dwells permanently within the holy Shechinah, for the King is always to be found in His palace.

Ya'acov added a further tikkun in that he rectified the holy Shechinah in the aspect of *yirah* [reverence]. This is the gateway to the dwelling. For *yirah* is the doorway, both to the consciousness of the Shechinah as a house, and to the consciousness of the Shechinah as a palace, as in the inner meaning of the verse, "How full of *yirah* is this place, this is the gateway of heaven" (Gen. 28:17).

Once a person has completely taken upon himself to behave according to these three *tikkunim* of the fathers, then he may know the measure of that which is already rectified in the holy Shechinah. Then he can enter the Beit Knesset and pray his prayer, so he may rectify for the holy Shechinah whatever She still lacks.

Explanation of the Zohar: Avraham is the root of the virtue of *chesed* [loving-kindness] for the souls of Israel. He rectified the holy Shechinah to be a vessel for the *Or d'Chassadim,* [the joy that comes through giving unconditionally] and he received this light on behalf of all the souls of Israel to their fullest capacity.

If the tikkun had been left at that, then all Israel would have been in dvekut with God permanently, and the holy Shechinah would have been the dwelling of the Malchut [the collective soul of humanity], filled with all good and joy, and no one would have wanted to be separated from Her, even for a moment.

The tikkun that Avraham did, was that he made a perfect receptacle for the *Or d'Chassadim* without any possibility of defect at all. He raised the holy Shechinah to the aspect of giving pleasure to God, in affinity of form with our Creator, may He be blessed, in that we give to the Creator without receiving any gratification for our selfish love at all.

This is the ultimate measure of the light of loving-kindness and its vessel, as the sages of the Mishnah taught: "One who says, 'What is mine is yours, and what is yours is yours, is a person of loving-kindness.'"[9] Such a person does not ask for anything for his own self-gratification at all.

Since all the constrictions and the grasp of the *sitra achra* that prevent us from receiving the light of God apply only when we desire to receive for ourselves alone, we see that Avraham has completely removed all the sickness of the *klipot* and of the *sitra achra* and has rectified the holy Shechinah in the utmost purity.

However, this did not bring the Purpose of Creation to its complete fulfillment. For the Creator's main purpose in His creation is to give pleasure to the created beings. Furthermore, the measure of pleasure that the created beings feel in God's light is entirely dependent on the magnitude of their desire to receive it.

Therefore, although the Shechinah was already rectified [by Avraham], She was rectified with only a vessel of giving; not receiving anything from the Holy Blessed One, but only giving to Him. Therefore, Avraham's tikkun does not fulfill the Purpose of Creation, as this can be achieved only through the great desire to receive.

The inner meaning of, "and Avraham begot Yitzchak" (Gen. 25:19) is that although Yitzchak found the Shechinah to be in the ultimate of fulfillment and satisfaction with respect to the *Or d'chassadim* (the light of loving-kindness) through the tikkun of Avraham, nevertheless, he felt the lack that the Shechinah still had, in that She was not yet fit to receive all that is included in the Purpose of Creation.

Therefore Yitzchak's tikkun additionally rectified the Shechinah as a receptacle for receiving the light that God wants to give us according to His Purpose of Creation—the *Or d'Chochmah*. Indeed, Yitzchak awoke within the Shechinah the desire to receive from the Holy Blessed One, but Her receiving may be carried out only as receiving with the intention of giving. This means that we need to have a great desire to receive, but we need to receive only because it is the Creator's desire that we do so. If the Giver does not desire it, then we should not wish to receive at all.

Receiving only with the intention of giving is considered as pure giving, and thus the *sitra achra* has no hold on this type of receiving. So the holy Shechinah was rectified by Yitzchak in all Her great and final rectification. Now She is fit to receive all the pleasantness and gentleness with which the Creator thought to give pleasure to the created beings when it arose in His thought to create them. Thus, the Shechinah is designated as the Palace of His holiness, may He be blessed, because now the King dwells within Her in all His splendor and glory as a King within His palace.

Through the tikkun of Avraham, the Shechinah is designated as only a house—that is to say the house of Malchut—for, at this point, all the glory and splendor of the King has not yet been recognized; for the glory of the King is recognized only in His own special palace.

Yitzchak rectified all the vessels of receiving within the souls of Israel. This means he enabled the sweetening of the strict judgments that occur according to the Divine Providence. For all the contractions, suffering, and punishments that happen in the world come about only in order to correct the souls' vessels of receiving, so that they should be fit to receive all the good that is included in the Thought of Creation. Since Yitzchak rectified the Shechinah in this perfection, all the vessels of receiving were rectified at that time. The souls had, for the moment, come to their desired purpose.

But Yitzchak's tikkun did not endure because the world was not yet fit for the final tikkun. Esav came forth from Yitzchak, and he spoiled Yitzchak's tikkun. Esav did not abide by the rule of receiving only for the sake of giving in the way that Yitzchak had rectified, but he went astray, receiving for himself alone. Even when it was clear to him that the Giver did not wish him to receive, he, nevertheless, wanted to receive for his own pleasure. Therefore the *sitra achra* and the *klipot* took hold of him. Thus Esav brought the lower aspect of the Malchut once more into the domain of the *klipot*, in the inner meaning of the verse, "Her latter end is death and her steps support hell" (Prov. 5:5).

When Ya'acov saw the ruin that the wicked Esav had brought about, he rectified the holy Shechinah in the attribute of *yirah*. This is the inner meaning of the Scripture, "... and his hand had hold on Esav's heel, עקב; and his name was called Ya'acov, יעקב" (Gen. 25:26), on which the sages of the Zohar state that when Ya'acov saw the ruin that Esav had brought upon the Shechinah—represented at the beginning of Ya'acov's name by the letter י—he rectified himself in great *yirah*, until he had raised the Shechinah to a crown over his head.

In this way, Ya'acov grasped the rectifications of both Avraham and Yitzchak simultaneously, and no defect came forth from him.

However, this rectification does not yet qualify as the *gmar hatikkun* [end of the tikkun], for the *yirah* that Ya'acov rectified is the fear of committing a sin. For it was the heel of Esav that gave rise to this *yirah*, that we should not sin as Esav did.

But at the end of the tikkun, when the heel of Esav will be nullified, according to the inner meaning of the Scripture, "And death will be swallowed up forever" (Isa. 25:8), then the basis of the *yirah* will be reverence for God; that is, a person will feel *yirah* only because God is great in loving-kindness and governs all.

It is certain that Ya'acov himself definitely attained this true *yirah*, but for the general community of Israel, this tikkun is left for the generations following Ya'acov to complete, until we reach the end of the tikkun.

This is what the sages of the Zohar said, **"As for me, in the abundance of Your loving-kindness I will enter Your house,"** refers to Avraham, for Avraham rectified the Shechinah in the aspect of a house filled with all good in the light of loving-kindness. **"I will bow down to the palace of Your holiness" refers to Yitzchak,** for Yitzchak rectified the Shechinah in the aspect of the palace of holiness, as is fitting for the splendor and glory of the King, may He be blessed. **"In your *yirah*" refers to Ya'acov,** for Ya'acov rectified the holy Shechinah in the aspect of *yirah*. In this way, Ya'acov rectified the holy Shechinah as a receptacle for both the *tikkunim* of Avraham and Yitzchak together.

A person should first include himself in the *tikkunim* of the holy fathers. For how would he know what there is yet to correct in the holy Shechinah if he does not include himself in these three *tikkunim* that our forefathers already corrected? "Including himself" means that he should take upon himself to behave according to the holy fathers' *tikkunim*. This determines that he is included in the fathers' attributes. Only when he has included these three rectifications of our holy fathers within himself can he begin to rectify the Shechinah at the consciousness where Ya'acov our father left off. Only then can he raise up the level of *yirah* to the *yirah* due to the exaltation of the Creator, which is *yirah* because He is great in loving-kindness and the Governor of all.

Then he can enter the Beit Knesset and pray his prayer. This means that the person should pray and draw to the holy Shechinah the higher lights associated with the *yirah* of the Creator's supremacy, which will bring the holy Shechinah to the end of the tikkun, as it is written: "And He said unto me, 'You are My servant, Israel, in you I will be glorified" (Isa. 49:3).

His Foundation in the Holy Mountains

The light of Atzilut, elevated and clear,
Glories in the vessels of giving and of receiving.
Directing over the splendor of Briyah,
Yet it guards the foundation of Yetzirah.
Fed from His most precious light
It is formed to stand strong.
He hovers over it like a crown of light.
He gave His vineyard to the keepers;
It will get cleansed from the fragments, from the excess.

He sits me down and raises me up in His splendor;
He will show me wonders in His Torah,
As He does, for all who know the true nature of His innerness.
And my eyes will behold some of the splendor of His sovereignty.
Yes! I have heard Him,
And I have seen Him as He receives glory.
Here I am and all God's goodness,
We will stand together.
Taste and see,
For my futures, I will hasten.
Surely as He is gracious to me,
Choose you, the One.

Oh! Would that I had a companion
From those who find favor, the people of delight,
Who know the meaning of everything,
Who have labored in His innerness and found results.
Yes! They are His witnesses,
And happy are they
That the Omnipotent filled their hands
With all that their thoughts desired
And all they yearned for.

The most hidden and the most High,
Above every mystery.
Where there is Chochmah,
There He is!
I have beheld the wellspring of all wisdom,
And before I understood, I found Him, and searched Him out.
Please, the One who teaches humankind understanding,
To You is the praise,
Have pity upon me and say a word.
The wisdom and the knowledge is Yours.
You are the Worker of every action.

My guilt is much,
And more than that is my shame.
I forgot man and angel both.
Will they forgive my sin?
Will they comfort me in my sorrow?
Yes, I do have understanding that there is none other than Him,
And one who finds understanding has found faith,
And with his finger, he will show God
That for which he yearned.
Who gave him delight in his labor?
And who is like Him that answers
Sin with love and shame with pride?

In whose hand are all my futures,
From Him comes all my joy and all my sorrow.
He had mercy on me
And carried me quickly to my redemption.
Since then I am lovesick.
My Beloved remembers what is in the hearts,
The light of my delight
Awaits at the cornerstone;
And between Him and me
There are words of love.
My redeemer lives,
The drops of my sweetness He will number.

He will account according to my years,
And my spirit will not be injured.
He hid me and I do not know how,
And how He renews my youth as an eagle
And the wisdom flows.
My dust will be enriched with milk,
And my sheaf of corn will become a standing crop.
His loving-kindness strengthens from within the house,
From without, and from my surroundings.
May my falling down, my vicissitudes,
Be to attain my delights.
Let the clouds of my darkness at times
Hide my arrogant acts.
I will always contemplate them,
After all, they were the desires of my high places.

The heavens cannot contain Him,
And in my tent He is willing.
From all His aspects and His sides there is playfulness
    and affection.
His delight is established in my heart as a flame
That catches alight as of itself, and goes up, and is not extinguished.
True life have I tasted, from the Temple hallway,
    and within, it is built.
In it, I did not labor, and all is built according to His design.
I have uttered His mighty acts,
And His secrets fill my belly.
And like a shadow
I am drawn into the inner room,
Into the established Kingdom.

Yehudah Halevi Ashlag
Jerusalem, *Cheshvan* 8, 5689
(October 22, 1928)

Chapter Fourteen

In the Presence of the Sage

It was while Rabbi Ashlag was writing the *Perush haSulam* in Tel Aviv that a young rabbi by the name of Aharon Shemesh bought Rabbi Ashlag's books that had already been published. He contacted Rabbi Zalman Lemburger and begged him to obtain permission from the Sage to be allowed into the lessons. At first, this was refused, as Rabbi Ashlag permitted only those who demonstrated a strong desire to serve God and who were capable of self-sacrifice to join the beit midrash as students. But Rabbi Shemesh refused to give up, and eventually, he was allowed to participate in the lessons.

At first, Rabbi Shemesh couldn't understand a word. He came from a Sephardi family, so he did not understand Yiddish, which, at the time, was the language Rabbi Ashlag used in the shiurim. When the Baal HaSulam asked him if he had followed the lesson, he answered, "My soul understands." But from then on, the Sage taught in Hebrew. To help Rabbi Shemesh progress, the Sage organized for him to learn *Talmud Eser haSephirot* with Rabbi Yehudah Tzvi Brandwein and Talmud with his grandson Rabbi Shmuel Ashlag.

Eventually, Rabbi Aharon Shemesh became one of the most important of Rabbi Ashlag's students and the Sage valued him greatly. Each morning, he came to pray in the beit midrash, which was situated in the Sage's house, because he felt its holy atmosphere.

Rabbi Zalman Lemburger:

> Once I was standing behind the Sage. I saw him talking with excitement to Rabbi Aharon. Suddenly, he turned to me and said, "I have a special joy in the faith of Rabbi Aharon."

Rabbi Aharon gave much money to help print the books. He simply didn't consider his own needs at all; he gave all he had.

The Lessons

During the period when the early morning shiurim still took place, before Rabbi Ashlag suffered his first heart attack, Rabbi Zalman Lemburger would offer the students a hot drink when they arrived. But during the shiur itself, he did not get up. The Baal HaSulam would teach the Zohar at the very place he was working on in his commentary, the *Perush haSulam*. He did not go back for new pupils, but the older ones would teach the newer ones, and in that way, they progressed.

Rabbi Baruch Shalom:

> During my father's lessons, the students did not write down what they heard. Only after the shiur was finished would they write it down. If you write at the time the words are said, you can hear only with the intelligence, but you cannot hear with the spirit.

In the shiur itself, the Sage would usually confine himself to the substance of the lesson. Only occasionally would he digress on a matter of the service of God, not connected with the material they were studying at the time. Questions on the service of God pertaining to the individual were asked by the pupils privately, usually before the Sage ate breakfast or, in the period after the heart attack, before he went to rest.

"Let the Awe of the Sage Be Like the Awe of God"

Rabbi Zalman Lemburger:

> The Baal HaSulam conducted himself with the utmost simplicity. Outwardly, he did not display anything of his inner thoughts. His dvekut with God was so continuous that it was completely natural to him. One could definitely feel that he was not of the

consciousness of this world and that he did not live for himself. Indeed, every single moment, it was palpable that he lived only for the sake of God. During prayer, his face would change colors and it was possible to see that in his spirit he was very far from his physical location.

The Sage would sit in his room and when he needed me, he would ring the bell that had been provided for him. It was very frightening to be in his presence. I really cannot describe the tremendous awe he inspired. It was clearly perceptible that here is standing a man who actually isn't here.

The Baal HaSulam's grandson, Rabbi Shmuel Ashlag:

The awe and fear that my holy grandfather inspired were very great. Everyone really felt that they were in the presence of an angel of the Lord, who was connected unceasingly with the living God. After the youngest of my grandfather's children had married, it became necessary for one of the family to be present with my grandfather on Shabbat. But the difficulty this entailed was immense because it was really frightening to be in his presence. It was a fear that was hard to control. I remember one Shabbat when I was present; I was so afraid I could not eat anything. When my grandfather turned around for a minute, I quickly ate everything on my plate in one gulp. But after that, I could not be with my grandfather again at the Shabbat meal.

Once, Rabbi Avraham Ashkenazi asked the Baal HaSulam a question on the material of the learning. It was midnight. The Baal HaSulam answered that he was busy and could not answer him, but that he could turn to Rabbi Yehudah Tzvi Brandwein for the answer. Rabbi Avraham did not wait till the morning but immediately set out for Rabbi Brandwein's house. The distance from the beit midrash to Rabbi Brandwein's was very great, but this did not deter him, nor did the fact that it was raining heavily. He got to Rabbi Brandwein's house, woke him up, asked his question, and when he received the answer he went straight back to the beit midrash. On his arrival, the Baal HaSulam said, "That is what I call a soldier!"

While living in Tel Aviv, the Baal HaSulam would hold a *tisch* each Shabbat, whereas when he had lived in Jerusalem, he generally had done so only on the festivals. The students who lived in Jerusalem made great efforts to come to the *tisch* on Shabbat even though it meant leaving their families. At these meals, the Sage would give over Torah, speaking fluently for four or five hours. He spoke with great precision on the dynamics of the light and the vessel in the higher worlds and their connection with our inner work of serving our Creator.

The importance of the *tisch* can be learned from the following conversation between the Rabbi and himself, recorded by Rabbi Binyamin Sinkovsky:

> We talked about the shiur, and while we were talking, the Rabbi said to me, "You still don't understand me. You still don't have attainment in me."
>
> I said, "I know that."
>
> I mentioned to him that he used to hold a *tisch* on Shabbat, but now, after the second heart attack, he no longer did so.
>
> He said to me, "It is indeed a great loss for you. Because I no longer hold the *tisch*, you lose **eighty percent of the connection with me;** and you lack that very much."
>
> I had, in fact, mentioned this issue to him on several occasions, but he was adamant, "I'm too weak to hold a *tisch*."
>
> Since the Rabbi had already spoken on my attainment of him, I told him that, also for me, the Shabbat was not the same as it had been because of the weakness of the Rabbi, may he live a long life.
>
> But the Rabbi responded straight away with energy, "Thank God, I myself don't suffer. For me, the Shabbat is exactly as it always was. For myself, I have enough, but I am too weak to give out. Once, the light poured out of me, and then it was enough for you as well. Today, the light does not pour out of me. However, for myself, I have everything."
>
> The Sage continued, "If the Holy Blessed One wants me to arrange the *tisch*, He will give me the strength for this. Indeed, I hope that when I finish volume fourteen of the Zohar, we will try to hold a *tisch* again." [1]

Journeying to the Rabbi

When Rabbi Ashlag lived in Tel Aviv, the students who lived in Jerusalem would delegate at least one of them to travel specially to be in his presence on Shabbat. That student would take messages and requests to the Sage from those who were unable to travel.

One time, it was the turn of Rabbi Yitzchak Agassi. One of his relatives asked for a blessing for his livelihood, but since it was not the custom of the students to ask for material things from the Sage, but only for spiritual help, Rabbi Agassi felt extremely embarrassed. When the Baal HaSulam approached him and asked him if he had any requests for him, Rabbi Agassi told him that he had, but that he was ashamed to ask it. But the Sage said that since he was only the messenger, he must carry out his mission. Hearing this, Rabbi Agassi confessed that one of his relatives had asked for a blessing for his livelihood. The Sage replied, "Ah! Of this matter, I, myself, have not had experience for a very long time!"

Rabbi Moshe Baruch Lemburger would travel every Shabbat to Tel Aviv to spend the holy day in the presence of the Sage, from whom he could not bear to be parted. His wife did not always agree that he should go and tried to prevent him from traveling by hiding his *shtreimel*. But Rabbi Moshe Baruch could not reconcile himself to staying away, so each time he would borrow a *shtreimel* from the shop.

Friday Morning

Friday morning, before dawn,
Breathing in the clear air,
The barrier is lifted, blown away, past.
Now His salvation is forever.

His delights pour forth, unending.
The light! He shows, like that! with a finger.
He will show me wonders in His Torah,
I will be satiated by His delights all my days.

Yehudah Leib Ashlag
Poem given to Rabbi Binyamin Sinkovsky
with the words, "This is for you!"

Chapter Fifteen

The Real Miracle—
The Inner Transformation

Rabbi Zalman Lemburger:

Once, at a Shabbat meal, Rabbi Ashlag was asked if he would give a blessing to one of the student's sons, that he should grow up in Torah with *yirat shamayim* [reverence for the Creator]. The Sage replied that he could bless the boy with all the blessings in the world, but what determines the issue is the person's own work. Only that can determine whether the blessing will be fulfilled and the child merit to the attribute of *yirat shamayim*. One cannot bless someone else that he will put in the work because only the person himself can do his own work.

Once Rabbi Ashlag told his students:

If I only knew that my toil on your behalf would be of use to you, then I have the strength to work for all of you. But this is not the case. Each one of you must work and labor for himself.

Once a certain woman approached one of the students, Rabbi Menachem Edelstein, pouring out her heart to him because every child she gave birth to died within a short period, leaving her childless. Rabbi Edelstein turned her away, saying he couldn't help in the matter. But she came back several times in great distress. Finally, he told her to go to his teacher in Jerusalem; maybe he could help. So she traveled to Jerusalem to Rabbi Ashlag, telling him that it was Rabbi Edelstein who had sent her. She asked to be blessed with children who would survive. He blessed her, and the blessing was upheld. But when Rabbi Edelstein arrived in due course, the Sage said to him, "Don't send me work. I have enough without that."

Explanation: The Baal HaSulam did not hold with working miracles. He followed the school of Kotzk, who taught "Signs and wonders belong to the land of the children of Ham," means that such things are not necessary for the Jew, who has to come to God through faith. The Sage taught that we need to accept the yoke of *Malchut Shamayim*, (serving God) out of belief in the greatness of God; a belief that is above the paradigm of knowledge. He did not believe it appropriate for people to base their Judaism on wonders or miracles and thus exempt themselves from doing their own inner work.

Nevertheless, since Rabbi Ashlag was a man of God, the students did sometimes see miracles.

When Rabbi Yitzchak Agassi became engaged to Rabbi Baruch Shalom's daughter, he approached the Sage and told him about his sister, who was no longer young, but for whom they still had not managed to find a suitable mate. The Sage replied, "Don't worry, she will be engaged and married before you." And so it was.

Once Rabbi Yosel Weinstock's son became severely ill and needed a dangerous operation. Rabbi Yosel went to the Baal HaSulam who instructed him to take upon himself to try and distribute the Zohar with the *Perush haSulam*. Rabbi Yosel did so, and immediately, to the doctors' astonishment, his son recovered.

Once Rabbi Yosel Weinstock himself became seriously ill and the doctors said he needed a difficult operation. He came to the Baal HaSulam and told him the situation. Again the Sage told him to take upon himself the distribution and selling of the books. So Rabbi Yosel redoubled his commitment, even though he was ill. After only a few days, the doctors were amazed to see no sign of his illness. After that, Rabbi Yosel continued to make great efforts selling and distributing the Zohar with the *Perush haSulam*. In his later years, he was to write, "Thanks to the Creator, who gave me the merit, even in my old age, to travel throughout the world, publishing and distributing 3,500 sets of the holy Zohar with the *Perush haSulam* and more than one thousand sets in Israel. In this way, I was able to help our holy teacher fulfill his purpose when he wrote the books."[1]

When Rabbi Yosel's grandson, Yoseph, became sick with meningitis, the doctors did not expect him to live. His mother turned for help to the Sage. That day Rabbi Ashlag prayed the afternoon service without joining the minyan and her son recovered.

Once, Rabbi Azriel Lemburger, the son of Rabbi Moshe Baruch Lemburger, became ill before Yom Kippur with an illness that had a very high mortality rate and had already killed many people. Rabbi Moshe Baruch turned to the Sage for help. The Sage blessed him that his son would recover. When his son was well again, Rabbi Moshe Baruch told him, "From now on you are not my son, but you are the son of the Rabbi, because he is your 'reviver of the dead'!" The Baal HaSulam also said that it was possible to make the blessing, "Blessed are You, Oh God, who revives the dead."

We see here two opposite approaches: on the one hand, no one took account of the miracles, not the Baal HaSulam himself, and not Rabbi Baruch Shalom Ashlag. We never heard the students speak of them, for these things didn't interest them at all. Only the question, how can a person deal with his nature and transform it to come closer to God, occupied their thoughts.

All the closest students of Rabbi Baruch Shalom testify that they never once heard him tell of a miracle wrought by his father. He would speak on his father's customs or on events in his father's life, but he never spoke of miracles. Indeed, the Baal HaSulam once told his wife that he did not want the students to have more awe of him than they had of God, so he did not want to perform miracles and did not give them any importance.

On the other hand, as some of the incidents related here show, there were indeed miracles. Because when we have such a man of God, who is cleaving to the living God, then he does have it in his power to heal the sick or to raise the dead. Indeed, the Baal HaSulam said that anyone with some connection with the service of God can work miracles. So miracles were not taken as indicators of a person's inner work.

The real miracle

Outwardly, the Sage acted simply. Here is an example:

One night a certain person had a bad dream and when he got up in the morning he felt depressed because of it. He began to ask various Rabbis to interpret his dream, but then he didn't know which interpretation was correct. Then he heard of the Baal HaSulam as being a Sage, completely immersed in the study of Torah. So he came to the Baal HaSulam and told him his dream and asked for its interpretation. The Baal HaSulam told him that since he was a simple Jew, he should act in accordance with the simple instruction from the Talmud—he should interpret his dream before three people. The man took his advice and immediately felt better.

Moral of this story: There are many "Kabbalists" who give advice using all types of counseling, according to the expectations that people have of one who knows Kabbalah. Such "Kabbalists" do this for money or for honor. But the Baal HaSulam did not hold with any such wonders, neither real nor imaginary. He held that a person needs to serve God with all his strength, and to conduct himself simply, modestly, and not in any way that will draw the attention of people. As the Zohar states, "Blessing is only found in something that is hidden from the eye."

There is a well-known story of the Sage of Kotzk: Once, some disciples came to him and told him about a certain Master who performed different miracles. The Kotzker said: I want to see if he can do one miracle. Can he take a man, and make him a Jew?

The meaning of this is: The only reason for us to be in the world is to find how we can come to dvekut with the Creator of the world; that is, just as He is merciful, so should we be merciful. That is the meaning of being a Jew. However, within us there are two conflicting forces, the force of the ego and the force of the soul. Whoever enters this work comes to know and feel that the work of becoming a Jew in the highest sense is beyond our ordinary human strength and is only achieved through divine grace. This, then, is the real miracle. All who endeavor to serve the Creator yearn for this grace, this miracle.

Chapter Sixteen

The Foundation of a Just Society

Within the core of every being—indeed, within every entity in existence, whether spiritual or physical—lie the Sephirot, the most subtle vessels for the divine light. Their nature, like the nature of all spiritual vessels, consists of the desire to receive God's goodness.

The goodness of the Creator is termed "the light." The light of the Creator has one constant desire that never changes. This desire is to give of itself, thus giving pleasure and enjoyment to all created beings. It is this desire of the light's that is called "the Purpose of Creation."

The Purpose of Creation manifests at the very highest spiritual level, the Ein Sof (the Infinite.) Here the light, wishing to bring the Purpose of Creation into reality, creates a desire to receive the light. This desire to receive all the pleasure, sweetness, and gentleness that is the light of God, is called "a vessel." The vessel for the light is the only created aspect of reality; whereas the light of God, His goodness, is not created but simply is. The vessel for the light of the Ein Sof is called the "Malchut." It is from the Malchut that all the myriad vessels of creation come.

Although the Malchut is fully formed in the Ein Sof, its emergence from the light occurs in stages. These stages are included within the Malchut and form intermediate vessels for the light. These, together with the Malchut, are called "the Sephirot." The Sephirot all embody varying degrees of the desire to give—the desire of the light—and the desire to receive—the desire of the vessel. The Sephirot, being the primary vessels for the light of the Creator, form the building blocks of creation.

As creation unfolds from world to world, the Sephirot are arranged according to the specific desires they embody.* Some Sephirot, having the desire to give, attract to themselves and are fulfilled by the pleasure and joy of giving. This pleasure is termed the *Or d'Chassadim* (the light of loving-kindness).** These Sephirot constitute the spiritual vessels that make up "the right-hand line of consciousness." As their nature is that of desiring to give unconditionally, the vessels of the right-hand line are in affinity of form with the Creator. Thus they form the basis for the framework of holiness.

Other Sephirot, whose desire, like that of the original vessel of the Ein Sof, is to receive the light of God, form the vessels of "the left-hand line of consciousness." They attract the *Or d'Chochmah*, the divine light of goodness with which God wants to give all created beings pleasure. These Sephirot have therefore the potential of fulfilling the Purpose of Creation.

But following the early event in the unfolding of the worlds called the *Tzimtzum*, simply receiving the light of God now causes opposition of form and separation from the Creator. Therefore, in order for the vessels of the left-hand line to remain in affinity of form with the Creator and within the framework of holiness, they need, on receiving the light, either to give it back, or to combine with the vessels of the right-hand line and receive the light only for the sake of giving pleasure to the Creator.***

If the vessels that desire to receive do receive the light without attempting to be in affinity of form with the Creator, they enter the framework of evil. The framework of evil is made up of vessels that are used to receive solely for themselves. Such receiving causes opposition

---

* For a fuller discussion on the *Tzimtzum* and the unfolding of the worlds, see the Talmud Eser haSephirot pages 336–342. Also *A Tapestry for the Soul*, (Nehora Press) Lesson Eight.

** Although the light of God is one, it receives different names according to the vessel that attracts it and is fulfilled by it.

***The phrase "receiving for the sake of giving pleasure to the Creator," refers to the fact that the Purpose of Creation can only be fulfilled if the vessel both receives the light and is simultaneously in affinity of form with the light.

of form with respect to the Creator and thus separation from Him. Then, in any case, they cannot receive the light that God wants to give.

All spiritual entities other than the human being belong to either the framework of holiness or the framework of evil. Uniquely, the human being is made up of vessels from both frameworks. Thus, at any moment, he has a choice on whether to use his desires in accordance with the framework of holiness or in accordance with the framework of evil.

How does this function in practice? In any circumstance, a person may choose to respond to the situation by simply refraining from using his desires to receive for himself alone. Alternatively, he may choose to use the situation to manifest his desire to give unconditionally. In either case, he remains in the framework of holiness. If, however, he reacts to the situation with his desire to receive for himself alone, then he joins with the framework of evil. In this state he is unable to receive the true light intended for him and he suffers emptiness and lack.

Does the receiving of our basic needs separate us from God? The answer to this question is no. We all have to receive food, shelter, clothing, and such-like. Receiving that which is necessary for our physical, earthly existence neither causes us to become distanced from God, nor does it bring about closeness with God. It is neutral. We become separated from God when we go beyond that which is necessary to fulfill our basic needs, especially if by doing so we are exploiting someone else.

Opposition of form between the spiritual vessels and the Creator, which leads to complete separation, first arose prior to the creation of human beings when spiritual vessels of the framework of holiness received more of the divine light than they could handle and began to receive for themselves alone. This event is known as sh'virat hakelim (the shattering of the vessels) wherein spiritual vessels first fell into the framework of evil.* From this point on, the possibility for humans to receive for themselves alone, and thus separate from the Creator, became real.

---

* This event took place in the spiritual world called the *Olam HaNikkudim*. For further information, see Rabbi Ashlag's Works, page 340 .

As human beings, our desires to receive are embodied in the physical, emotional, mental, and spiritual realms. Together, these constitute the ego. The basic substance of the physical body is a source of many of our simpler desires to receive. But more powerful ones are found in the emotional realm, such as desires for appreciation and control. The desire for knowledge constitutes the will to receive in the mental realm and is an extremely powerful desire in the human being. A blind desire for knowledge has led the human race to develop technology that has brought us to the brink of self-destruction. Even greater than this is the will to receive in spirituality, which is a desire to know God directly and to usurp His light. When misused, the will to receive in spirituality is a potent cause of wars and holocausts.*

These vessels of receiving, when used only for the sake of enhancing our selfish love, bring us into opposition of form with the Creator and cause us to remain in the framework of evil. However, by becoming aware of them and reigning them back, these vessels may enter the framework of holiness. It is indeed in the very act of moving elements from the framework of evil to the framework of holiness that we fulfill the purpose for which we, human beings, were created.

The soul, the divine essence within us, endows us with the desires to give unconditionally—either to give altruistically to our fellow or to place our faith unconditionally in the Divine Providence. These vessels are always in affinity of form with the Creator and form the right-hand line of the framework of holiness. The left-hand line is formed by the vessels to receive, when, instead of using them in their original form, we simply let go and decline to use them as we do not wish to be separated from the Creator. An example of this could be when somebody provokes us, but we decline to allow our anger to overtake us.

In a harmonious fusion between the vessels of the two lines, the right-hand line—the desire to give altruistically—and the left-hand line—the desire to receive, which we simply let go of—a third, middle line emerges, in which the vessels of receiving can now be used to receive for the sake of giving pleasure to the Giver. In such receiving, these vessels enable the Purpose of Creation to come to fruition.

---

* For a more complete discussion on the nature and development of the will to receive, see A Tapestry for the Soul (Nehora Press) Lessons 10–11.

When all our work of moving elements of our will to receive from the framework of evil to the framework of holiness will be complete, then receiving for the sake of giving will prevail as the dominant consciousness of humankind. This heralds a double benefit: (1) the finite vessels of receiving, the vessels of the left-hand line, become infinite channels for the light of the Creator, fulfilling the Purpose of Creation, and (2) they will simultaneously be in complete affinity of form with the Creator.

The arrangement of the vessels of the framework of holiness into these three lines of consciousness: the right-hand line, the left-hand line, and the middle line, is the root of our own spiritual work. It forms the basis with which we may form a correct relationship with God and with each other.

We can describe the functioning of the right-hand line and the left-hand line in this way: "Give unconditionally as much as you are able for the benefit of the other (the right-hand line) and receive only according to your needs (the left-hand line)." If these principles of giving and receiving in affinity of form with the Creator were to be followed by many people, then human society, being made up of many individual relationships, would follow similar harmonious and holy lines in dvekut with the Creator, and we would be able to establish a just, humane, and God-conscious society.

The phrase, "Give as much as you are able, and receive according to your needs" was also articulated by the philosophers of the socialist and communist movements. Karl Marx and others [1] formulated the phrase, "give as much as you are able and receive according to your needs" to describe a particular relationship of the individual to society that is imposed on the person by an external government. They failed to allow for the freedom of the individual to choose whether to act in opposition of form or in affinity of form with the Creator—a choice that is every person's right. Furthermore, they did not relate the phrase, "give as much as you are able and receive according to your needs" to its spiritual roots or relate to the two lines of consciousness as channels of connection with the Creator.

Such a formulation can be but a partial truth and doomed to failure in practice, because it does not accommodate the human being's basic nature of receiving for himself alone, his selfish love, which, being implanted in us by the Creator, is part of every human being, manifests as his ego, and provides him with the raw material for his spiritual work.

Since, above all, the ego likes rest, in general, a person will not work or exert himself in any way unless he believes that by so doing, either his lot will improve, or, if he fails to do so, his lot will deteriorate. As we see, the failure to take the nature of the ego into account caused the collapse of communism in the Soviet Union. The communist regime did away with economic incentives to work and so it could only maintain itself through punishments. Then Soviet Russia, which is a country of vast resources, fell into economic degradation.

Only if a person has a totally different basis for his motivation—that of contributing to society and giving benefit to his brethren because he wishes to come to affinity of form with the Creator—will he have a basis with which to work, as such a motive is not based on monetary rewards or on fear of punishments. Such an altruistic motive may, rarely, be inborn, but for the majority of people, who are endowed with egoistic tendencies, an altruistic nature needs to be acquired slowly, through the patient application of conscious, inner work of coming to affinity of form with the Creator.

Eventually, when all members of society will act from altruistic motives, then each individual will have hundreds of people looking out for him! Society would then flourish in peace and harmony.

Rabbi Ashlag:

> We have said that nature obliges the human species to live a societal life. That is clear. So we have to consider the laws of nature that we are obliged to keep, looking at how they apply to the life of the community.
>
> In general, we find that we need to interact with the society in which we live from the perspective of only two laws. We may define these two laws as "receiving" and "giving benefit." That is, every member of a society must receive his needs from society, and he is also obliged to contribute to society through his work. If he does not obey these two fundamental rules, he definitely will suffer the consequences.

Regarding the law that nature obliges us to receive from society, we do not need to consider this aspect to any great extent, because it is clear that failure to do so causes immediate harmful consequences. Therefore, no one neglects this. However, regarding the second rule, which is that of giving benefit to the society, the consequence of its neglect comes about in an indirect manner and is not immediately perceived. Thus, this rule is not kept properly, and humankind continues to simmer in the dreadful skillet of war, hunger, and their consequences, from which we suffer even now.

The most amazing thing is that nature acts like a seasoned judge, punishing us precisely according to our development. For we bear witness to the direct relationship that exists between humanity's development and the measure of affliction and suffering we undergo in order to attain our sustenance and ensure our existence.

We have here, in front of our eyes, the basis for scientific evaluation: Divine Providence has commanded us to fulfill the requirement of giving benefit to our fellow with all our might, such that none of us may lessen our work in bringing about the success and happiness of society. So long as we are lazy, not fulfilling our role to the required extent, nature will not cease to inflict the consequences on us and wreak its vengeance on us. We need to consider not only the blows we receive in our own time, but also those that hang as a drawn sword held over us in the future. The conclusion we are forced to come to is that nature will defeat us, until ultimately, we are compelled to unite to fulfill the mitzvot of the Creator in the measure that is asked of us.

One who argues with my words may raise a question, in that I have only proven the necessity of working for the benefit of our fellows. Where is the practical proof that we need to undertake this mitzvah of serving others for God's sake? However, history itself has provided incontrovertible direct proof before our very eyes. Look at the great state of the Soviet Union that has a population of hundreds of millions and a land mass greater than that of the whole of Europe, possessing unsurpassed natural resources. The people of the Soviet Union agreed to live a communal life—even to the extent of nullifying personal property—deciding that all should work for the sake of the society itself, such that, according to our human intellect, they appeared to have attained the attribute of giving benefit to their fellow in its fullest meaning. Nevertheless, look at what happened to them! Instead of ascending over the capitalist countries, they sank ever lower, until not only were they unable to ensure a better living standard for their people than that which the workers in capitalist countries enjoy, but even their daily bread became scarce and their minimal needs hardly met.

Indeed, this fact seems extremely strange, for according to the innate prosperity of the state and the number of its members, common sense dictates that it should not have reached this low level. But this nation committed a fundamental error that Divine Providence does not forgive them: all their precious and exalted work of giving benefit to their fellow man was based on working for the sake of humanity and not for the sake of God. Since their work was not for the sake of God, it had no chance to survive, from the rules of the Divine Providence itself.

Try to imagine how it would have been if every member of that society had cared deeply about fulfilling the Scripture, "And you shall love the Lord your God with all your heart, and with all your soul, and with all your might"? Accordingly, everyone would have been concerned to fulfill the mitzvah, "Love your neighbor as yourself, I am the Lord" (Lev. 19:18) to the utmost, fulfilling the needs of his fellow exactly as he would have wished his own needs to have been met, as the target of all his work would have been God.

Every worker, while he was working for the happiness of the society, would know he was working for the Creator. The worker would expect that, through his work for the society, he would merit to unite with God, the source of all truth and goodness, the source of all pleasantness and gentleness. There can be no possible doubt that within a few years, the prosperity of such a state would have been greater than that of all the other nations put together, for they would have been able to utilize their rich natural resources, and would have been a wonder among the nations. They would have been called, "Blessed ones of the Lord."

However, when the foundation of working for the benefit of the other rests solely on the welfare of the society, the basis of such work is shaky. For who will compel the individual to increase his labor for the community? Even sophisticated people find it impossible to find the energy with which to overcome their inertia from a dry principle that has no life force.

Therefore, the question stands: where will the worker or the farmer get sufficient motivation to work, unless he himself stands to benefit from his own labor? If, for example, a person moves his hand from his chair to the table, it is because it seems to him that if he were to rest his hand on the table, he will gain more pleasure. If this did not seem to him to be the case, he would leave his hand where it was. In fact, he would not move throughout his entire life unless he felt he had something to gain from his effort! If this is the case with respect to a small movement, how much more must it be true for something that involves real work?

If you were to say that the solution is to place overseers or inspectors over the workers, so they could punish anyone who does not fulfill his quota by taking away his rations, then I would ask you: from where will the overseers obtain sufficient motive for such work? For supervising someone else is hard work and may even prove harder than doing the work yourself. Work in such a condition is like trying to move a motorcar without providing any gasoline.

Therefore, such a state is doomed as a natural consequence. The laws of nature will ensure this because the workers do not adapt themselves to fulfill the requirement of giving benefit to their fellow as part of their service to God. Only through service to the Creator could they come to the fulfillment of the Purpose of Creation, which is brought about through their affinity of form with the Creator.

We have already explained that as the worker acquires affinity of form with God, so there comes to him a measure of His bounty, which is pleasant and full of joy. This further increases until the worker has a sufficient measure of such bounty, whereupon he is elevated to recognize the truth of God. This increases and develops until he merits to the great joy that is hinted at by the sages in the inner meaning of the Scripture, "The eye has not seen it, O God, only You" (Isa. 64:3).

Imagine for yourself if farmers or workers would feel this purpose to be their utmost priority when they are working for the welfare of society. They would, then, definitely not require any overseer to supervise them, for they would have great motivation to labor to their utmost until they were able to raise society to the heights of happiness.

It is true that to understand these matters in this way requires a lot of care and the correct means, but all see that we survive only through this rule, as nature is unyielding and does not brook any compromise.

I have clearly proved from our experience seen throughout history, that there is no possible remedy for humanity unless we accept on ourselves the command of Divine Providence of giving benefit to our fellow in order to serve God, according to the measure implied in the two scriptural injunctions: "Love your neighbor as yourself, I am the Lord" (Lev. 19:18), and "You shall love the Lord your God with all your heart and with all your soul and with all your might" (Deut. 6:4). The injunction "Love your neighbor," embodies, not only the essence of the work itself, but also implies that the effort we put into giving benefit to our fellow must be not less than that which we put out in caring for our own needs. On the contrary, we need to promote the needs of our fellow before those of our own.

The second injunction, "And you shall love the Lord your God with all your heart and with all your soul and with all your might," is the purpose that must be present before our eyes when we work to fulfill the needs of our fellow. It is on His instruction that we act and labor to come to affinity of form with the Giver, may He be blessed. He spoke, and we do His will, may He be blessed.

If we are willing and listen, then we will eat of the goodness of the earth; for the poor, the oppressed, and the misused will cease from the land and the happiness of each person will ascend higher and higher beyond measure. But if we refuse, and don't want to come to the covenant of the service of God in all the measure that has been explained, then nature and its rules stand, in all their explicit measure, and will take vengeance from us and will not let us go, but will vanquish us until we accept its rule in whatever it commands us, as we have explained.

So I place this practical research in the analysis of human experience before you and have proven the complete necessity for all the created beings to accept the service of God upon themselves with all their heart and with all their soul and with all their might.[2]

Rabbi Ashlag wrote much on his vision for the establishment of such a just human society that would fulfill its purpose, bringing benefit to all—a society in which the vision of the prophet, "nation shall not lift up sword against nation"(Mic. 4:3) would be fulfilled. His perspective included the whole of humanity, giving detailed step-by-step moves for us to take. He envisaged the establishment of small communities whose members follow the principles of the right-hand line and the left-hand line of the framework of holiness, giving according to their ability and receiving only according to their needs. Each such small community would embody an ideal society. Once established, such small communities would act as models for people who would see the beauty of a life lived in accordance with altruistic principles in affinity of form with the Creator, thus fulfilling the purpose of the human being, in accordance with divine will. Such communities would multiply until the entire country would follow these principles. These principles would also then be established as the norm in relationships between countries.

The motive of serving God has to be the foundation for the establishment of such communities, as any other basis is too weak to provide sufficient motivation to overcome the natural demands of the ego.

From Rabbi Ashlag's unpublished writings:

Indeed, it is for the establishment of such a just society that the nations look to Israel, and it is what they expect of the Jewish community in the Land of Israel. For such wisdom does not belong to other nations. Other wisdom we may learn from all the nations, but in the Torah of righteousness and peace, they are our students, for this wisdom comes through the Torah.

The Jewish nation is in danger, for before the economy will stabilize many will leave. Not everyone is able to bear poverty when he has the possibility of living well in other countries. The Jewish nation may, God forbid, be swallowed up by the Arabs that surround them. Danger also threatens the kibbutzim, whose establishment is built on ideals, which, in the natural course of events, will diminish, because altruism and ideals are not inheritable traits. Indeed, the kibbutzim will disintegrate first of all, for their existence is built upon ideals that from their nature will lessen with the generations, for ideals are not inborn.

But if we walk in the way of Torah, we come to the middle line. The middle line emerges as a synthesis of the right-hand line and the left-hand line and enlightens the soul. Then each person will have the ability to bear the burden.

Once the economy of the country is stabilized it will attract the ingathering of the exiles from all other nations, who will then have an extra push to come and return to their land, where they may live in tranquility and justice.

If all Israel were to accept on itself this idea of working in order to attain affinity of form with God, according to the holy Torah, then it will be possible to build the Temple and restore all its ancient glory. Furthermore, such work certainly proves the just claim of Israel over that of all other nations in Israel's return to their land, even over all the Arabs. This is not the case regarding the secular return of the Jews to the Land of Israel as it exists today. This makes no impression on the nations of the world and one must fear that the secular Jews may sell the independence of Israel or let go of Jerusalem for their own needs.

The basis for governance in practice is the Torah of the Kabbalah, which we may ponder, and which provides the philosophical and ideological basis for the leaders of the community so they can establish the correct direction for society.

Meetings with the Leaders of the Secular Community

Rabbi Ashlag met with the heads of the secular Jewish *Yishuv*, hoping to elevate the socialist basis of Zionism, and particularly that of the Kibbutz Movement, to one in which the individual's service to God as an essential element of his service to his fellows is recognized.

These meetings took place from 1940 onwards. David Ben-Gurion, who became Israel's first prime minister, came to visit Rabbi Ashlag on three occasions, as did Moshe Sharett, Israel's foreign minister. They formed a close connection with the Sage, and, from time to time, would consult him on different issues.

Rabbi Ashlag was interested that the new state should be run according to socialist principles because the main thrust of socialism consists of giving to our fellows and of equality among citizens. Thus, there was a possibility that the practice of socialism could be a step on the path of establishing a rectified and just society. But in order for socialism to be a viable system of communal governance, each individual would have to overcome his natural egoism. This is not possible without belief in the Creator; and although socialism, as such, does not have reference to the Creator and is therefore faulty, nevertheless, the Sage saw it as a possible preliminary step through which the consciousness of working to serve God might penetrate society.

Meetings with David Ben-Gurion and Moshe Sharett were set up with the help of Professor Dan Sedan, then the editor of the *Dvar* newspaper. Afterward, Rabbi Avraham Brandwein met with Professor Sedan who told him what had transpired:

> I asked the Sage, "Why do you want to meet with the secular leaders of the community? You have nothing in common with them!" He answered, "I want to meet with them because the Holy Blessed One has handed the management of practical matters pertaining to the Land of Israel into their hands."
>
> I can further state that the Rabbi told Ben-Gurion that true giving between people is actually material. If, for example, a person teaches his fellow mathematics, then he still has his own grasp on the subject. But if he gives him a loaf of bread, then he is left with less himself. Indeed, it is important that the spiritual work

that flows from the wisdom of the Kabbalah is actually expressed materially. Therefore, the most important way a person can give to his fellow is by helping him with his material needs.

Ben-Gurion then asked the Rabbi if he believes in devils. The Rabbi responded, "Devils are only ideas that don't come into any practical expression. So what is the difficulty in believing in such things?"

Rabbi Zalman Lemburger:

When Rabbi Ashlag met David Ben-Gurion in the Haas Hotel in Tel Aviv, Ben-Gurion stated: "I am a heretic. I don't have anything to do with the Torah. What does the holy Rabbi want with me?" But the Sage responded, "The faith of a person who was a heretic and has returned to God, may ultimately prove to be greater and more important than one whose faith stems from education. For education causes faith to become a habit which thus may lack life. But faith that comes from within has life."

The Sage asked Ben-Gurion to ensure that the Shabbat would be honored as a free day for working people. Despite the fact that Rabbi Ashlag made his request quietly and calmly, Ben-Gurion became very agitated at this. He jumped up and paced back and forth in a great passion, saying, "How can I tell others to do what I myself don't do? I cannot lie!" Rabbi Ashlag answered, "Lies and truth are, to some extent, relative. If a lie leads to good, then it may be true."

Indeed, some years after this talk, Ben-Gurion proclaimed the Shabbat as the national day of rest in the State of Israel.

In his later years, Rabbi Ashlag tried to influence the Kibbutz Movement. He said, if people are already working in an idealistic way for the benefit of others, then they need only change the reason they are doing this work to working for the sake of Heaven. He sent his son Rabbi Baruch Shalom to talk to Zalman Shazar [later, president of Israel]. They discussed the ideas for several hours. Finally, it was decided to make a meeting between one of the heads of the Kibbutz Movement, a certain Mr. Chazan, in order to move the project onto more practical lines. But two days after their meeting, Mr. Chazan was killed in a helicopter accident over Tiberias. The Sage said that this was a sign from Heaven that the world was not yet ready for this step.

During his previous sojourn in Tel Aviv, Rabbi Ashlag had been in touch with Chaim Nachman Bialik, the national poet of the Jewish *Yishuv*. Bialik had been a yeshivah student in his youth, but had left the religious world and become completely secular. Now, after meeting with the Sage on several occasions, he told him he wanted to return to Judaism and asked to be accepted as a pupil. But first, he had to travel to Vienna to undergo an operation. Unfortunately, he died there on the operating table. The Sage said that if he would have returned, he would have come back to his Judaism completely. But it was not to be.

The Conscious Way of Peace as Opposed to the Way of War

Rabbi Ashlag:

> The will to receive, ingrained in every created being, is the basis of his difference of form with respect to the Creator. Therefore, a person's soul is separated from the Creator, like a limb is separated from the body; for change of form in spirituality separates spiritual entities like a blade separates physical entities.
>
> So it is clear that what God wants of us is to come to affinity of form with Him. Then we will again be one with Him, just as we were, prior to our created state.
>
> In explanation of the command to cleave to God, the Sages taught, "Cleave to His attributes! Just as He is merciful, so you be merciful." This means that we need to transform our ingrained attributes, which are based on our desire to receive, and instead, adopt the attributes of the Creator, whose only desire is to give benefit. In that way, all our actions will be directed only toward giving benefit to our fellow and being of use to him to the extent of our ability. Thus we may come to achieve the purpose for which we were created, which is dvekut with Him, and which implies acquiring affinity of form with Him.

That which a person does for his own needs, out of necessity, in the minimal measure for his own and his family's upkeep, is not considered to cause a difference of form between himself and the Creator. What a person needs to receive out of necessity for his survival is neither denigrated nor is it praiseworthy.

The work of transforming our nature to one of giving is the tremendous revelation that will be fully manifest only in the days of the Messiah when all will accept this teaching. Then we will merit the full redemption.

I have already spoken on this. There are two ways to come to this full revelation: either through the way of Torah or through the way of suffering.

Therefore, the Holy Blessed One has given knowledge of technology to the children of men, culminating in their discovery of the atom bomb and the hydrogen bomb. If the massive destruction these weapons are liable to wreak on the world is still not sufficiently clear to the people of the world, they will have to wait for the third world war or the fourth world war, God forbid, until the bombs do their work. The remnant, who survive such destruction, would have no choice open to them but to transform their nature. At such a time, neither the individual nor the community would work for themselves alone except to supply the necessities for their existence. The rest of their efforts would be directed for the benefit of their fellow. If all the nations of the world would agree to this, then wars would be abolished, for each would be looking out for the benefit of his fellow, rather than putting his own self-interest first.

This law of affinity of form is the Torah of the Messiah, as the Scripture says, "And it shall be at the end of days, the mountain of the Lord's house shall be firmly established at the top of the mountains, and it shall be raised above the hills, and peoples shall stream upon it. And many nations shall go, and they shall say, 'Come, let us go up to the mountain of the Lord and to the house of the God of Jacob, and let Him teach us of His ways, and we will go in His paths, for out of Zion shall the Torah come forth, and the word of the Lord from Jerusalem. And he [the Messiah] shall judge between many peoples and reprove mighty nations, even those distant... '" (Mic. 4:1-3).

The Messiah will teach how to serve God in affinity of form, which is the instruction and the law of Messiah. He will reprove the mighty nations that if they do not accept the work of God on themselves, all the nations will be destroyed by wars, God forbid. But if they do accept his teaching, then, " ...they shall beat their swords into plowshares, and their spears into pruning hooks; nations shall not lift sword against nation; neither shall they learn war anymore." (ibid.)

We see that if we go in the way of Torah and accept the teaching of Messiah, then all will be well. But if we don't receive his teaching, then we will go the way of suffering, and then, God forbid, nuclear wars will manifest in the world. Only then will all the nations of the world seek a way to escape these wars. Then they will come to the Messiah in Jerusalem, and he will teach them this Torah.[3]

Chapter Seventeen

The Establishment of the State of Israel

O n Friday, May 14, 1948, (*Iyar* 5, 5708) the State of Israel came into being. Although, in general, the Sage hid his feelings, when the students came and told him of the proclamation, all could see tremendous excitement on his face, and he said, "Yes, I do feel somewhat the feeling of a *chag* (Jewish festival) today!"

Rabbi Menachem Edelstein:

> The Baal HaSulam added, "This is the beginning of the process of the *Geulah* [the redemption]." He said that the State of Israel will endure until the coming of the Messiah, may he come speedily, Amen. He further said that if it were not for the establishment of the State of Israel, many Jews in the Diaspora would assimilate and Israel would lose more children than Hitler had managed to destroy. It was the establishment of the State of Israel that would encourage many in the world to keep their Judaism at any price and not assimilate.

> Indeed, during the First World War, when anti-Semitism in Poland was on the increase and Poles were routinely attacking Jews on the streets of Warsaw, Rabbi Ashlag had said it was a sign from God that the Jews need to pack their bags and leave Europe for Israel. Again, when he journeyed to Europe for the last time, he repeated his warning, but it was not heeded.

Rabbi Ashlag:

> We need to understand clearly that the redemption and the coming of the awaited Messiah (may he come speedily and in our days, Amen!) implies our attainment of a whole and total connection with the light of God. As the Scripture says, "No longer shall a person teach his neighbor or his brother, saying, 'Know the Lord,' for they shall all know Me, from their smallest to their greatest, says the Lord. For I will forgive their iniquity and I will no longer remember their sin" (Jer. 31:33).
>
> … When the Children of Israel will have a complete connection with God, then the wellsprings of understanding and knowledge will burst beyond the boundaries of Israel and give water to all the nations of the world, according to the Scripture, " …for the earth shall be filled with the knowledge of the Lord as the water covers the seabed" (Isa. 11:9). Also, "For the Lord has ransomed Jacob and redeemed him from the hand of one that is stronger than him. And they shall come and sing in the height of Zion, and they shall flow to the goodness of God, to the corn and to the wine, to the oil and to the young of the flock and of the herd; and their soul shall be as a watered garden and they shall not pine any more at all" (Jer. 31:10-11).
>
> This increase in the connection with God is a consequence of the influence of the Messiah spreading out to all nations. It negates an idea held by coarse people who cling to the power of the fist, and who imagine this influence of Israel over other nations as meaning some type of physical governance in which others are ruled. Such people take reward in their great pride, lording themselves over the peoples of the world. What shall I say to them, seeing that the sages have already rejected them and those like them from the congregation of the Lord? For the sages of the Talmud have said, "Regarding the proud, the Holy Blessed One says, 'he and I cannot dwell in the same dwelling.'" [1, 2]

In Spirituality, the Time of Giving and the Time of Receiving are Separate.

The Baal HaSulam wrote:

In physical matters, the receiving of something occurs simultaneously with its being given. But in the realm of spirituality, the time of giving is one event, and the time of receiving is a separate event.

When the Creator gives anything to the one who receives it, He actually gives only the opportunity to receive. The receiver does not yet receive anything until he has purified himself and separated himself from the unclean, as is fitting. Only then will he merit to receive that which God intends to give him. Thus, between the time of giving and the time of receiving, there may be a great delay.

Has this generation already reached the spiritual level indicated by the Scripture, "And the earth will be filled with the knowledge of the Lord as the water covers the seabed"(Isa. 11:9)? We can only say yes, in the sense that we have been given the opportunity for attaining a whole connection with the Creator, but as for receiving such a great light, certainly we have not, and we will not reach that point until we purify and sanctify ourselves, study, and labor in the service of God in the required measure. Only then, will come the time of receiving, at which time the Scripture, "and the world will be filled with the knowledge of the Lord," will be upheld.

It is known that the fact of redemption and our complete attainment of the knowledge of God are two elements that are intimately bound up with each other. It is a wondrous thing that all who are drawn to the innermost aspects of the Torah are also drawn to the Land of Israel. Therefore, the prophecy that the land will be filled with the knowledge of the Lord cannot be fulfilled except at the end of days, that is, at the time of the redemption.

Just as we have been given only the opportunity for dvekut with the Creator, but we have not yet attained it, likewise, we have been given only the opportunity for the redemption, but have not yet received it. For the fact is that although the Holy Blessed One has taken our holy land out of the possession of non-Jews and given it back to us, we still have not yet **received** the land to our governance, because we have not yet come to the time of receiving. God has given us the land, but we have not yet received it, for we do not have economic independence; and there cannot be political independence unless we have economic independence.

Furthermore, there cannot be redemption of the body without redemption of the soul, and while most of the people of Israel are captive to foreign cultures of the other nations and are not adjusted at all to the religion and culture of Israel, so the bodies are captive under the forces of foreigners. In this sense, the land is still in the hands of foreigners.

It is a wonder that no one seems at all excited by the redemption, as we should be, after two thousand years. Many who live in the Diaspora are not moved to come and enjoy the redemption. Even a large part of those who have been redeemed and are now dwelling among us wish to be rid of this redemption and look with longing to return to the lands of their dispersion! So even though the Holy Blessed One took the land out of the possession of the nations and gave it to us, nevertheless we have still not received it and we do not enjoy it. But in this giving, the Holy Blessed One has given us the **opportunity** for the redemption that we may purify ourselves, sanctify ourselves, and take upon ourselves the service of God in Torah and mitzvot for its own sake. Then the Temple will be rebuilt, and we will receive the land to our domain. Then we will sense and feel the joy of the redemption. But until we have come to this, nothing will change. There is no difference in the manners of the country now, compared with what they were when we were under the rule of strangers; not in the justice system, nor in economics, nor in serving God. And so we have only the opportunity for redemption.

Nevertheless, our generation is the generation of the Messiah. Therefore, we have merited the redemption of our holy land from foreign powers. Likewise, we have merited the revelation of the book of the Zohar, which is the first step in the fulfillment of the Scripture, "And the earth will be filled with the knowledge of the

Lord, as the water covers the seabed" (Isa.11:9). Also, "No man will teach his neighbor or his brother, saying, 'Know the Lord!' For all of them will know Me, from the smallest to the greatest" (Jer. 31:33). But regarding these two aspects of redemption, we have, as yet, merited only to have been given the opportunity for them from God, but we have not yet received them into our hands.

Still, we have been given the opportunity through this gift to begin the service of God; to practice the Torah and the mitzvot for their own sake. Then we will merit great success in all that the generation of the Messiah is promised; that which no other generation before us knew. Then we will merit the era of receiving on both these counts: the complete attainment of the knowledge of God and the complete redemption. [3]

The War of Independence

Rabbi Zalman Lemburger:

The students of the beit midrash maintained that the Baal HaSulam's greatness was no less than that of the Holy Ari. They held him in such high esteem that they felt he had the power to influence events. This accords with the idea, "the righteous decrees and God fulfills," [4] an idea based on the Scripture, "You will make a decision and it will be accomplished for you, and light will shine on all your ways" (Job 22:28).

Each day during the War of Independence, Rabbi Ashlag would sit with his pupils in front of a map of Israel spread out on the table. He would show them exactly how the war was being conducted and where the Jewish soldiers were going into battle. Once he said that a certain place they entered was not good. Rabbi Moshe Baruch Lemburger asked the Rabbi if he should go at once and tell Ben-Gurion, but the Rabbi answered there was no need as they had already discovered it for themselves, and what would come to pass, would come to pass. And indeed, the events unfolded as he foresaw.

Each day the Sage would hint at what would come to pass on the morrow in the conduct of the war. The students grasped that the entire proceeding of the war was taking place in the inner consciousness of the Rabbi and that the process within him had a direct influence on the outer conduct of the war.

This is possible to understand according to what the Baal HaSulam wrote in his *Introduction to the Zohar*:

Individuals, through their deeds, can cause an elevation or degradation of the whole world. There is an unalterable law that the macrocosm [the totality] and the microcosm [the individual] are as like to each other as two drops of water. The same procedures that occur with respect to the macrocosm occur with regard to the individual and vice versa. Furthermore, it is the individual components themselves that make up the macrocosm, and thus the macrocosm is only revealed through the manifestation of its individual components according to their measure and their quality. So certainly, the act of a single person, according to his capacity, may lower or elevate humanity as a whole. [5]

Rabbi Zalman Lemburger:

There came a time during the war when it seemed possible for the soldiers to enter the Old City of Jerusalem and try to recapture it. But the Rabbi said it would be of no use for the time had not yet come for this, and so it proved in practice.

During the war, there was tremendous shelling of the city by the enemy. We asked the Sage, "When will the shells stop flying?" He answered, "When we will read in the *haftarah*, [the weekly reading from the prophets] '…and the children of Ammon were subdued before the Children of Israel'" (Judg. 11:32). Indeed, it came about that on the Shabbat of *Parashat Chukat*, when we started to read the *haftarah*, the shelling increased greatly at first, but when we read that specific verse, the shelling ceased.

The Establishment of the State of Israel

Rabbi Baruch Shalom:

> When we captured the Negev, the desert area in the south of the
> country, my father was extremely happy. I asked him why, and he
> replied, "Now the Jews will come to settle in the Negev!" I con-
> tinued, "But there is no water in the Negev." My father answered,
> "When the Jews will come to live there, they will pray for rain, then
> rain will come." I asked him again, "But the Jews who will settle
> there will be secular Jews." He answered me, "Prayer is not the
> words you say with your mouth, prayer is a demand of the heart."

Chapter Eighteen

Dvekut

Tradition holds that Rabbi Shimon Bar Yochai, the great Talmudic sage who brought the Zohar into being, finished his teaching on the day he departed this life. Each year, these great teachings are celebrated on the anniversary of his passing on the festival of Lag b'Omer, when thousands of Jews gather at his grave in the village of Meron, dancing and singing. So when Rabbi Ashlag—Rabbi Shimon's spiritual heir—finished the *Perush haSulam,* his commentary on the Zohar, he decided to hold a meal of thanksgiving on Lag b'Omer at the site of Rabbi Shimon's tomb.

That year, 1953, Lag b'Omer began on *Motzei Shabbat* (Saturday night), so Rabbi Ashlag and his students traveled on the Friday to the village of Meron where they spent the Shabbat. That Shabbat eve, the Rabbi held a *tisch* in which he, like Rabbi Shimon, centuries before him, gave over very high teachings composed of inner meanings of the Torah. The Rabbi's face shone with a palpable and holy joy.

On Lag b'Omer, they held the meal of thanksgiving at the gravesite of Rabbi Shimon Bar Yochai at which Rabbi Ashlag spoke on the entire purpose of our work in Torah and mitzvot, which is to come to *dvekut* (unity) with the Creator. All the pupils felt the great holiness that enveloped the Sage as he spoke. Their joy burst forth like an overflowing spring and they broke into dance. One of the students, Rabbi Avraham Ashkenazi, took all eighteen volumes of the books and raising them above his head, danced with them. "Whoever did not witness such joy, never saw joy in his life!" [1]

Here is an excerpt of the talk that Rabbi Ashlag gave in Meron:

> It is known that the purpose of all our work in Torah and mitzvot is to come to dvekut with God, may He be blessed, according to the Scripture, "But surely, keep all this commandment that I am commanding you to do, to love the Lord your God in all His ways, and to be in dvekut with Him" (Deut. 11:22). But what does dvekut [unity with God] mean? How can we unite with God when the Scripture affirms, "for the Lord your God is a consuming fire" (Deut. 4:24)?
>
> The sages of the Talmud interpreted the injunction to unite with Him as meaning, "Unite with His qualities. Just as He is merciful and gracious, so you be merciful and gracious."[2] Still, we need to ponder, if that is the case, why didn't the Torah simply tell us to unite with His qualities? What does uniting with God mean?
>
> When we are talking about physical entities we understand dvekut as implying physical proximity between them. Separation between two physical entities means there is a distance between them.
>
> But for spiritual entities that do not occupy any space at all, unification or separation between them is not determined by whether they are in physical proximity to each other or distanced from each other, but by whether or not there is affinity of form [similarity of desire] between them.
>
> Affinity of form brings about dvekut [unity], whereas change of form [difference in desire] causes separation between spiritual entities. Just as a blade cuts a physical object—splitting it in two as it separates one part from the other—so does change of form divide one spiritual entity into two, separating the parts from each other. If the change of form between the entities is small, then we say that they are only slightly distanced from each other, but if the change of form between them is great, then we consider them as being much further away from each other. If they are in opposition of form, then we say that they are utterly remote from each other.
>
> For example, when two people hate each other, we say they are as far from each other as the east is from the west. If they love

each other, then we say they cleave to each other—in dvekut—as if they were one. We are not talking about physical closeness or distance, but we are talking about whether they embody affinity of form [similarity of desire] or change of form [difference in desire].

Now we can understand how right were the words of the sages, who interpreted the commandment of being in dvekut with the Creator, as cleaving to His attributes. The sages were not adding an interpretation of the Scripture, but simply explaining it. For spiritual dvekut cannot be envisaged in any way other than affinity of form. Therefore, through our equating our form with the form of God's attributes [that is wanting what He wants, which is to give good unconditionally] we attain dvekut with Him. And this is what the sages said, "Just as He is merciful...," that is to say, just as the purpose of all His deeds is only to give benefit and help to the created beings, and not for His use at all—for He, may He be Blessed, has no lack that would need to be fulfilled and from whom could He receive?—so should our acts be directed only toward giving benefit and help to others. In this way, we make our form equal to the form of the attributes of the Creator. This is spiritual dvekut.

... Prior to its creation, every soul is included in the essence of God. But through the act of creation, the soul obtains the desire to receive pleasure. This causes the soul a change of form that separates it from God, as His desire is only that of giving benefit. For change of form separates spiritual entities, just as a blade separates physical entities.

We find that the soul is now likened to a limb that has been severed from the body and is separated from it. Even though prior to the separation, the limb was part of the body as a whole and they were one, exchanging thoughts and feelings with each other, now that the limb is severed from the body, they have become two domains, not knowing the thoughts of the other or the other's needs. Indeed, once the soul has been clothed in the body that pertains to this world, all the connections that it had before its separation from the Creator's essence, have ceased, and the soul and the Creator have become two separate domains.

Thus the virtue of a person who has again merited to acquire dvekut with God is self-evident. He has merited affinity of form with the Creator, may He be blessed. Through the power of the Torah and the mitzvot, he has transformed the will to receive that is stamped within him, which had separated him from God's essence, into the will to give benefit, such that all his deeds are now performed only for the sake of giving benefit and use to his fellow. In this way, he has made his form equivalent to that of his Maker. He is like a limb that was once cut off from the body and has now rejoined the body. He again knows the thoughts of the body just as he did before he was separated from it.

So it is with the soul. Once it has acquired equivalence of form with the Creator, may He be blessed, then it again knows His thoughts just as it did before it was separated from Him by the change of form caused by the desire to receive. Then the Scripture is fulfilled, "Know the God of your father" (I Chron. 28:9). For then the person merits to receive full *Da'at* [connective knowledge], which is divine *Da'at*, and he merits all the inner meanings of the Torah. For God's thoughts, are the inner meanings of the Torah.

... In truth, the whole Torah, whether revealed or hidden, consists of the thoughts of the Holy Blessed One without any difference at all between the different parts of the Torah. This may be likened to a man drowning in the river whose friend throws him a rope. If the drowning man catches the rope by the end closest to him, his friend can save him by pulling him out of the river. Likewise, the entire Torah consists of the thoughts of the Holy Blessed One and is like a rope that the Holy Blessed One has thrown to humankind to save us and get us out of the forces of evil. The end of the rope that is closest to humankind is the revealed Torah, which does not require any intention or thought. Not only that, but even if the action of a mitzvah is done with an unworthy thought, such practice is still acceptable to the Holy Blessed One, as the Sages taught,

"A person should always occupy himself with Torah and mitzvot, even if practiced not for their own sake, for by doing them not for their own sake he will come to do them for their own sake."[3]

The Torah and mitzvot are the end of the rope that everyone in the world is able to grasp. If we grasp the rope strongly then we will merit to practice Torah and mitzvot for its own sake, that is, we will merit the practice of Torah and mitzvot for the sake of giving satisfaction to our Creator and not for our own purposes. Then the Torah and mitzvot will bring us to affinity of form with the Creator, that is, to dvekut with Him, as we said above. We then merit to attain all the thoughts of the Holy Blessed One, which are designated "the secrets of the Torah" and "the inner reasons of the Torah." These inner aspects of Torah belong to the portions of the rope that are farther away from us initially and to which we do not merit until we come to full dvekut with the Creator.

We liken God's thought—the inner meanings of the Torah and the reasons for the mitzvot—to a rope, because there are many levels of affinity of form with the Holy Blessed One. There are, correspondingly, many levels in the portions of the rope; that is, many levels of attainment in the inner meanings of the Torah within each one of us. These portions of the rope within us refer to our attainment of the inner meanings of the Torah. These accord with our stage of affinity of form with the Creator and correspond to the five levels of the soul available to us, which are: *Nefesh, Ruach, Neshamah, Chayah,* and *Yechidah.*

These levels of soul are also referred to as "worlds," as the sages of the Talmud have said, "in the future, the Holy Blessed One will bequeath 310 worlds to every tzaddik."*[4] The reason that the levels of attainment of the light of the Holy Blessed One are called "worlds" is that there are two meanings to the word "world": (1) All the inhabitants of a world are equally endowed with senses and feelings, such that what one person sees, hears, and feels, all others can equally see, hear, and feel; (2) the inhabitants of one world cannot know or grasp anything of another world.

---

* See page 79 for full discussion of this idea.

Likewise, we find that these two definitions apply to attainment: (1) Whoever merits a certain spiritual level knows and attains that which everyone who comes to that specific spiritual level attains—whether he is of the same generation, or of past or future generations. He shares with them a common attainment as if they are all in one world. (2) All who come into that spiritual level cannot know anything about what is to be found in a different spiritual level—just as we, in this world, can't know anything about the next world, the world of truth. Thus, these spiritual levels are called "worlds." [The Hebrew word for "world" is עולם which comes from the root עלם meaning "hidden."]

The spiritual masters were thus able to compose books and to write of their attainments in hints and parables that are understandable to anyone who has merited the same level of spirituality of which they are speaking. But whoever does not share the author's spiritual level will not understand anything.

Complete dvekut and the complete attainment of God's light may be divided, generally speaking, into one hundred and twenty-five levels. Before the days of the Messiah, it was impossible to merit these one hundred and twenty-five levels completely. However, the generation of the Messiah differs in two respects from all other generations: (1) Only in the generation of the Messiah will it be possible to attain all one hundred and twenty-five levels. (2) In all previous generations, those who merited attainment of God's light and dvekut were few, but in the generation of the Messiah, **every single person can merit to dvekut and attainment of the light of God,** as it is said, "And the earth will be filled with the knowledge of the Lord as the water covers the seabed" (Isa. 11:9). Also, "No man will teach his neighbor or his brother, saying, 'Know the Lord,' for all of them will know Me, from the smallest to the greatest" (Jer. 31:33).

Only Rabbi Shimon Bar Yochai and his generation, the Masters of the Zohar, merited all one hundred and twenty-five levels of attainment of God's light, even though they lived prior to the days of the Messiah. It was about Rabbi Shimon Bar Yochai and his pupils that the sages of the Talmud said, "a sage is preferable to a prophet,"[5] and thus we find stated in the Zohar that there will be no other generation like that of Rabbi Shimon Bar Yochai's until the generation of the Messiah. This is why his book made such a great impression on the world, for the inner meanings of the Torah that are contained in it encompass all the one hundred and twenty-five levels of attainment of God's light.

So it is written in the Zohar that only at the end of days will the Zohar be revealed: that is, in the days of the Messiah. For if the spiritual level of those who study it is not equal to the spiritual level of the author, that is they have not reached the level of Rabbi Shimon Bar Yochai and his companions, they will not understand the subtleties of his writing, as they do not share the same attainment. We, therefore, find that in the generations before the days of the Messiah there was no common spiritual attainment with that of the sages of the Zohar. So it was not possible for the Zohar to be revealed prior to the generation of the Messiah.

From here, we have a clear proof that our generation has come to the days of the Messiah. We see with our own eyes that all the explanations of the Zohar that preceded us explained, maybe, only ten percent of the difficult places in the Zohar, and in the small amount they did explain, their words are almost as impossible to understand as those of the Zohar itself. But in this, our generation, we have merited the *Perush haSulam*, which is a complete explanation of all the words of the Zohar. Not only that, but it does not leave anything incomprehensible in all the Zohar without explaining it. The explanations are formulated according to a normal student's intelligence, so that anyone of reasonable intelligence can understand them. Since the Zohar has been revealed in our generation, this is a clear sign that we are already in the days of the Messiah, in the beginning of that generation, of which it is said, "And the land will be filled with the knowledge of the Lord."[6]

That year, following the completion of the *Perush haSulam*, on the Shabbat on which we read in the Torah of the deliverance of the Children of Israel from Egypt (*Parashat BeShalach*, Exod. 13:17-17:16),

Rabbi Ashlag requested to be called up for the Levite's portion of the Torah reading. He asked the reader to continue straight through the story of the deliverance right until the end of the Song of Moses. The students were happy to acquiesce in his request, dividing up the rest of the *Parashah* in a shortened way among the others called up to the Torah that day.

Receiving Only for the Sake of Giving

The Baal HaSulam's purpose in revealing his own spiritual attainments was only to help the world progress to the fulfillment of its purpose. Rabbi Baruch Shalom told us that on one occasion his father expressed to him that if he had explained the Zohar to the required depth, it would have taken at least a thousand volumes! He had also wanted to write a commentary on the *Aggadot* (parables) in the Talmud and in the *Midrash*, but he did not manage this.

We really rejoice over the mighty gift the Baal HaSulam left us: twenty-one volumes of the Zohar with the *Perush haSulam* commentary; the six volumes of the *Talmud Eser haSephirot*; three volumes of the *Etz Chaim* of the Ari with the *Panim Meirot uMasbirot* commentary; *Matan Torah*; the book *Ohr haBahir*; the book *Sha'ar haKavanot*; three volumes of the book *Pri Chacham*; the introductions and essays.

We also have many poems and songs that the Baal HaSulam wrote, filled with the spirit of dvekut and joy in service to God, wreathed in the innermost meanings for the Torah and subtle manifestations of levels of divine light. Rabbi Ashlag composed many melodies saturated with longing for his Creator and filled with happiness on every manifestation of God. All this, in addition to the oral teachings faithfully recorded by his students.

When we look at Rabbi Ashlag's life's work, we cannot help but be amazed. We wonder, how did he merit to attain the ways of the spiritual worlds with the utmost dvekut that is possible for a man to achieve? On more than one occasion, Rabbi Baruch Shalom said that his father expressed to him that all these revelations had only one cause: he labored day and night with tremendous self-sacrifice. Each day he saw that his inability to understand only grew. Nevertheless, he continued to study with incredible devotion for fifteen years, until Heaven had mercy on him, and finally opened the gateways of the wisdom to him. From this, we see that our labor is the key to enter the palace of the King. We must not think that such great revelations can take place by chance, or that it is through such revelations that a person reaches spiritual heights. But we need to put forth our effort to the fullest possible extent, even beyond our human capacity, and give ourselves over to the work with all our heart and soul. After that, God is pleased to bring us near.

It was only after intense labor that our teacher merited the soul of the Holy Ari and the revelations of the wisdom that he was given. Indeed, the Baal HaSulam explained the verse, "The Lord is clothed in majesty" (Ps. 93:1) saying, "It is as if the Holy Blessed One is garbed in a type of pride that wraps Him, and He is not willing to allow anyone to draw near, except one who puts all his life, his heart and soul into his desire to cling to the King with a strong will, until nothing stands in his way. The seeker doesn't look to the right or to the left, but has only one aim—dvekut with God—and this aim is continually in front of his eyes."

Song

Oh my God, I embrace You,
As one who is drowning struggles to reach the harbor.
Yes, I yearn for Your footsteps as I wrestle with myself.
You say now to come to dvekut with You,
That is well.
What is my hope, if I am serving myself,
Since You have demanded to give me dwelling?
Surely my soul is stirred up and my belly; how You grind my will
    so small—
What is pleasing to You of my deeds?
What will be fit for You as a meal offering and as a gift?
Please, my Maker, tell me!
Then I will find favor with You,
He, who raises me up.

Yehudah Leib Ashlag
Cheshvan 4, 5697 (1936)

Chapter Nineteen

"My Father! My Father!—
The Chariots of Israel and Their Riders!"

(Kings II 2:12)

After the Baal HaSulam had finished writing his commentary on the Zohar itself, his health began to worsen. Nevertheless, he continued, writing a commentary on the *Zohar Chadash*. * But his strength was greatly lessened and he was no longer able to teach much, confining himself to one shiur a week.

Rabbi Binyamin Sinkovsky:

The 5th evening of Parashah Metzorah 5714 (8th April 1954)
When I came to him at an earlier time than usual, I found him sitting bent over the *Zohar Chadash*. I was sorry. I had not wanted to waste his precious time. But he, may God bless him, turned to me saying that he was suffering terribly from rheumatism. It caused him great psychological suffering because he didn't have the desire even to take up his pen to write Torah. Only the tablets that he took once every eight hours gave him some relief, but they began to work only after three hours.

I said to him, "But if you want, surely you can help yourself? You do not live for yourself; you are my Rabbi and you need to do much for the students. Is it not permissible for you to rid yourself of the illness by miraculous means?" But on this, he replied, "The

---

* The *Zohar Chadash* is a part of the Zohar that was not included in the Zohar's original printing in the sixteenth century.

way of nature is a very good way. One does not need recourse to supernatural means, since natural means are sufficient and considered. The Creator, may He be blessed, created nature so that it will suffice, and it is good. One does not need to go beyond nature. One needs to do one's own work. That is better and healthier and produces better results. [1]

When the students saw the Rabbi's health failing, they wrote a letter requesting him to begin all the work with them anew. For their part, they were prepared to take on themselves everything he would tell them to do, just as if they were new students starting out. All of them signed the letter and presented it to him, but the holy Rabbi said it was too late.

Rabbi Zalman Lemburger:

In the latter years of his life, our holy Rabbi never went out of his house, and it was very rare that he would organize a journey to the holy places. I remember only two such occasions: The first was on the completion of the *Perush haSulam,* and the second was in the month of *Adar,* in the last eighteen months of his life. Then the holy Sage traveled to Safed, where the students hired a hotel and made a great *seudah* [holy meal].

Our Rabbi did not say then what this seudah was for, only one or two of the pupils knew that it was, in essence, a farewell seudah for the students. At this seudah there was a tremendous feeling of joy, greater than the students had ever felt in all their days; a joy that is impossible to describe. It was the holy Rabbi who now gave this tremendous joy into the heart of each and every one of the students.

In the midst of the dancing and the happiness, the students decided to stage a play: At that time Stalin reigned over the Soviet Union with a reign of dread. It was rumored that he was plotting to deport all the Jews of the Soviet Union to huge concentration camps in Birobidjan, an area of Siberia, close to the Chinese border, where the natural conditions are harsh and the temperature in winter can reach minus twenty degrees centigrade. Jewish survival was in great jeopardy. So the students staged a play, putting Stalin on trial. It lasted about half an hour and all the students took part. At its end, they "killed" Stalin. During this time, the Rabbi was sitting in his room nearby, but he knew all about the students' activities. Two days later, they heard that Stalin's health was in a critical condition, and subsequently, he died.

From Safed the Rabbi journeyed to Meron, where Rabbi Shimon Bar Yochai is buried. As was his custom, he stayed only three minutes in prayer at the tomb.

Following his return to Jerusalem, the Rabbi told the Rabbanit that the students would not rejoice like that in the near future.

That last year, Rabbi Ashlag called to his assistant, Rabbi Moshe Baruch Lemburger, telling him: "You must be quick to ask me anything you want to ask." Indeed, from that time on, Rabbi Moshe Baruch went into the Rabbi's presence and asked as many questions as he was able.

Rabbi Azriel Chaim Lemburger told of what he heard from Rabbi David Mintzberg, that on the last Succot of Rabbi Ashlag's life, the students were amazed and concerned to see that his face shone with a great light. Unlike his usual custom, he spoke on many things that had happened to him in his life. He also told Rabbi David Mintzberg, "You see I have a very beautiful succah? Next year it will be even more beautiful." Rabbi David asked him, "But surely the Rabbi's succah is always more beautiful than the year before?" Rabbi Ashlag answered, "That is true. But next year it will be one of unparalleled beauty." To Rabbi Binyamin Sinkovsky, to whom he was particularly close at this period, he said, "Next year the succah will be so beautiful! It will have the aspect of 'No eye has seen it.'"*

After Succot, Rabbi Ashlag told the Rabbanit, "The students will not rejoice with me much longer, only one more year." When Rabbi Moshe Baruch heard this he was troubled by it, but afterwards he forgot it.

---

* This is a reference to the Scripture, "And whereof no one has ever heard, has ever perceived by ear, no eye has ever seen, besides You, O God, who acts for one who waits for him" (Isa. 64:3).

Rabbi Azriel Chaim Lemburger:

> During the last summer, the students asked the Rabbi if he would write a continuation of the *Perush haSulam* for the *Tikkunei haZohar*, but he refused, saying he did not want to start something he would be unable to finish.

Each year, as the holiday of Succot approached, the students would search out a beautiful etrog for the Rabbi. They began their search on *Rosh Chodesh Elul*, six weeks ahead of time. However, in the Rabbi's last year, he told the students, "This year, don't search for an etrog for me; it is better you should look for a beautiful etrog for yourselves."

Rabbi Yehudah Tzvi Brandwein prayed as the *shaliach tzibur* (prayer leader) on that Rosh HaShanah. Rabbi Avraham Brandwein: "My father told me later that the holy Rabbi told him explicitly, 'You should know that I will leave this world in another ten days.'"

Rabbi Azriel Chaim Lemburger:

> A neighbor by the name of R. Peretz Albom lived opposite the Rabbi and would sometimes come to visit him. Before Yom Kippur, when Rabbi Ashlag was on his sickbed, and it was now clear that he was leaving this world, Reb Peretz came in and asked him, "What shall we do without the Rabbi?"
>
> The holy Rabbi answered him explicitly saying, "Afterwards, whoever wants will have more than he has now."

Rabbi Zalman Lemburger (who had been the Baal HaSulam's assistant):

> The holy Rabbi was always in constant grasp of the higher worlds; despite this, he performed all outward actions in the usual way even though his words were always directed to the higher worlds. But three days before he passed away, he said to me, "Give me the slippers of *Abba and Ima* [a spiritual stage of the world of Atzilut related to the Sephirot of Chochmah and Binah]. Normally, he would just say to me, "Give me the slippers," but now, when he was so close to his departure from this life, he was unable to hide his intentions.

"The Day is Leaving, the Sun is Sinking, Let Us Come Into Your Gates."[2]

The day that the Baal HaSulam departed this life, Yom Kippur, 5715, fell that year on a Thursday. The Sage asked for the prayer service to start two hours earlier than usual. So instead of beginning at 8:30 a.m., the students started prayers at 6:30 a.m. The sky was overcast and rain began to fall. The students felt terrible. The day had come—the day that they had hoped and prayed would not come.

The leader of the prayer was Rabbi Moshe Baruch Lemburger. When he got to the verse, "I will satisfy him with length of days and I will show him My salvation," he could not get the words out of his mouth, and he repeated the words, again and again, until they called him into the room of the Rabbi. It was at those words, 'I will satisfy him with length of days," that Rabbi Ashlag's holy and pure soul had left and rejoined its Source.

The Rabbi was sixty-nine years old when the song of his life ceased. It was a life that had been entirely dedicated to pleasing the Creator, may the One be blessed.

The students wept uncontrollably. It was as if the holy Shechinah had left, as if a pillar of light and manifestation of God's light and divinity had departed, as if a web of life dedicated to the service of God with untold self-sacrifice had ended. How would the world continue now? How would it continue without the teacher and guide for those who seek dvekut with God?

Rabbi Baruch Shalom:

> The feeling among us was hard and painful. You really cannot imagine it, and it is impossible to describe. It felt as if we were living through the destruction of the Temple itself. It was a feeling of bereavement, of being fatherless. From that moment on, until the end of his life, Rabbi Moshe Baruch Lemburger was unable to revive his spirits. He just couldn't get over the loss. Indeed, for all the students it was a time of change, and we needed a period of tremendous perseverance until we were able to open a new page in the service of God.

The funeral took place on the morrow of Yom Kippur, on the Friday. Rabbi Ashlag was buried on Har Menuchut, close to where he had served as rabbi in Givat Shaul. Indeed, once, when contemplating the hills surrounding Jerusalem, he had remarked, "It will be good that here I will rest." The students were glad to fulfill this last wish.

Rabbi Shmuel Mintzberg:

My father, Rabbi David Mintzberg, the Sage's faithful student, dealt with the details of the burial and buried the Rabbi's holy and pure body himself.

The students wished to build a small building over the grave, similar to the one that houses the grave of Rabbi Shimon Bar Yochai in Meron. But the *chevrah kadishah* [the burial society] objected because there was no such precedent in Jerusalem. Nevertheless, in the middle of the night, Rabbi Baruch Shalom and the others took blocks and cement and built the marker over the grave with their own hands.

Rabbi Moshe Baruch Lemburger:

A few years after the passing of our holy teacher, Rabbi Moshe Yair Weinstock had to undergo an operation on his throat in the United States. Following the operation, he wrote to me: "When they took me to the operation, I saw the Baal HaSulam. He said to me: "You should know that I am light-years away from you, but when you need me I will always be present."

May his merit guard us and all Israel, Amen

Dayeini

It Would Have Sufficed Me

Happy is the man whose strength is in You, and God forms the pathways of his heart.

Happy is the man who obeys Your commandments and Your Torah, and he places Your word on his heart.

You are He who brings forth light and creates darkness, who makes peace and creates everything.

If you had inclined a listening ear to me, You, in profound, eternal love, but had not shown me how Your eyes see from one end of the world to the other, it would have sufficed me.

If You had promised me that I would attain all Your secrets and be among those who may approach You, but had not clothed them within me as an actual present reality, it would have sufficed me.

If You had clothed me in your secrets, as an actual present reality, but I had not attained the awareness that the respect owed to You cannot be compromised and that nothing limits You—not even levels of spiritual consciousness—it would have sufficed me.

If I had attained the realization that levels of spiritual consciousness do not limit You, but You had not made of me a receptacle for prayer to receive all my needs from Your hand, it would have sufficed me.

If I had merited Your call and merited to be answered—as a man demands from his fellow—on all that my heart wishes, but You had not amazed me by the birth of the land in one day, and the begetting of a nation at one moment, it would have sufficed me (From Isa. 66:8).

If You had shown me the secret of the One who looks out over the land from His dwelling place (from Deut. 4:35), but You had not set me on my feet in the very beginning, so I may feel Your presence within my heart, it would have sufficed me.

If I had merited to feel all Your lights within me as *Or Pnimi*, [inner light], that gives me the light of Your revelation, but You had not made known to me that this is the purpose that You want for all Your creation and it is all Your joy, it would have sufficed me.

If You had made known to me Your unique joy that awaits all the work of heaven and earth, but You had not taught me to know how You have blessed it above all the days and sanctified it above all the times, it would have sufficed me.

If I had merited the blessing of all the days and the sanctification of all the times—past, and future together—but You had not troubled to pacify me with much wisdom and friendliness, to remove the shame from me, it would have sufficed me.

If I had merited to be purified like the heaven itself and its host, according to the inner meaning of "my prayer beseeches You" [that the vessel is equivalent to the light], but You did not ask of me, "if your children keep My covenant," (after Ps. 132: 12) it would have sufficed me.

If I had heard from Your mouth the oath that you swore in Your holiness, "Surely I will not be false to David; His seed shall endure forever, and his throne as the sun before Me" (Ps. 89:36–37), but You had not taught me that apart from it being Your delight, it is also my delight, it would have sufficed me.

If my palate had let go of all wisdom and all desire, and all my yearning was only for Your light, but You had not clarified for me that I have nothing left to add and that I am permitted to leave this world, it would have sufficed me.

And if I had understood with all my intelligence that I have to leave this world immediately, and You hadn't awakened me to look for some work within my abilities and I hadn't found anything, it would have sufficed me.

And if You had awakened me to know that Your desire lies in hard work and not only in pleasure, and you had not awakened me with a welcome and some consciousness of understanding in the holy books, it would have sufficed me.

And if You had not awakened me to yearn after the understanding in the books, but You had not taught me that the most important thing is the certainty and the cleanliness of the heart and that the light, of itself, has no value, it would have sufficed me.

And if I had attained that there is no importance to the light, only the certainty of faith and the purity of the heart, but You had not granted me to long for You, and that it is not possible to receive the light without causing a defect in the respect owed to You, it would have sufficed me.

And if I had departed this world in the fulfillment of all my purpose, but I had not merited to attain the inner meaning of the Scripture, "Let not a sage boast of his wisdom" (Jer. 9:22), and thus the ability to receive the renewal of the vessels for faith, it would have sufficed me.*

From this stage on in the poem, the Baal HaSulam talks of different levels of attainment of the light of faith and the illumination of the Or d'Chochmah that he had the merit to attain. It is clear from his

---

* At the time when a person attains a revelation of the *Or d'Chochmah* he needs to nevertheless let it go and prefer the light of faith. (See the letter to Rabbi Joshua Horovitz, page 83-94, and the teaching of the Rabbi of Belz, page 13).

description that every stage he attained is separate and individual, and that the attainment of every stage required him, each time, to let go and return to the light of faith, which gives the lesser light of the Or d'Chassadim. This is very difficult to achieve.

The latter part of the poem is filled with allusions to these stages as described in the Zohar. But I do not understand these and they are beyond my capacity to translate. Y. C.

The poem finishes:

How much incredible untold bounty I have merited!

I have merited to all the above, even to the resurrection of the dead, in great mercy, to draw me close, in *teshuvah shelemah* [perfect repentance] in *yirah* [reverence] and in love of You and in true service.

And You have brought me again close to the community of all Israel and to Your Torah in great love and faith. What can I give back to You for all Your goodness to me?

Yehudah Leib Ashlag

Chapter Twenty

Swifter than Eagles,
Stronger than Lions

(Samuel II 1:23)

The connection between a true sage* and his student is a dynamic relationship that changes as the student grows and matures in his spiritual work. This relationship develops in distinct stages, similar to those we go through in our own relationship with God. By considering how the student's relationship with his sage develops, we can also learn how our own relationship with the Creator grows. These stages are described by the Holy Ari as the embryo, the nursling, and consciousness.

In the stage of the embryo the student is still, to some extent, bound up with his desires to receive for himself alone. He doesn't yet have the correct desires (vessels) with which he can receive the light of God. Therefore he needs to put aside his own desires and instead, use his faith in his teacher as his guide for his thoughts, his actions, and his speech. Then, like the embryo, which receives its nourishment from its mother, he may receive the light of God through the vessels of his sage. The more he believes in the greatness of his sage, and the more he can adapt his own thoughts, speech, and actions to accord with his sage's example, the more he may receive the light of God and be

---

* For the question of who is a true sage, see the discussion that appears in the letter that Rabbi Ashlag wrote to his father, page 129.

fulfilled. At this stage of development, the student is completely carried by his teacher, who, for his part, is happy to give to him. As the sages of the Talmud said, "More than the calf wants to nurse from its mother, the cow wants to suckle her calf." [1]

As the student progresses, he begins to recognize how much his teacher is giving to him. Likewise, he becomes cognizant of the role of Divine Providence in giving goodness in his life. This awakens within him the desire to come to affinity of form by giving unconditionally to his teacher and to God. This is the stage of the nursling.

Now that the student has reached the stage in which he desires to give unconditionally to others and to God, he starts to contemplate deeply on the question, "What can I give to You?" He realizes that there is nothing he can give to God, because God is the root of all and lacks nothing. Finally, he internalizes the Purpose of Creation, that God's only desire is to give benefit to all created beings. He sees that by using his vessels of receiving only in order to give the Creator the pleasure of fulfilling His purpose, he is thereby giving to Him. This is the stage of consciousness.

Because the student's relationship with the sage develops in parallel with his relationship with God, the sage may use his relationship with the student as a means to help the student progress in his connection with the Creator. We saw an example of this in the letter that Rabbi Ashlag wrote to Rabbi Joshua Horovitz (page 83).

The effect that the sage has on the student's development is not, however, the only outcome of the student-sage connection; the student also has an effect on the sage. It was the needs of the students in their struggle to understand the material and their difficulties in putting the principles into practice that gave Rabbi Ashlag the impetus to receive the wisdom more deeply in order to amplify his teaching. Anyone who studies the *Perush haSulam* may see how the same concepts are explained, again and again, each time from a different perspective, with clarity and with patience. It is a clear example of how the love between sage and student mutually enhance each other.

Rabbi Ashlag studied the works of the Ari and the texts of the Zohar with the students. It was from the content of the early lessons that his first book, the *Panim Meirot uMasbirot*, was composed. But when the Sage saw that the students did not understand the book, he began again and wrote a more detailed work, the *Talmud Eser haSephirot*. Thus we see how it was the students' need and their questions that awoke in the Sage the channels with which he could bring these great lights down for our generation.

When we see the important role the students played in the creation of these works, we get a glimmer of understanding as to how they were willing to sacrifice themselves, and even their families, over and over again, to publish the books for the benefit of all humanity. They understood that just as they had been helped and their lacks assuaged by the light in these works, so others would be helped.

The Baal HaSulam taught only men whose desire for serving God in truth was of paramount importance. He gave personal direction to the students depending on each one's unique character. To the students who tended to criticize themselves harshly, he emphasized the role of faith and joy in the service of God. To others, he emphasized the need for self-inquiry to uncover the bitter truth of our selfish love.

Some of the stories we read about the students are hard for us to understand in these days of relative material affluence. At this distance in time, it is hard to assess how much of the poverty and of the sacrifice the students made on their own behalf and on behalf of their families was due to their dedication to their Rabbi, and how much was a part of the economic stringency prevailing in the country in the early years of the British mandate after the First World War, and then later, during the Depression.

Unlike many of their contemporaries from the chareidi community, the students of Rabbi Ashlag did not spend their entire day in study, but endeavored to earn their living; their study being conducted at the expense of their sleep. Despite this, there was opposition to the students' connection with the Sage from their wives and their families. Part of this opposition seems to have originated from the fact that the wives did not understand the work in which their husbands were engaged, nor could they recognize its importance, as Rabbi Ashlag was not, at that time, known or appreciated in the wider community. And, of course, part of the opposition stemmed from the fact that it was the wives and families who had to deal with the practicalities of life.

What follows below are not full biographies of the students, but sketches intended to illustrate aspects of their personalities, their individual connection with the Sage, and their particular approach to his teachings.

Rabbi Moshe Baruch Lemburger

Rabbi Ashlag gave Rabbi Moshe Baruch a job: to wake him up every night at one o'clock in the morning. Rabbi Moshe Baruch's son Rabbi Azriel Chaim relates:

> Many times it happened that until my father had finished all he had to do, it was already eleven o'clock at night before he reached home. His time was short, for at midnight he needed to wake up and hurry to Rabbi Ashlag's house, which was about an hour's walk away—Rabbi Ashlag lived in Givat Shaul, whereas we lived in the Old City. Despite this, my father would first sit down and learn Gemara with me for about thirty minutes to check that I was learning properly, and at eleven-thirty, he would lie on his bed for about a half hour, until midnight. However, to make sure he did not oversleep, he would get up several times during this half hour and ask if it was twelve o'clock already.
>
> At exactly twelve, he would get up and start to walk in the direction of Givat Shaul. At that time there was no transport and there were no streets. The ways were dirt paths, and at night there were packs of feral dogs that were dangerous. But nothing stopped him—not the freezing winter nights, not the rain, and not the hot summer nights.
>
> But the truth remains that my father never managed to wake Rabbi Ashlag, for, always, when he got to Givat Shaul, Rabbi Ashlag was already sitting over his books! But at least he merited to make him a cup of coffee each night. Then he would return home and learn till the light of day.

Rabbi Avraham Ashkenazi:

> Once, I was on my way to a private shiur with Rabbi Ashlag. It
> was one o'clock in the morning and the weather was stormy.
> Thick fog covered Givat Shaul. I walked quickly, intent and full
> of expectation, to my meeting with the Sage. Suddenly, emerg-
> ing from the fog, I saw a figure marching along. I wondered to
> myself, "Who can this be, wandering around Givat Shaul at this
> time of night?" As I got nearer, I saw it was Rabbi Moshe Baruch
> Lemburger going home after having made the Sage a cup of coffee,
> as he did every night.

A Soul Dancing Before the Creator

Frequently, at times of simchah, Rabbi Ashlag would tell the students
to dance. In order to dance, a person needs an uplift of spirit. However,
this is not always easy for people who are treading the path of true
service to God. These are people who are fiercely critical of themselves
and who constantly measure to see if they have progressed in their
faith in God and in His Divine Providence. For faith in God does not
mean paying lip service; it means behaving, thinking, and speaking
exactly as we would if we could perceive the Creator with our senses.
If we check ourselves according to this criterion, which of us can truly
say that we have faith in God? The students, who were on the path
of wanting to truly serve God, therefore needed to make great efforts
to overcome their fierce self-criticism and to simply let go and dance.
Nevertheless, their dance was filled with joy and uplift of spirit.

But of all the students, Rabbi Moshe Baruch stood out. Dance
was an inseparable part of him. When he danced, it seemed as if his
physical body wasn't present, only a soul full of longing to unite with
its Source. He didn't need other people to dance with him; he was
able to dance completely alone. He would dance for hours, sometimes
as much as four hours. Rabbi Yitzchak Agassi said of Rabbi Moshe
Baruch that he was a servant of God of the highest level, such as had
been known in the generation of the Baal Shem Tov.

Poverty and Self-Sacrifice

The times were harsh, and economic hardship and distress were widespread in Jerusalem. There was literally not enough to eat.

Rabbi Azriel Chaim Lemburger tells:

> Once, my uncle came to our home and shouted in despair at my mother, "Nechamah, why do you let him go to the Sage? He doesn't finance the household and the children have nothing to eat!"

In the Sage's own house, the poverty was tremendous. The Sage was completely involved in spiritual work and in writing the holy books. His son Rabbi Baruch Shalom used to joke that on Shabbat they had to close the windows when they served up the chicken, because it was so small they worried that every little wind would blow it away! Where could money come from? Nevertheless, Rabbi Moshe Baruch Lemburger dedicated his life to the Baal HaSulam: he would give over anything he owned to help finance the books, even selling the contents of his house more than once. He supported himself with difficulty by selling wines, but whenever he had any money, he brought it straight to the Sage. He would also bring food to Rabbi Ashlag's family, even when the poverty in his own house was just as bad.

Later on, when the Baal HaSulam moved to Tel Aviv, Rabbi Moshe Baruch also stayed there during the week. However, since Rabbi Ashlag had requested him to carry on with the wine business in order to help finance the books, and since most of the sales were on Friday, he would travel to Jerusalem to work in the shop all Friday. This prevented him being with the Sage on Shabbat, but he deferred his own wishes to fulfill the request of his teacher.

Rabbi Pinchas Brandwein:

> Rabbi Moshe Baruch did all he could to help finance the books. He sold his share in the bus company that the students had set up that ran between the Old City and Givat Shaul. Furthermore, when they would sell the *aliyot* to the Torah on the festivals [as is customary in many communities in order to raise money for the synagogue], Rabbi Moshe Baruch would buy the mitzvah for

huge sums; sums that in today's currency would amount to more than half-a-million shekels, despite the fact that in his house there was hardly anything to eat. In order to give the sums of money he had promised, he used to borrow from friends and from charities. He was in debt all his life. His only purpose was to ensure the flow of money that would enable the printing of the *Perush haSulam* on the Zohar to continue.

Rabbi Moshe Baruch brought his two sons, Rabbi Zalman and Rabbi Azriel Chaim, to the Baal HaSulam, so they could also act as his assistants. This they did faithfully.

Deference to the Sage

Rabbi Azriel Chaim Lemburger told me that the Baal HaSulam once asked him, "Have you ever talked with your father about spiritual matters? He does not regard his own ego at all. He thinks only about how he can serve his fellow man." Indeed, whenever the Baal HaSulam used to receive any of the students privately to discuss their inner work with them, or when other people would come to speak to the Rabbi, he never asked Rabbi Moshe Baruch to leave the room, since Rabbi Moshe Baruch put his own self aside to the extent that it was as if he wasn't there at all.

Rabbi Moshe Baruch took great pains over the mitzvah of the lulav and etrog on the festival of Succot, and would always purchase a beautiful etrog for a high price, even as much as three hundred dollars. However, on the first day of Succot he would put his own etrog aside and make the blessing on the etrog of his teacher.

Rabbi Azriel Chaim Lemburger:

Once, the son-in-law of the Baal HaSulam Rabbi Isaac Shia Verdiger approached me, saying," I am so amazed at your father. He is in the presence of the Baal HaSulam constantly, yet every time he needs to enter the room, he checks his clothes and his beard to ensure they are tidy. He enters with great awe and trembling, just as if it were the first time."

Sometimes, my mother would ask my father to mention the name of a sick friend to the Sage, asking him to intercede with the Almighty on her behalf. Afterwards, she would ask, did you mention her to the Rabbi? He would shrug his shoulders uncomfortably, saying, "I can't just speak to the Rabbi at any time, whenever I want. He needs to come down to my level to speak with me."

Love of Friends

Rabbi Yisrael Miller:

Once there was an argument between Rabbi Yitzchak Agassi and Rabbi Moshe Baruch on the content of the study. The argument was sharp and penetrating. They did not reach an agreement, so they left and went home. It was late at night, Rabbi Yitzchak was already in bed, when, suddenly, there was a knock at the door. He got up sleepily, and Rabbi Moshe Baruch was standing there. He said, "*Bist gerecht* [you are right]," and turned to go. But then Rabbi Yitzchak invited him in and the two sat in love and friendship, studying until the morning.

The Baal HaSulam once said to his son Rabbi Baruch Shalom:

It is written in *Pirkei Avot*, "One who is pleasing to his fellow man is pleasing to God. But one who is not pleasing to his fellow man is not pleasing to God." If any of the students wants to know if he is pleasing to God, he should look to see if he is pleasing to Rabbi Moshe Baruch Lemburger, for he is one of those who are pleasing to God.

The place where all the students gathered together, when not in the beit midrash, was in the cramped home of Rabbi Moshe Baruch. Rabbi Baruch Shalom related, that when the Sage was abroad, the students would gather at Rabbi Moshe Baruch's house to study before dawn, even though he only had one room and a kitchen. The family slept in the one room and the students learned in the little kitchen. Despite—or maybe because of—the tight space, they learned together in love and companionship and the atmosphere was one of pure spirituality.

Emphasis on the Inner

Rabbi Zalman Lemburger:

> Once my father came to me and asked me why I sway backwards and forwards when praying. He disliked intensely any outward show of spirituality, as it detracts from channeling all one's energy on the inner intention. Rabbi Baruch Shalom taught that the sages' injunction, "Do not look at the container, but at what is in it"[3] should be applied to oneself. If someone is praying with fervor, he should ask himself, what is compelling him to this fervor?
>
> However, such an inquiry is relevant only for those who wish to work on their inner service of the Creator. For one who does not so wish to work, it is better to stay with the outer form.

One time, when Rabbi Zalman was young, Rabbi Moshe Baruch came to find his son in the Beit Knesset. There was a certain Jew there whose function was to supervise the children to see that they prayed properly. When he saw Rabbi Moshe Baruch, he thought he had come to check on his son, so he went up to him and told him that he had nothing to worry about, for the child was praying beautifully. Whereupon Rabbi Moshe Baruch asked, "How do you know that he prays beautifully? Have you entered his heart?"

Where Has My Beloved Gone?

Rabbi Baruch Shalom:

> Following the passing of my holy father, there followed a period of great darkness for us all. We were enveloped by a great pain that had no relief. From then on, Rabbi Moshe Baruch, who always used to murmur passages of the Zohar that he knew by heart, would now accompany them with a heavy sigh. It was obvious,

right up to the day of his death, that he was a man from whom his beloved had been taken, and he was not able to find any succor for the dreadful loss.

Rabbi Moshe Baruch Lemburger passed away on *Adar* 5, 5740 (February 22, 1980). He was a servant of God of the highest degree. His faithfulness and self-sacrifice for his teacher are beyond our comprehension.

Rabbi Moshe Baruch Lemburger used to jot down the teachings that he heard from the Baal HaSulam, including the content of personal instruction he received from the Sage. These notes, under the name *Bircat Moshe*, have been published as part of the work, *HaShem Shamati Shimecha*, a collection of the writings of the students of the Baal HaSulam.

Rabbi Joshua Alexander Sender Horovitz

When Rabbi Joshua was a young man, the sage Rabbi Mordecai of Rachmastrivka, a grandson of Rabbi Nachum Twerski of Chernobyl, lived in Jerusalem. When walking in the Jewish Quarter on his way to the Western Wall, he was set upon by bandits who injured him mortally. He was on his deathbed when Rabbi Joshua came to him, begging to be shown the way to truly serve God. Rabbi Mordecai was deeply moved, for he understood what Rabbi Joshua meant, but he said, "It is too late for me. But soon you will have a true teacher who will show you the path."

Indeed, not long after this episode, Rabbi Joshua met the Baal HaSulam. Rabbi Joshua was studying at the Chayei Olam Yeshivah when he discerned the distinctive character of Rabbi Ashlag, who was studying and meditating on the holy Zohar and on the works of the Ari. Rabbi Joshua understood for himself that this was the man of whom the Sage of Rachmastrivka had spoken.

One day, he plucked up his courage and approached Rabbi Ashlag, asking him to accept him as his pupil. The Sage answered that if he would gather together a group of pupils who, in all seriousness and sincerity, wanted to advance in their inner work and service of God, then he would be prepared to teach them on a regular basis. Thus it came about that Rabbi Joshua gathered around him the first nucleus of students.

Rabbi Joshua clung to the Sage with all his heart. Together with his companions, he would walk every night to learn with Rabbi Ashlag, first in the Old City, and subsequently in Givat Shaul.

Hardships

Like many others, Rabbi Joshua's mother did not approve of his getting up in the middle of the night to learn with Rabbi Ashlag, and she expressly forbade him to continue. But Rabbi Joshua replied saying that he absolutely needed a sage to instruct him. Turning to his mother, he told her, "You should know that there are two great teachers of Torah in the world. One is our rabbi, Rabbi Ashlag, the other is the Rabbi of Belz in Poland. If you do not let me go to Rabbi Ashlag, I will have to leave the country and travel to the Sage of Belz, because I cannot live without learning Torah that is taught together with the service of God." Despite the risk to his life that would be incurred by traveling to Poland at that time, Rabbi Joshua immediately started to pack his belongings. When his mother saw this, she relented.

It was told that Rabbi Joshua said, "If the holy sage Rabbi Ashlag would order me to jump into the fire just one time, I would do this without a second thought. But he orders me to do so every month, and to this, my ego strongly objects!"

Deference to the Sage

Following the death of the Baal HaSulam, Rabbi Joshua deferred to Rabbi Baruch Shalom as his teacher, even though he himself was of a very high spiritual stature and had been part of the first nucleus of students. He often came to learn with Rabbi Baruch Shalom, and for his part, Rabbi Baruch Shalom would travel every week to Rabbi Joshua's flat in Jerusalem where he would give a shiur. A tremendous friendship grew between them.

When Rabbi Joshua passed away, Rabbi Yitzchak Agassi said of him that he had achieved the fullest expression of the potential of his soul. He passed away *Sivan* 12, 5732 (May 25, 1972). His son Rabbi Tzvi Shlomoh Horovitz also became a devoted student of the Baal HaSulam and subsequently of Rabbi Baruch Shalom Ashlag, as did his son after him, Rabbi Baruch Halevi Horovitz. Rabbi Baruch Horovitz wrote down all the teachings that he heard from Rabbi Baruch Shalom Ashlag in a work called *Otiyot d'Liba*.

Rabbi Moshe Yair Weinstock

Rabbi Moshe Yair Weinstock was a descendant of the chasidim of Karlin and of Lelov. Even in his youth, he was known for his prowess in learning Torah. He was drawn to the Zohar and to the writings of the Holy Ari and was able to recite many passages from the Zohar by heart. When Rabbi Ashlag arrived in the Holy Land, Rabbi Moshe Yair was the leading pupil at the Chayei Olam Yeshivah, and they immediately connected with each other. They decided to study every night from one o'clock in the morning, and thus began an incredible web of relationship between Rabbi and disciple woven through eight hours of intimate study every night.

Rabbi Moshe Yair lived in Jerusalem in the district known as Batei Warsaw, which was quite a distance from the Old City, where Rabbi Ashlag lived at the time. But the distance did not deter him from his study. Neither was there any interruption in his devotion to the Sage when Rabbi Ashlag moved to Givat Shaul. As witness to the great love Rabbi Ashlag had for Rabbi Moshe Yair, there exist the many letters he wrote to Rabbi Moshe Yair from London.

When the Sage moved to Bnei Brak, Rabbi Moshe Yair would travel to him constantly.

Rabbi Menachem Yoseph:

> At that time, my father often traveled to Bnei Brak to the holy Sage.
>
> Once when I was still a youth, my father took me with him. He went into the room of the Baal HaSulam and left me by the

door. I waited for him to come out, but he didn't come out for the next three days. I have no idea what took place between the Sage and my father during those three days. I know only one thing: that I did not see my father once in all that time. Thankfully, the Rabbanit had pity on me and gave me some food to eat and a place to lie down at night.

Throughout his life, Rabbi Moshe Yair wrote down his studies on the Torah, ultimately publishing eighty-four books on all aspects of the Torah—truly, a fountain that never ceased to flow. It was from his years with the Baal HaSulam that he drew all his knowledge of the hidden Torah. Whenever he mentioned the Baal HaSulam it was with awe and trembling. It was clear that all the days of his life, he was nourished by the impressions he received while in the presence of the Sage. Some of his writings on the innermost aspect of the Torah that he gained specifically from the Baal HaSulam have been published under the name *Chavat Yair* and form part of the collection, *HaShem Shamati Shimecha*.

Rabbi Moshe Yair died *Av* 9, 5742 (July 29, 1982)

Rabbi Yehudah Tzvi Brandwein

For many years Rabbi Yehudah Tzvi Brandwein would get up before dawn to study the holy Zohar and the writings of the Ari. When the Baal HaSulam first arrived in Jerusalem, it happened that the family rented an apartment in the same house where Rabbi Yehudah Tzvi lived. It did not take long before Rabbi Yehudah Tzvi connected with the Baal HaSulam and eventually became one of his greatest pupils. After the death of his first wife, he became further connected to the Baal HaSulam through his marriage to Leah, Rabbi Ashlag's cousin and sister-in-law. The Baal HaSulam wrote to his uncle concerning this marriage, "My cousin, Leah, is awaiting marriage in these days. Her fiance is a great Torah scholar and teacher, and is known as a God-fearing man. He comes from a great family, being the grandson of the Sage of Stretin and is descended from the Maggid of Mezeritch. His parentage encompasses almost all the disciples of the Baal Shem Tov, may his memory be a shield for us."

According to Rabbi Binyamin Sinkovsky, the Sage once said that only two of the pupils grasped his teaching completely: his son Rabbi Baruch Shalom and Rabbi Yehudah Tzvi. It is therefore not surprising that the Sage sent Rabbi Yehudah to give shiurim in Tel Aviv and Tiberias. Once, Rabbi Yehudah said to Rabbi Moshe Baruch Lemburger, "Everything that Rabbi Chaim Vital testified concerning the Ari, I can testify concerning the Baal HaSulam." Such was his closeness to the Sage.

Desperate Poverty

The poverty in Rabbi Yehudah Tzvi's home was terrible. Rabbi Ephraim Mintzberg:

> With great difficulty, Rabbi Yehudah Tzvi opened a printing press, *Yehudah v'Yerushalayim*, specifically to publish the Baal HaSulam's books. One morning, Rabbi Yehudah Tzvi's wife came to the press. She cried, saying there was nothing at all in the house to eat: no bread, no milk. She had sent the children to school without anything, and she herself felt faint with hunger as she had not eaten anything for a very long time. Rabbi Yehudah Tzvi sighed, but told her he didn't have a single coin to give her. A passerby, seeing their distress, gave them a small sum. So she bought some *sus* [a drink made of licorice and other herbs] with which to revive herself and went home.

Rabbi Yitzchak Baruch Mintzberg:

> At Rabbi Ashlag's request, Rabbi Yehudah Tzvi would travel to Tiberias to give shiurim on the Sage's teachings. Rabbi Avraham Ashkenazi and Rabbi Menachem Edelstein took part in these shiurim. Rabbi Yehudah Tzvi would travel from Jerusalem on Sunday and come back on Thursday.
>
> Once, on his return one Thursday, Rabbi Yehudah Tzvi came to our house. He met my father with great love, and whispered something in his ear. Afterward, our father told us that he had whispered to him that during the entire week in Tiberias, he had

hardly eaten anything at all and he felt he was going to collapse. Immediately, my father got a meal together for him from the food that had already been prepared for Shabbat, and he sat and ate. He felt visibly better. Unfortunately, it was only too clear why he had come to us and not gone to his own home: he knew that at home the situation was dire, and anything he ate would deprive his wife and children.

In 1932, to earn their living, Rabbi Baruch Shalom and Rabbi Yehudah Tzvi worked as laborers, building the police station in Hebron. These were lean years and whoever did not work simply could not survive. The following year, they built the beit midrash in Bnei Brak.

Publishing the Works of Rabbi Ashlag

Besides opening the printing press, *Yehudah v'Yerushalayim*, Rabbi Yehudah Tzvi helped enormously in the publication of Rabbi Ashlag's works on the Torah of the Ari. He copy-edited and proofread the *Talmud Eser haSephirot* and the *Beit Sha'ar haKavanot*, working day and night, until these great lights went out into the world.

His work was equally indispensable in bringing the *Perush haSulam* to its finish. He did the copy-editing necessary before the work was printed, and proofread it after the first galleys were made. He also compiled the references to the scriptural sources referred to in the text of the Zohar, and noted cross-references as they occurred, listing them on every page under the title, *Masoret haZohar*. He also noted variant readings of the Zohar on each page of text.[*]

Even in the lifetime of the Baal HaSulam, the chasidim of Stretin requested Rabbi Yehudah Tzvi to become their sage, a request to which he acceded. The Stretin chasidim would meet at Rabbi Yehudah Tzvi's house on Hillel HaZaken Street in Tel Aviv, where he held his beit midrash and where also there was a mikveh.

---

[*] Nowadays with the assistance of the computer and the internet, these tasks do not seem to us as particularly extraordinary. But when we see the actual work involved, and remember that these references were compiled in the pre-internet era, we realize the encyclopaedic knowledge Rabbi Yehudah Tzvi Brandwein had of the Zohar and of the works of Rabbi Ashlag. We can only marvel.

Perush Ma'alot haSulam

Following the death of Rabbi Ashlag, Rabbi Yehudah Tzvi started to write the commentaries on the additional parts of the Zohar that the Baal HaSulam had not managed to finish. In 1956, he wrote the commentary *Ma'alot haSulam* (Rungs of the Ladder) on the *haShmatot haZohar*. These are small sections of the Zohar not included in the main version. Then in 1960, he continued the commentary, *Ma'alot haSulam,* onto the first volume of the *Tikkunei haZohar,* which he published.

In his introduction to the *Ma'alot haSulam,* Rabbi Yehudah Tzvi writes:

> When the holy sage Rabbi Yehudah Leib Ashlag, may his memory be for a blessing, finished his commentary on the *Zohar Chadash,* he prepared to continue with the *Tikkunei haZohar.* But his illness grew and his soul departed on Yom Kippur 5715.
>
> I determined to begin the commentary on the *Tikkunei haZohar;* indeed, I had already written the commentary on most of the introduction to the *Tikkunei haZohar.* But I heard some criticism that the twenty-one volumes of the *Perush haSulam* on the Zohar were still incomplete, because the variant texts of the Zohar as well as the *haShmatot haZohar,* had not been included. Likewise, the articles in the *Zohar haChadash* needed organizing. So I set all aside and arranged the *Perush* on the *haShmatot.* This I called, "*Ma'alot haSulam*" [Rungs of the Ladder] because this commentary consists entirely of what I received from the Baal HaSulam and from his commentary, the *Sulam.*
>
> I am like one who ascends the rungs of a ladder, but I did not, myself, make the ladder. All that I write is from what I received from my holy teacher, may his memory be a shield for us. I merited to serve him for more than thirty-two years, and in all those years my hand did not move from his hand.

Rabbi Yehudah Tzvi intended to carry on with his commentary on the *Tikkunei haZohar,* but in the following year, Rabbi Aharon Shemesh came to him with a suggestion that he publish the works of the Holy Ari. So he left off the commentary on the *Tikkunei haZohar* and began to edit and reference all the works of the Ari. Included in this edition were citations of the Baal HaSulam's commentaries. This work took him until 1966. He then turned once more to the *Tikkunei haZohar* in order to continue with the commentary *Ma'alot haSulam*, but on *Nisan* 18, 5729, (April 6, 1969), he died suddenly of a heart attack. His son Rabbi Avraham Brandwein published *Ma'alot haSulam* after his death.

Rabbi Yehudah Tzvi Brandwein was undoubtedly one of the greatest of the Baal HaSulam's students. He had a complete grasp of the Sage's teaching. His notes on the oral teachings of the Baal HaSulam have been published under the title *Tzvi la Tzaddik* as part of the collection *HaShem Shamati Shimecha*.

Rabbi David Mintzberg

Rabbi Shmuel Mintzberg:

> In those years, the Chayei Olam Yeshivah in the Old City was a great institution. It included both a yeshivah for young men and a kolel for married men. As a young man, my father learned in the yeshivah, and as a graduate, he taught there.
>
> My father was very well known in Jerusalem. He was a direct descendant of the Holy Jew [Rabbi Yitzchak Ya'acov Rabinovitz of Peschischa], of Rabbi Moshe Lelover, and of Rabbi Tzvi Hirsch of Zitidchov, known as the *Ateret Tzvi*. My father was known to be an extremely wise man and if, God forbid, there happened to be a problem of *shalom bayit* [marital disagreement] my father would be called on to find a solution.

Rabbi Moshe Yair Weinstock had already connected with the Baal HaSulam, and he introduced Rabbi David Mintzberg to him. Rabbi David would come to Rabbi Ashlag's shiurim at one o'clock in the morning, study till dawn and then, following the morning prayers, teach in the Chayei Olam Yeshivah until the afternoon. He would then return to learn again with the Baal HaSulam, returning in the late afternoon to teach again in the yeshivah. He saw his home only for a short time every evening.

Rabbi Baruch Yitzchak Mintzberg:

> My father told me that the first time he came to the Baal HaSulam he said to him, "It is written that we need to learn Kabbalah in secret," whereupon the Baal HaSulam got up and closed the curtain saying, "Now we may learn!"

Everlasting Love

Rabbi Shmuel Mintzberg:

> My father, Rabbi David, was very close to the Baal HaSulam and loved him deeply. Unfortunately, my mother's health was extremely poor and she would be hospitalized for months at a time. But there were small children in the house who needed attention; sometimes one of us was sick. Nevertheless, my father would somehow or other get to the Baal HaSulam every day at two in the morning even when the Baal HaSulam had moved to Givat Shaul and we lived in the Old City. On Shabbat he would do this journey twice. All his life, my father served the Sage with great love, and in his turn, the Baal HaSulam greatly loved my father. My father would often seek the Sage's advice on his inner work.
>
> My father passed this great love of the Sage on to me also. Once, when Rabbanit Rivkah Raiza was ill in hospital, I stayed in the ward for hours, as I wanted the doctors to see that there was always someone from the family by her side. Afterwards, the Sage turned to me and said to me *"Bist a feine bochur"* ["You are a good boy."] I felt he valued me very much.

Rabbi David Mintzberg suffered greatly because of his connection with the Baal HaSulam. He was a teacher in the Chayei Olam Yeshivah, for which he received a modest salary. But when it became known that he was a student of Rabbi Ashlag, the administrators fired him on the spot, maintaining that he could not possibly teach properly during the day since he was awake learning at night! But Rabbi David carried on his study with Rabbi Ashlag, without allowing this to disturb him.

Rabbi Zalman Lemburger:

> One time, Rabbi David Mintzberg came straight after the morning prayers to the beit midrash to speak to the Sage on some pressing matter. But the Baal HaSulam was unable to meet with him just then. So Rabbi David stood and waited. In the meantime, the Baal HaSulam had to go somewhere. When he came back, Rabbi David was still waiting. After a short while, the Baal HaSulam asked me to please call in Rabbi David. He had waited from the morning until well into the afternoon. Eight hours! I saw Rabbi Mintzberg go into the room. He took, at most, a minute of the Baal HaSulam's time. When he came out, his face was shining and so happy! It was worth it to wait eight whole hours for one minute with this holy man of God.

Rabbi Menachem Edelstein was a frequent guest of the Mintzberg family:

> I would see Rabbi David learning the books of the Baal HaSulam. If someone who did not belong to the group of disciples came into the room, he would change the words until the stranger had left, because of the importance of the Baal HaSulam and his writings. This could be likened to someone talking over a matter of importance with a close friend who lowers his voice or changes the subject if anyone comes near.

Visit to Poland

Once, after Rabbi David had become a student of the Baal HaSulam, he had to journey to Poland on behalf of the Warsaw *Kolel* in Jerusalem. Naturally, he wanted to meet the sages of Poland, and in particular the sage of Porisov, Rabbi Ashlag's teacher. The sage of Porisov received him with great respect. Rabbi David told him of the shiurim in Jerusalem and what the Baal HaSulam was teaching. The

Sage asked, "And who gave him permission to reveal all this? All this he took from me!" But Rabbi David answered him, "I don't need to justify my teacher. In my eyes, all that he does is done in righteousness and in correct judgment."

Rabbi Shmuel Mintzberg:

When the Baal HaSulam moved to Tel Aviv, my father traveled there to see him every week. My father was then working as a building contractor and had many responsibilities, but he didn't take account of that at all, only of the possibility of being together with the Sage.

Each day before dawn, Rabbi David would give over shiurim in his home in Jerusalem. The pupils who would gather with him were: Rabbi Yitzchak Agassi, Rabbi Aharon Lemburger, Rabbi Zundel Hagar, and, later on, Rabbi Eliezer Vishpitz and my elder brother, Rabbi Ephraim Mintzberg.

In his last days, Rabbi David lay on his bed learning the holy Zohar. Rabbi Ephraim would read it aloud and he would listen. They reached the verse, "And Jacob concluded commanding his sons, and he drew his legs [up] into the bed, and expired and was gathered to his people" (Gen. 49:33). At that, Rabbi David breathed his last and returned his holy soul to his Maker, on *Nisan* 5, 5734 (March 28, 1974)

Rabbi Avraham Ashkenazi

"With everlasting love, I have loved you, for I have drawn you to Me with loving-kindness" (Jer. 31:2).

Rabbi Avraham Ashkenazi:

I was born in Tiberias into a family whose roots stretch back. My mother was the seventh generation of the Slonim Chasidim, some of whom had established a community in Tiberias in the early nineteenth century. From my youth, I learned in the Yeshivah Beit Avraham of Slonim, and I cleaved to the sage of Slonim.

I married my first wife in 5685 [1925]. She was descended from Rabbi David Biderman of Lelov. After the wedding, I chanced to be in Givat Shaul; I was looking for an elderly blind man by the name of Rabbi Shmuel Andron, who was famous as having tremendous knowledge in the Talmud and in the *poskim* [those who decide halachah]. I wished to discuss my learning with him.

While searching around, I chanced upon a house in Rechov Najara. There, on the ground floor, I saw a strange sight. In a small beit midrash, there sat a Jew wearing a shtreimel of the type common among the Gur chasidim. Around him sat a group of men who were drinking in every word that came out of his mouth with tremendous thirst. It was a wondrous sight. I drew closer and closer to this group, the sight of which filled me with amazement. As you have guessed, this Jew was the angel of God, the holy sage, my teacher, the Baal HaSulam, may his memory guard us. He turned to me and said, "Why are you standing outside looking in? It is better for you to come inside and look out."

I came into the beit midrash, the pupils made room for me, and I sat down. The Sage taught from the *Etz Chaim* of the Holy Ari. It was on the material of these lessons that he subsequently composed his commentary, the *Panim Meirot uMasbirot* on the *Etz Chaim*. This was the beginning of my everlasting connection with my rabbi, the Baal HaSulam. It is a connection that continues to this very day. I didn't need much in the way of words from him; I immediately felt that this was my place. I sensed a powerful connection with him and I sensed the godly light that radiated from within him with wondrous spiritual brightness. From then on, I clung to him with all my heart and soul.

I would come to the beit midrash every day at two o'clock in the morning and sit with the other students, with whom I received the Torah of the living God from the mouth of the living Ari. I was so united with Rabbi Ashlag that I completely forgot this world. It was as if I entered another world completely, a world in which only the existence of God has any reality, a world of endless longing to fulfill the will of the living God, as a fire aspires to the heavens. I can still picture the form of the holy Rabbi, and his words have stayed alive within me until this very day, even many years after he has departed from us.

You must know that the students of the Sage were all, without any exception, servants of God of extremely high spiritual stature. The holy Rabbi received as students into his beit midrash only those who were great workers for God.

Even though I lived in Tiberias, I didn't spare any effort. I traveled regularly to hear the Torah from this man of God. After a period, during which I had become close to him with the true dvekut that pertains between a sage and his pupil, I received a letter that he sent to me to Tiberias. At the top of the letter, he wrote, "To Rabbi Avraham: 'With everlasting love I have loved you.'"

The Beit Avraham of Slonim and
Rabbi Yoel Teitelbaum of Satmar

My first wife died young, so I married again. Two months after the wedding, which took place after I had already become connected with the Baal HaSulam, I traveled to Bialystok, the seat of the Sage of Slonim, the *Beit Avraham*. When I arrived in his presence I made the *shechechyanu* blessing* with God's name. The Sage of Slonim drew me very close to him throughout the entire period that I stayed with him, sitting me next to him.

After I had been half a year in Bialystok, I returned to Tiberias. At the end of each week, I would travel to Jerusalem to spend Shabbat in the presence of the Baal HaSulam. At that time, I prayed in the beit midrash of Rabbi Yoel Teitelbaum, the sage of Satmar. Once, when I arrived there, he told me that he urgently needed a large sum of money. [The Rabbi of Satmar was known to be concerned with many charitable endeavors, especially for refugees.] I told him I would give him whatever he needed. He sighed and said he needed about 400 lira—a huge sum in those days; one could buy many properties for this sum. I didn't ask him why he needed the money and I didn't ask for any blessing.

---

* This blessing is recited, among other occasions, when a person experiences an especial joy.

I could have requested wealth or a blessing to get *yirat shamayim* [the quality of reverence for God], but I didn't want to receive anything in exchange. I just gave him the money without requesting anything at all.

Self-Sacrifice

Throughout this period, I remained connected with the living Ari, the Baal HaSulam. I undertook many journeys from Tiberias to see the light of his face and to find shelter in the shade of his holiness, even though the journeys were very hard indeed—long and exhausting hours of bumpy rides in the heat and the cold. Nevertheless, I didn't weaken in my resolve to visit my teacher.

Once, I didn't have any ready money, but I dearly wanted to travel to him, so I went to the street leading out of Tiberias, and there I stopped a lorry carrying bales of cotton tied to its back. The bundles reached a huge height and I had the "honor" of sitting on their very top. When we reached the hairpin bends in the vicinity of Nazareth, the bundles started to sway in a most alarming manner. I felt that at any moment, the cotton bundles were about to fall over the edge, and I with them. I held on with all my strength. I thought every moment was my last. When I eventually arrived in the Baal HaSulam's presence, he asked me, "Why are you so pale?" I told him about the journey. He then said to me, "In the same measure that you experienced fear when you saw the depths open before you, so you should fear being separated from God."

When I was in Tiberias, I would sit and study in the yeshivah that is situated above the grave of Rabbi Meir Baal HaNess. The day after I had returned from my journey to the Rabbi, I was walking in the direction of the yeshivah, when, suddenly, an enormous viper came out of the bushes by the side of the road. It stood opposite me. I knew that if it bit me, that would be my end. Then I remembered the words of my holy Rabbi. I felt that God was giving me a chance for me to give my life for Him. So I closed my eyes and thought, "This is how I need to be afraid of being separated from the Creator." When I opened my eyes, the snake gave a jump and disappeared in the direction from which it had come.

"Be wholehearted with the Lord your God" (Deut. 18:13)

I would often get requests for monetary help from my companions, the other students of the Baal HaSulam, when the poverty got so dire that they could no longer cope. I would also receive requests in connection with the printing of the Zohar with the *Perush haSulam*. Once, Rabbi Yehudah Tzvi Brandwein sent me a letter asking urgently for help. I went to the bank to inquire into the state of my account. I found that I had sixteen lira. I sent him a check for the full sum. When I came to the Sage in Tel Aviv, he asked me, "Why did you send that particular sum, sixteen lira?" I answered him, "I will tell the Rabbi the truth. This was the exact sum I had in the bank. Actually, it did cross my mind to make an effort and add another lira to make it up to the sum of the word *tov,* טוב (good), [the letters of which add up to seventeen according to *gematria*] or to add another two lira, which would make the word *chai,* חי (life) [whose letters add up to eighteen]. But then I reflected and thought, "Why am I trying to mix my accounting with those of God's? All I need to do is to fulfill the will of my Rabbi and no more." When he heard this, the Rabbi got up from his seat in great excitement and shouted, "Be wholehearted with God" (Deut. 18:13). He paced up and down the room all alight with an inner flame. He called out several times, "Be guileless with God." His face changed colors from red to pale and from pale to red. I saw before me an angel of the living God—a mighty soul. Since the day that God created the heavens and the earth, there was none like him on the planet.

The needs were many and the price for printing the books with the high cost of the ink and the paper was enormous, and none of us had any money. Everyone, without exception, made superhuman efforts, and myself with them. When the final volumes came to be printed, I spared no effort and labored very intensely to get the money. I gave a fantastic sum, equivalent to what you would need to buy an apartment! When the printing was finished, the holy Rabbi arranged a festive meal of thanksgiving at Meron. Tremendous joy filled all the hearts of the students, and I was among them. I was overwhelmed with happiness. I took all eighteen volumes of the Zohar and waved them above my head, dancing with all my heart and soul.

The last Yom Kippur, I traveled to my teacher, my Rabbi, to spend the holy day in his presence. When I arrived, I gave the Rabbanit five lira for *kaparot*, and I went into the holy Sage's room. He was lying in his bed in a state of extreme weakness. I said, "Please God, the Rabbi will hold many *tisch* in the coming year." But the Rabbi answered me in his clear and truthful way, "I will never hold a *tisch* again." On the following day, on Yom Kippur itself, his holy soul ascended on high. May his memory defend us and all Israel, Amen.

Following the death of the Baal HaSulam, Rabbi Avraham Ashkenazi recognized Rabbi Baruch Shalom as a sage and became his pupil, even though he himself was of a high spiritual stature and could have taught pupils himself.

Rabbi Yitzchak Heller:

Rabbi Avraham told me that the first time he gave a *kvitel* [a note requesting a spiritual blessing] to Rabbi Baruch Shalom, as is customary between chasid and sage, he felt a tremendous elevation of spirit, just as he used to in the days of his holy father, the Baal HaSulam.

On every Rosh Chodesh and festival, Rabbi Avraham used to come from Tiberias to visit Rabbi Baruch Shalom. He would sit close to the Sage at the table, and it was clear that when Rabbi Baruch Shalom spoke on the service of God, his words were often addressed to Rabbi Avraham.

Rabbi Menachem Edelstein

His name was Menachem, which means "the one who comforts," and he was the son of Simchah, whose name means "joy." Like his name, so was his nature.

The Baal HaSulam teaches that the concept of "father and son" implies cause and effect. And so it was in this case: the cause of Rabbi Menachem's deeds and thoughts was his simchah, and it was through his joy that he comforted many after the two great sages, the Baal HaSulam and his son Rabbi Baruch Shalom, had left this world.

Rabbi Menachem's joy was indeed witness to his great spiritual stature, for it is not easy to remain joyful amid the difficulties of this world. True joy springs from the belief in God and that all He does is good. Rabbi Menachem radiated this joy to all who came into contact with him. It was impossible to remain sad in his presence. He simply would not allow such a state to exist.

Rabbi Mintzberg Brings Rabbi Edelstein to the Baal HaSulam

Menachem was born on *Rosh Chodesh Av* in the year 5070 (1910) in the city of Lublin, Poland.

In 1921, his father, Rabbi Simchah, left Poland for the Land of Israel, and the following year brought his family to join him. They settled in the Old City of Jerusalem. Rabbi Menachem learned in the Chayei Olam Yeshivah as a pupil of Rabbi David Mintzberg. Their connection extended far beyond the normal teacher-pupil relationship, and the young Menachem became very close to Rabbi David, such that when he had finished his studies in the yeshivah, he became a regular member of Rabbi David's household, eating and sleeping in his home. Several times, the young lad asked Rabbi David to wake him at midnight and thus he merited to see Rabbi David's great service to God. When Rabbi Menachem had grown and matured, Rabbi David brought him to the Baal HaSulam.

As it is known, the Baal HaSulam did not accept students easily, so he made a condition with Rabbi Menachem that he would get up for three months each night at midnight and learn alone. If he could manage to do this, without missing one night, then he would be willing to include him in the band of students. Rabbi Menachem fulfilled this condition and was then accepted as a student.

After his marriage, Rabbi Menachem had to leave Jerusalem and move to Tiberias to comply with his wife's wishes. But he did not sever connections with the Baal HaSulam. Each week he would travel to the Sage from Tiberias to Tel Aviv. Even though the way was arduous, he never missed a shiur.

In Tiberias, both he and Rabbi Avraham Ashkenazi dwelt in the chareidi section of the city. Rabbi Menachem often sat and learned in the yeshivah of Rabbi Meir Baal HaNess where he became friendly with Rabbi Avraham Ashkenazi. The Baal HaSulam then told Rabbi Avraham that he should take Rabbi Menachem as a *chevruta* (study companion).

The relative positions of Rabbi Avraham and Rabbi Menachem within the chareidi society of Tiberias were very disparate. Rabbi Menachem was considered a "nobody." He hid his real spiritual stature, so people thought he was simple and even called him derogatory names, whereas Rabbi Avraham had a respected lineage in Tiberias.

The two men would meet at midnight and learn from the *Talmud Eser haSephirot* of the Baal HaSulam. However, wherever holiness starts to flourish, disturbances soon follow, enabling us to serve God unconditionally and not for our own personal enjoyment. These disturbances took the form of the wives of the two men, who, for some reason, did not view this *chevruta* with favor.

Not being content with making their views known in the privacy of their homes, the two women would rise with their husbands at midnight and, together, would make their way to the place where the men learned. This was not easy, for the way was steep and involved climbing up a rocky hillside. But they were undeterred! On their arrival, the two women would try to disrupt their husbands' study. This, however, the rabbis would not allow, and they continued their *chevruta* with great concentration.

Rabbi Menachem:

"Once, I came to the holy Rabbi three weeks before the High Holidays in order to spend the entire period of the festivals, until the end of Succot, with the Sage. At home, this provoked a war with my wife that she never forgot, even when we were both old! However, this period proved to be one of great spiritual richness. I had the privilege of spending many hours with the Baal HaSulam, talking to him privately on spiritual work on a daily basis.

Once he rebuked me: He asked me, "Menachem, do you remember what I told you yesterday?" I answered him truthfully that really I didn't remember anything. Then the Rabbi said, "I have spoken with you for hours upon hours, but since you valued my words only as you would value a small coin, it all got lost. If you had valued my words in the way you would value even one lira [which in those days was quite a large sum of money] you would not have forgotten them!"

Rabbi Menachem further told:

Once, the Sage spoke to me about selfish love: concerning eating, drinking, and other physical pleasures, that even when a person eats and drinks, he is separated from the Life of all lives. Therefore, the Holy Blessed One commanded us to make a blessing before we eat, to ensure that our eating is not so materialistic.

Rabbi Menachem filled his life with the impressions he retained from the times he spent with the Baal HaSulam. Through these impressions, he would pour life and joy into his everyday life. Even many years after the Baal HaSulam had passed away, when he wanted to feel the unity and joy again, he would close his eyes and remember the face of the Sage, and again he would be filled up with the spirit of holiness and exaltation.

Once the Baal HaSulam wrote to him:

I received your letter, and I take great pleasure in the knowledge that you are learning my books. You should know that through your connection with the consciousness in the books, you connect also with me. And this is the surest way of all to come to your purpose. It all depends on the inner work.

After the Baal HaSulam died, Rabbi Menachem became the pupil of Rabbi Baruch Shalom. He moved house to live close to the Sage in Bnei Brak. He would arrive every night at two o'clock in the morning to study with the Sage, with whom he would study again in the afternoon. These times of study with Rabbi Baruch Shalom were fixtures that he allowed nothing to disturb. If Rabbi Menachem was invited to a simchah, he first went to the beit midrash to learn as usual and then went on to the place of the simchah, even if it was situated at a distance.

His custom was to go to the mikveh at one o'clock in the morning, then, on his way back, he would wake up the other members of the group. Nothing stopped Rabbi Menachem. Not financial worries, health issues, or physical tiredness, and not old age. Even when he was over eighty, he continued in the same pattern and didn't give up. Even when he sometimes felt short of breath or experienced pains in his chest, he never complained and never gave in or gave up.

On Fridays, Rabbi Menachem would come to the beit midrash, a few hours ahead of time to prepare for Shabbat. He would spread white cloths on the tables and blue velvet cloths on the lecterns. He would then make coffee and tea essence and arrange the books neatly. Once he had done that, he would sit with Rabbi Baruch Shalom learning the *Sha'ar haKavanot* of the Ari on the special Kabbalistic intentions for Shabbat. Even when he was advanced in years, he was as full of life as a young lad just beginning his way. He didn't hold himself above any of the other students, but was as connected with the youngest as with the oldest. He didn't talk much and was often silent, speaking only after great thought. He was modest, and everything he did was done quietly.

Many times we heard Rabbi Baruch Shalom exclaim that the simchah of Rabbi Menachem that always shone on his face was a real gift from God and not a small thing. Such joy testified more than anything to his continual closeness to God.

I remember that Rabbi Menachem would arrive first to the beit midrash in the early hours of Shabbat morning. He would open the door, his face shining with light and with a tremendous shout of *Gut Shabbas!* he would wave his hands to the walls and furniture of the beit midrash.

"This is the Torah: a man when he dies in a tent." (Num. 19:14) This scripture refers to the tent of Torah. One Wednesday, when Rabbi Menachem was sitting learning together with the other students, he did not feel well and was taken to hospital. He died a few days later at the age of eighty-four, on *Cheshvan* 28, 5754 (November 12, 1993).

Rabbi Baruch Shalom Ashlag

Baruch Shalom, the firstborn of the Baal HaSulam, was born in Warsaw, Poland, on *Shvat* 7, 5667 (January 22, 1907). Even as a child, it was clear that he was gifted. When he was only nine years old, his father let him join a group of select students with whom he learned *Choshen Mishpat* of the *Shulchan Aruch*. Rabbi Ashlag used to take the young Baruch with him on his journeys to the Rabbi of Porisov and to Rabbi Yissachar Dov of Belz.

In 5681 (1921), the family left Poland and emigrated to Israel, settling in Jerusalem. As a young man, Baruch Shalom learned in the Torat Emet Yeshivah of Chabad, where he would learn for twelve hours at a time without a break, just placing a few pieces of fruit on his desk to quiet his hunger.

Even though his father had forbidden unmarried students to come into the Kabbalah lessons, the young Baruch Shalom would take advantage of his assignment of preparing the coffee by serving it to the students extremely slowly, so he could hear as much of the lesson as possible.

In 5685 (1925) at the age of eighteen, Rabbi Baruch Shalom became engaged to the daughter of Rabbi Yechezkel Elimelech Linder from one of the most important families of Jerusalem. After his marriage, the Baal HaSulam allowed him to join the students on a formal basis. At age twenty, Baruch Shalom was ordained as rabbi by Rabbi Yosef Sonnenfeld of Jerusalem.

When Rabbi Ashlag became the rabbi of Givat Shaul, Rabbi Baruch Shalom, like the other pupils, would rise at midnight and walk from the Old City to Givat Shaul. He did not allow anything to deter him, and never missed an opportunity to learn from his father.

When the Baal HaSulam moved to Tel Aviv, Rabbi Baruch Shalom continued to come to the lessons, even endangering his life to do so. Those were the days when Jerusalem was under siege, and the only way to get to Tel Aviv was to travel in an armored column for the sum of 3-5 *grush*, which, then, was quite a large sum. Although Rabbi Baruch Shalom didn't have the money, his desire to get to his father was so great that he decided to travel on the roof of a lorry, exposed to the sniper bullets. He was unharmed, but when he got to Tel Aviv he found his father standing outside on the balcony waiting for him. This was most unusual. Rabbi Ashlag said to his son, "Don't do that again! The whole time I carried you on my head." Shortly after this episode, Rabbi Baruch Shalom and his family moved to Jaffa, not far from his father.

During the period when Rabbi Ashlag sent some of the students to work, especially those who had *yichus* (lineage in Torah learning), Rabbi Baruch Shalom went to a work camp of Solel Boneh, Israel's road building company, where he volunteered to sleep in the kitchen. This required rising an hour before the other workers in order to prepare a hot drink for them, but he preferred this, as it was the only place in the camp that had a light burning. So, every morning he would rise at one o'clock, and learn Torah until it was time to prepare the drink and rouse the others. Then he would work together with the other workers.

At home, the family's poverty was great, so much so that they often didn't have enough money to light a lamp at home. At those times Rabbi Baruch Shalom would sit outside and learn by the light of the moon.

Rabbi Baruch Shalom cleaved to his father. He wrote down every oral shiur or talk that his father gave on serving God. These notes ultimately amounted to tens of notebooks and form an indispensable part of the Baal HaSulam's teachings—teachings that would have been lost if it were not for Rabbi Baruch Shalom's diligence. These were later published as the book *Shamati* ("I heard"), and form the basis of our understanding of the way of serving God in practice; the way that the Baal HaSulam taught orally to his pupils.

Rabbi Baruch Shalom had a phenomenal knowledge of his father's writings on the work of the Holy Ari and of the Zohar. He had the ability to penetrate the technicalities of the learning to the extent that he was able to express the principles in simple language. In his teachings, he demonstrates that even the most technical aspects of the study of Kabbalah are really about a person's relationship with the Creator.

In 5709 (1949) at his father's request, Rabbi Baruch Shalom started to teach the newcomers to the beit midrash. They would study for a period with him before they were permitted into the main shiur.

Rabbi Baruch Shalom remained devoted to his father and did not wish for any recognition on his own account. After his father died, on Yom Kippur 5715 (1954), he acceded to the pleas of both his father's and his own students to take upon himself the role of leadership and sage and to give the shiur in his father's stead. His service of God was always modest and hidden from sight. "Walk modestly with the Lord your God," was a watchword for him. Once he rebuked a student whom he saw learning from a book at a wedding, saying that it is possible to learn without the entire community seeing. Like his father, he avoided making political statements of any type, as he did not want these matters to distract him.

Rabbi Baruch Shalom continued his father's custom of rising each night at one in the morning to give over his shiurim until the light of dawn. On every day of the year, even on Yom Kippur, or after holding a *tisch* that had continued into the early hours of the morning, he would still get up to learn or teach, even if he had hardly slept. He would also teach a shiur for a few hours in the afternoons for the students who were not able to come to study in the early morning. At the end of the day, after about ten hours of teaching, he would be available to help the students with their problems.

For many years, Rabbi Baruch Shalom conducted the beit midrash as his father had, opening it only to those few who proved themselves to be true workers in the path of serving God. However, in the latter years of his life, Rabbi Baruch Shalom opened the beit midrash to a wider circle of students.

Rabbi Avraham Mordecai Gottlieb:

> Despite the fact that Rabbi Baruch Shalom was a godly man, he
> never kept a distance from his pupils, but acted toward us more
> like a father or a friend. On many occasions, he would sit among
> us, talking with us. He never behaved with any sense of superior-
> ity. Despite his great knowledge in both the revealed Torah and
> in the hidden Torah, he conducted himself with humility and
> with friendliness to all who surrounded him. At one o'clock in the
> morning, he himself would walk the streets of Bnei Brak waking
> up the students for the lesson!
>
> His most outstanding quality was his devotion to truth. Truth
> for him was the most important and dearest of all qualities. In gen-
> eral, a person is afraid to face the truth about himself, as the truth
> of his own lowliness is bitter and painful. Rabbi Baruch Shalom
> did not expose this truth about others; his work was only on him-
> self. But this work radiated out to us and inspired us. He used to
> ask, "Who are those who think they can give faith to others? They
> think that they themselves have so much faith that it is spilling
> over... ! But whoever really looks, finds, that within himself, he not
> only lacks faith, but it simply isn't there. For how can a person be
> said to have faith unless he thinks about God every moment of
> the day? How can a person have faith in God and not long to cling
> to Him at every moment?"
>
> Those of us who had the privilege of being with this man of
> holiness tried to absorb his principles and put them into practice.

Throughout his days, Rabbi Baruch Shalom devoted himself to giving
over his father's writings and teachings. He did not publish books of
his own, and what we have of his teachings are preserved from tapes of
his oral shiurim and from his own personal notebooks.

In the later years of his life, Rabbi Baruch Shalom taught himself
to type, and would painstakingly compose one essay a week to help the
students progress in their service of God. Each is based on a verse from
the *Tanach* (Bible), the Talmud, or the Zohar. These essays are written

in seemingly simple language, but are, in fact, extremely deep, showing how the inner aspect of the Torah consists of advice and instruction on how to come closer to God. They, at one and the same time, teach the principles of the service of God and speak individually to every person who reads them. These essays were later collected into four volumes and became known simply as the *Sefer haMa'amarim* (The Book of Essays). They occupy a unique place in all spiritual literature.

Rabbi Baruch Shalom and his family lived in an old flat situated in Bnei Brak, in which was set aside one small and narrow room for learning and prayer. In time, it became too small for the growing number of students, and so began the building of the synagogue on 81 Chazon Ish Street. With the erection of this building, the shiurim multiplied.

On *Cheshvan* 3, 5731 (November 2, 1970) Rabbi Baruch Shalom's son-in-law and close assistant, Rabbi Yitzchak Agassi, passed away. Rabbi Yitzchak Agassi had been a student of the Baal HaSulam, and after the Baal HaSulam died he clung to Rabbi Baruch Shalom. He was a man gifted with a perceptive mind and a warm heart. A few years later, Rabbi Baruch Shalom's eldest daughter, Rabbi Agassi's widow, also died. Rabbi Baruch said of her that she used to go into the Baal HaSulam's presence and he would teach her about the service of God. Despite these sorrows and others, Rabbi Baruch never looked back. He used to say, "Whoever looks backwards is a pensioner in the service of God!"

On the second day of Rosh HaShanah, in the last year of his life, Rabbi Baruch Shalom felt unwell and went out to rest. When he returned, the students sang the verse, "My heart whispered to me a good thing, it said, my deeds are for the King" (Ps. 45:2). Rabbi Baruch Shalom explained, "When a person can say that all his deeds are directed to serve the King, then he can say, 'my heart whispered to me a good thing'. This is easy to say, but hard to fulfill."

At the end of the festival, he traveled to the hospital, and there the doctors decided he should stay for some tests. However, on the Friday, *Tishrei* 5, 5752 (September 13, 1991) in the early morning, when he was looking over some writings that he had taken with him, his heart stopped and he returned his pure soul to his Maker.

May his righteous memory be for a blessing.

Afterword

The Love of Companions

First Steps on The Path

The Beit Midrash hummed with activity on a daily basis. Rabbi Baruch Shalom sat with us, advising us, helping us with our study, and teaching us by his own example how to serve God in the way that his father, the Baal HaSulam, had received from his teachers, the sages of Kalozhin, Belz, and Porisov. These basic ideas and teachings on how each one of us may serve the Creator in actual practice permeate all the Baal HaSulam's writings, and not a day went by without one or other of these ideas being taught or discussed in the Beit Midrash. Indeed, they were in its very atmosphere. Of course, we did not learn these steps in the service of God in an orderly way, but we learned them as they arose naturally out of the events of our lives or in the material we were studying.

Our purpose was to strive to come to serve our Creator unconditionally. Of all the ideas we were given to help us in this, one stands out above them all: the practice of loving our companions; a practice which is a preliminary step to loving all our fellow human beings. The Baal HaSulam spoke on the importance of this in almost every letter that he wrote to his students when he was away from them:

> I request each one of you to make all possible effort to love each of the companions as much as you love yourselves. This means that when one of your fellows is suffering you feel as sorrowful over his trouble as if it was your own; and that you join in your companions' happiness and joys to the greatest possible extent.

And I hope that you will fulfill my words in this and bring this matter to its completion.[1]

Yet again, I request you to make extreme efforts in the love of companions. Discover new ways to increase the love between each of you and also ways to nullify those appetites that the ego desires, because these produce only hatred—and among those who are trying to serve the Creator, hatred or jealousy have no place. On the contrary, only compassion and love should be present. This matter is simple.

I've written that each of you should show my letters to the others, for these matters are spoken from one unity [Rabbi Ashlag] to another unity [all the students as a whole]. You should have one Torah with which to subdue the ego and to sanctify the soul. Do not change anything, even inadvertently, as we are so liable to do when bribed by the ego. It would be fitting for you to consider my words deeply from this day forth, for they are your life and the length of your days, and it is not for my benefit that I seek this.[2]

A person who is sorrowful relates his trouble to his companions because it is impossible for him to hide his feelings or refrain. So I tell you now of my feeling of sorrow concerning all of you that "today" goes by into "tomorrow," and instead of "now" you say "later." There is no remedy for this except to make an effort and understand this grave error and distortion, for one who needs the salvation of God can be saved only when he needs this salvation today, whereas one who can wait till tomorrow may well find that he is waiting years, God forbid.

You have fallen into this trap through negligence in carrying out my request to you to make an effort in the love between the companions. As I have explained to you, in every possible term, there is enough light in this virtue alone with which to fulfill all your lacks. And even if you cannot ascend to heaven, I have laid before you pathways for your use on earth. Why haven't you redoubled your efforts in this work?

Besides, apart from the light that is hidden in this issue—whose greatness you cannot imagine—you need to know that in each member of the group are to be found many sparks of holiness. If you were to gather together all these sparks of holiness to one place, in one focused will, when sitting together in brotherhood, love, and friendship, then, certainly, together you would attain an important level of the light of holiness—the illumination of life. I have already spoken on this at length in all my letters to the companions. I have also requested that each of you should show every letter to his fellows. Do so now, and I beg of you from this day forth to understand me and obey me in this, at least in what you are able to do, for then God will be able to open to us His good treasure. [3]

In this world of the cellphone and the personal computer, individuals are more socially isolated than ever before. Nowadays it is perfectly possible, and often more convenient, to learn the teachings of Rabbi Ashlag by studying alone with a book or over the internet. However, if we do this as our sole contact with this teaching, we miss a vital component of the teachings, and that is our relationship with other students. When we learn together, we learn, not only Rabbi Ashlag's teachings, but we learn from each other's life experience and ways of putting the teachings into practice. We also learn other ways of understanding these teachings and gain new perspective on how to value the privilege of having this learning in our lives. We learn how to judge each other meritoriously, endeavoring to see only the good in each other and learning to overlook our companions' deficiencies. Furthermore, we unite in the common purpose of desiring to serve God and our fellow unconditionally.

Rabbi Ashlag wrote much on the attitude we need to adopt towards each other so that we can learn from each other. Here is what he writes in his book, *Matan Torah*:

A person who feels himself to be greater cannot receive from one whom he considers to be lesser than himself, especially with regard to being moved by his words. Only one who feels himself to be lesser may be influenced by one whom he esteems as being greater. Thus, every student needs to value and love his fellow student to the utmost, and to regard him with the same esteem as he would one who is the greatest teacher of the generation.[4]

Since we are not yet tzaddikim, and we all consist of mixtures of attributes, worthy and unworthy, being able to esteem our fellow on a continual basis, even when his or her faults seem glaring, requires effort and faith. We need to believe in the ultimate potential of each one of us, that all our unworthy attributes, including our own, are the seeds for great good. Indeed, the more we have faith in the worth of each of our companions, the more motivation we have to work to implement the Scripture, "Love your fellow as yourself" (Lev. 19:18).

The Baal HaSulam instituted the practice that all the students should meet together on a regular basis. At first, they convened once a month; later this became once a week. At this gathering, they were to discuss matters relating to the love of each other and to the service of God. They were also to discuss issues that would bring them to a closer understanding of each other, and each one was to endeavor to consider the merit of his companions and not their lacks, in order to bring the love and importance of each one of the companions into his heart.

Besides this main gathering, it was incumbent on each student to choose two or three friends with whom he was particularly close, and to direct his effort of loving his fellow towards them. This involved striving to implement the dictum, "Love your neighbor as yourself," in the fullest possible way, until he feels the same love for his fellow as he feels for himself.

It is not possible to achieve this level of love at the outset toward the whole world—we are not talking about a theoretical love, but one actually felt in the heart and acted upon—neither is it possible to achieve such a love initially with an entire community, but we can certainly strive to achieve this love of our fellow with people who are close to us. From there, we can widen the circle, until finally, we reach the desired spiritual state in which we love everyone as if he or she were ourselves.

Actually, the real effort in this work occurs when it seems to us that one of our companions is not acting properly toward us. Then we have to put ourselves and our own wishes aside and behave toward our friend exactly as we would behave toward ourselves, that is, just as we justify our own actions when we stumble—and we can find one hundred reasons to explain why we were right—so we need to justify our fellow. Why do we find this so difficult? It is because there is a general principle: "Love covers all sins" (Prov. 10:12). Since each of us naturally loves himself or herself we can naturally justify our own sins. Justifying the other person's acts is harder, as this natural love is absent.

The love of companions was a topic dear to Rabbi Baruch Shalom's heart, and it was with this topic that he opened his book, the *Sefer haMa'amarim*. This book consists of weekly essays that our dear teacher wrote for our benefit, toward the end of his life. The essays deal with how to put our learning into actual practice and come to affinity of form with the Creator as a practical living reality. Here are the opening essays of the book, all of which deal with the love of companions:

Purpose of the Group

Since we are created with a vessel that desires only to love itself—the ego—it follows that if we cannot foresee what we will gain by doing a particular action, then we don't have the motive to act, not even concerning the slightest thing.

Without nullifying this selfish love, we cannot come to affinity of form, that is to say, to dvekut with God. But nullifying our selfish love means working against our nature. So we need a group, the members of which will all be able to work together to nullify our will to receive solely for ourselves.

The will to receive for oneself alone is designated as being evil because it is that which prevents us from coming to the purpose for which we were created.

Therefore, the group needs to be composed of individuals, all of whom wish to transform the will to receive for themselves alone to the will to give benefit unconditionally. Together, the individuals combine, thus forming one big power, which each individual member of the group can use to fight his own will to receive for himself alone.

This great power is formed when each member's desire to transform his own ego is also composed of everyone else's desire for transformation. This depends on each person deferring to the other members of the group by looking at the virtues of his friends and not at their deficiencies; because one who considers himself superior to his companions will not be able to unite with them. By making his friends' desires also his, each individual member obtains a great and firmly based will for transforming his own will to receive.

During the meeting, we all need to be serious about the reason why we are meeting. There used to be a custom that for reasons of modesty, people would pretend to take their inner work lightly and would disguise their real intentions, when really a fire of passion for the service of God was burning within them. But this is not appropriate for people like ourselves; we need to take care not to speak words or act in ways that don't lead to the destination for which we came together, which is to find ways through which we may come to the unconditional service of God and thus arrive at dvekut.

Only if we are in the company of others who do not share our purpose, is it better not to show our true intention outwardly. This is the inner meaning of the Scripture, "and walk modestly with your God" (Mic. 6:8). Even though there are many lofty explanations on this scripture, its simple meaning is an important matter also.

Therefore, when we, as members of the group, gather together we should demonstrate that we share the same desire of coming closer to God. The group as a whole needs to take especial care not to enter into any spirit of mockery or cynicism because this would destroy the whole purpose of the group.

If someone comes who is not part of the group and who does not share its purpose, then it is best to leave the issue of how to come to dvekut as an internal matter and talk about other things while he is present.[5]

The Love of Friends

"And a man found him [Joseph], and behold, he was wandering in the field, and the man asked him saying, 'What are you looking for?' And he said, 'I'm looking for my brothers. Please tell me where they are herding the sheep'" (Gen. 37:16-17).

"The field" refers to the consciousness from which a person brings produce with which he can sustain his world. The work of the field consists of ploughing, sowing, and reaping. A field that God has blessed is designated as one in which "those who sow in tears will reap in joy" (Ps. 126:5). But a man may wander in the field, that is to say, he may become lost in his intellect until he does not know which way will bring him to his true purpose.

The man [the angel Gabriel] found him [Joseph], and asked him, "What are you looking for?"—in other words, "Can I help you?" And he answered, "I'm looking for my brothers."

[What is Joseph really asking for? It is as if he is saying,] if I were to band together with my brothers as one company, that is, if I were to be part of a group that is working on the love of companions, then I would be able to ascend the highway that leads to the house of God. This highway is called "the way of giving unconditionally." Since this path operates against our inborn nature, the only way we can achieve our goal of being able to give unconditionally in actuality, is through the love of our companions, wherein each one helps his fellow.

"But the man said, 'They [Joseph's brothers] journeyed from here.'" Rashi, the great Torah commentator, teaches, "They journeyed away from their brotherhood"; in other words, they don't want to join with you. This disunity was ultimately the cause of the exile of the Children of Israel in Egypt.

So, to enable ourselves to leave our own exile, which is caused by our use of our wills to receive for ourselves alone, we need to join a group that wants to work together on establishing love between all its members and then we will merit to leave our own inner Egypt and be fit to receive the Torah.[6]

The Love of Companions—
Questions We Need to Consider:

(1) Why do I need to work particularly on the issue of "the love of companions"?

(2) Why have I chosen specifically these companions? And why have these companions chosen me?

(3) Is it sufficient that each member of the group feels the love that he has for the others in his heart, working covertly and quietly for the sake of his friends, or should he openly reveal his love for his companions?

It is known that modesty is a very important virtue; but on the other hand, by this love being openly revealed, each one helps the other companions feel that every member of the group is working to strengthen the love within the group. In this way, each individual member receives greater motivation to work for the love of his companions, because the strength of each individual's love is amplified by being echoed in his companions.

We find that when love within a group is manifest, it multiplies. Instead of each individual having only his own strength of love with which to work on loving the other members, he also gains power from the others. If, for example, the company is made up of ten friends, then the love that each individual has for the others adds together, making ten units of power available to each. The individual thus has ten times his own innate strength of love available to him with which he can combat his own selfish love and use to work for the benefit of the others.

But if the love that each has for the other is not openly manifest within the group, then the company will lack strength, because in such a situation it is very difficult to judge one's friends as being meritorious. Each tends to think that he alone is righteous; only he is putting in the effort to love the others. We find that such a group has little energy with which to work for the love of their fellows. It follows, therefore, that within the group the work of loving one's companions needs to be manifest and not hidden.

We always need to bear in mind the purpose for which the group meets, as otherwise, the purpose of the group tends to get blurred. This happens because each person's ego naturally tends to be concerned with his own self-gratification. So we need to remember that the group was founded with the clear purpose of coming to love each other unconditionally, because such love is a springboard to the love of God.

The group fulfills its purpose when a person says that he needs the group so that he can learn to give unconditionally to his fellow without any recompense at all. But this won't be the case if he belongs to the group so that its members will give him material help, gifts, and so on. This will only give satisfaction to his vessels of receiving. A group that is built on such a basis of selfish love only enhances the members' vessels of receiving for themselves alone, because each person sees that there's a chance that his own personal wealth will increase because his friends are helping him in ways that increase his material satisfaction.

So we need to remember that the group is founded because its members want to learn to love their fellows unconditionally, and to learn to despise their own desire for self-gratification. The purpose of the group can only come to fruition when each can see that his companions are similarly trying to nullify their own selfish love and give unconditional love to their companions. When they can see this, each takes on the intentions of his fellows in addition to his own. [This is useful, for each person has different and unique ways of giving unconditionally, and we can learn these ways from each other.] We find that if, for example, the society is founded on ten members, and each member is working to nullify his own selfishness and trying to give unconditionally, then each individual can now acquire ten new ways.

(4) Does one need to know what each companion particularly lacks in order to know what he needs to do to fulfill it? Or is it sufficient that he occupies himself in general with the issue of the love of his companions? [7]

We need to understand that we can help each other only when we have something to offer that the other needs.

The one factor that is common to everybody is our state of mind. It is written in the Scripture: "Care in the heart of a man bows it down; but a good word makes it glad" (Prov. 12:25).

When we are feeling low, our wealth or our wisdom cannot help us, but another can help us when he sees that we are downcast. As the sages of the Talmud taught: "A person cannot release himself from prison." [8] Only a friend can help a downcast person raise his spirits. A friend can raise us up when we are disheartened and enable us to regain a spirit of life. Then we can again trust in life and in happiness and begin to feel again as if the purpose for which we are striving is attainable.

It follows from this that everybody does need to pay attention and think about how we can help each specific companion raise his or her spirits and how we can give him or her heart, because, in the issue of state of mind, everybody can help his or her companion. [9]

The Role of the Other Six Hundred and Twelve Mitzvot

What does the general rule, "Love your neighbor as yourself" (Lev. 19:18) give us? It is through practicing this general rule that we can come to the spiritual level of loving God. Since this is the case, what does our practice of the other six hundred and twelve mitzvot give us?

First of all, we need to know what the definition of a "whole" is. A whole is made up of many parts, without each of which there cannot be a whole. For example: We may talk about a congregation, by which we mean a number of individuals who have joined together to make a group, one of whom the members appoint to be the head of the congregation, and so forth. The congregation is called a *minyan*, which has to be made up of at least ten people. Then they can say specific prayers, such as the *kedushah*, that are said only in a *minyan*. Concerning this, the sages said, "The Shechinah rests on ten people." [10]

Likewise, the general principle of, "Love your neighbor as yourself" is made up of the six hundred and twelve mitzvot. That is to say, if we were to fulfill the six hundred and twelve individual mitzvot then we could come to the general principle of "Love your neighbor as yourself." We conclude that the fulfillment of the individual mitzvot allows us to reach the general principle, and then we will be able to come to the spiritual stage of loving God. "My soul has yearned, indeed it has pined for the courtyards of the Lord; my heart and my flesh will sing joyously to the living God" (Ps. 84:3).

But a person on his own is not able to fulfill all the mitzvot. For example, a father is not able to fulfill the mitzvah of *pidyon haben* [redemption of the firstborn son] if a daughter was born first. Equally, a woman is exempt from mitzvot that are time dependent.* However, due to the fact that all Israel are guarantors for each other, we find that all the mitzvot are upheld by the whole community. So we see that by including ourselves with everyone else, we do, in fact, fulfill all the mitzvot.

Thus, it really is the case that through the special merit of the six hundred and twelve mitzvot we may arrive at the general principle of "Love your neighbor as yourself." [11]

The Power of Working on Loving our Companions

"And you shall love your neighbor as yourself" (Lev. 19:18).

Rabbi Akiva says, "This is a great general principle of the Torah." [12] This statement of Rabbi Akiva means that if we can fulfill this general principle, we will be able to fulfill all the individual elements that constitute this general principle without any further trouble. So by fulfilling the general principle of loving our neighbor as ourselves, we wouldn't have anything further to add in order to fulfill the whole of the Torah.

However, we see that the Torah also tells us, "What does God ask of you, only that you have *yirah* [reverence] for Me..." (Deut. 10:12). This statement seems to imply that the only demand

---

* A woman is, in general, exempt from mitzvot that have to be performed at a specific time—her role as a mother often prevents her from doing so, but she is not prohibited from keeping these mitzvot if she so chooses.

made of us is to have *yirat HaShem* [reverence for God]. Indeed the Sages taught:

> Regarding anyone who has *yirat HaShem* within him, his words are heard, as it says in the Scripture, "In the end, all is heard: have reverence for God and keep His commandments, for this is the whole of man" (Eccles. 12:13). What does the phrase "this is the whole of man' mean?" Rabbi Elazar said, "The Holy Blessed One said, 'The entire world was created only for this.'" [13]

So if we were to fulfill the mitzvah of *yirat HaShem*, we would thus be fulfilling the entire Torah and mitzvot, including the mitzvah of loving your neighbor as yourself!

This conclusion appears to contradict the words of Rabbi Akiva that we learned above, which implied that if we were to keep the mitzvah of "Love your neighbor as yourself" then we would be fulfilling the whole of the Torah, including the mitzvah of *yirat HaShem*.

Furthermore, in a different section of the Talmud, the sages teach that the main principle we need to have is faith: "Habakkuk came and established the whole of the Torah on one principle alone, according to the Scripture, 'The tzaddik will live according to his faith' (Hab. 2:4)." [14] The Talmudic commentator, Rabbi Shmuel Idelish explains: "Faith is the one unifying principle for all the Children of Israel, at all times." From what he says, it follows that the most important principle for us to embrace is faith in God and in the goodness of His Divine Providence. According to this dictum, it appears that if we were to have complete faith we would then be fulfilling all the mitzvot, including those of *yirat HaShem* and loving one's neighbor!

How can all the above be true? In order to understand this we need to contemplate more deeply: Firstly, what constitutes faith? Secondly, what constitutes *yirat HaShem*? And thirdly, what constitutes loving one's neighbor as oneself?

To answer these questions, the most important thing we need to remember is what the Purpose of Creation is. It is known that the Purpose of Creation is to give goodness to the created beings. Since God wants to give good and joy to the created beings, why do we need these three principles: faith, *yirat HaShem*, and loving one's neighbor? The answer is that we need these three principles so that we can correct our vessels of receiving to vessels that are able to receive the good and joy that the Creator wishes to give us.

How do these three principles help us do this? Let us first take the element of faith: the element of faith includes trusting God. We need faith because, prior to anything else, we need to believe that God does want to give goodness to the created beings. We need a basic trust so that we can promise ourselves that we, too, will be able to arrive at this destination. We need to have a basic faith that the Purpose of Creation is not intended only for remarkable people, but that the Purpose of Creation will be fulfilled and belongs to all people without any exception at all. One does not need to be an especially talented individual with extraordinary powers of perseverance or courage and suchlike, but the Purpose of Creation will be fulfilled and belongs to every single human being. This is in accordance with what the Baal HaSulam writes in the *Hakdamah l'Talmud Eser haSephirot* [The Introduction to the Study of the Ten Sephirot]: "The Holy Blessed One said to Israel, 'By your life! All this wisdom and all this Torah is a very easy matter! Whoever has *yirah* [reverence] of Me and acts on the words of the Torah, all the wisdom will be found in his heart.'"[15]

So we see that we need the virtue of faith so that we will have that basic security that each one of us is able to reach the purpose for which we were created, to enable us not to despair in the middle of the work or run away from the inner struggle. But we need to believe that God is able to help, even those as lowly as ourselves. We need to have faith and believe that God will bring each one of us close to Him and that we will be able to merit affinity of form with Him.

In order to merit such faith, first of all, we need to work on our *yirat HaShem*, as Rabbi Shimon Bar Yochai teaches:

Zohar

Yirat HaShem is the first mitzvah, for it is the gateway to faith, and on this mitzvah, the whole world stands."[16]

Perush haSulam

The mitzvah of *yirah* includes all the mitzvot of the Torah within it since it is the gateway to a person's faith in God. According to the awakening of a person's *yirah*, so he is inspired with the light of faith in God's providence. Therefore, we must not forget *yirah* in every single mitzvah that we undertake."[17]

What does this *yirah* consist of? The Baal HaSulam teaches that *yirah* is the concern we need to feel regarding our ability to give satisfaction to the Creator. That is to say, we need to question: maybe we won't be able to act in a way that is unconditionally giving and thus not be in affinity of form with the Creator. True *yirat HaShem* implies that we are not concerned with fulfilling our own selfish love. It follows, that the gateway for faith is *yirat HaShem*, because without *yirat HaShem* we cannot come to faith in God.

But to reach this high level of *yirat HaShem* we need to first obtain the desire and the will to give unconditionally. Only if we have already acquired this will of giving unconditionally is it possible to worry about whether or not we are able to fulfill the commandment of *yirat HaShem*.

Since we tend to be more concerned with whether or not we will be able to fulfill our selfish love, we are not usually concerned over whether or not we will be able to give unconditional love to the Creator. So, from where can we attain these new attributes of a) wanting to give unconditionally, and b) not wanting to receive for ourselves alone, when, surely, both of these are diametrically opposed to our inborn nature?

Sometimes we may receive some thought or desire that we need to leave our selfish love. This thought may come to us because we heard it from a teacher or because we read it in a holy book. But this type of input gives us only a very small level of motivation, and so this idea is not always shining for us to the extent that we can say that we value the attribute of giving unconditionally.

However, there is one piece of advice that works. If several like-minded people, who, individually, have only a small power of motivation of wanting to leave their selfish love, were to gather together and defer to each other, forming one group, then, since each one has, at least, the potential for loving the Creator, then their individual strengths can combine together. This would give each member of the group a much stronger motivation with which to attain his goal. If there were, for example, ten members of the group, the group would now have ten times more strength with which to work than one person has as an individual.

This strategy would work, providing that when the members gather together, each one thinks about the fact that he has come to this group for the explicit purpose of nullifying his selfish love. In other words, we mustn't be thinking about how to fulfill our own will to receive, but we must be thinking now as much as possible how we can love our fellow. Only in this way will we be able to attain this new attribute, the will to give unconditionally.

It is from this love of companions that we will be able to arrive at the desire to give unconditionally to the Creator and be in affinity of form with Him. This desire is termed "Love of the Creator." So we see that only through working with the love of companions do we acquire the understanding that the issue of giving unconditionally is something important, and then it becomes a necessity for each one of us.

Only when we have acquired this desire of coming to affinity of form with the Creator can we be concerned with *yirat HaShem*. This is the concern that maybe we won't be able to give unconditionally to God. So we find that the foundation on which we are able to build this holy building is the general principle of, "Love your neighbor as yourself." It is through working on this mitzvah—firstly with other like-minded individuals—we are able to receive the need to give unconditionally to the Creator. Then, through the need to give to the Creator unconditionally, we come to *yirat HaShem,* which forms the gateway for the light of faith and trust in God.

Accordingly, we see that we do have three general principles: the first one is that of Rabbi Akiva, which is of that of loving your neighbor, because, before this, there is nothing that could possibly give us any motivation to move at all from our selfish love. Only then can we come to the second general principle, which is that of *yirat HaShem,* because without *yirat HaShem* there isn't any place for *emunah,* faith. And it is through faith, the third principle, that we can feel that the Purpose of Creation is to give good to the created beings and that it belongs to each and every one of us.[18]

May we all merit to progress, hand-in-hand with our companions, on the pathway to the unconditional love of our fellow and to the love of the Creator, and hasten the redemption when the whole world will come to harmony, and the light and love of God will be manifest to all.

Avraham Mordecai Gottlieb
Kiryat Ye'arim

Yedidah Cohen
Tsfat

Dates in the Life of the Baal HaSulam

+ 1885 (*Tishrei* 5, 5646) Rabbi Yehudah Leib Ashlag is born in Warsaw, Poland

+ 1903 (5664) The young Yehudah Leib first meets the holy Rabbi Dov Issachar of Belz.

+ 1904 (5665) Rabbi Ashlag receives *semichah* (rabbinical ordination) from the greatest of the rabbis of Warsaw.

+ 1905 (5666) Marriage to Rivkah Raiza Abramovitz.

+ 1907 (*Shvat* 7, 5667) The birth of Rabbi Ashlag's firstborn son, the sage Rabbi Baruch Shalom Halevi Ashlag, who follows in his father's footsteps.

+ 1921 (*Erev Rosh Chodesh Elul* 5681) Rabbi Ashlag and family leave Poland.

+ 1921 (*Tishrei* 16, 5682, *Chol haMoed* Succot) Arrival in Israel. Rabbi Ashlag is thirty-six years old. The family lives in the Jewish quarter of the Old City of Jerusalem and Rabbi Ashlag learns at the *Chayei Olam Yeshivah*.

+ 1923 (5684) Rabbi Ashlag moves to Givat Shaul where he serves as local rabbi and rabbinical judge.

+ 1924 (5685) Rabbi Ashlag returns to Warsaw to fetch the children who had been left there.

+ 1926 (5686) The Sage travels alone to London, where he stays two years. He composes his work, the *Panim Meirot uMasbirot* on the *Etz Chaim* of the Ari z"l.

+ 1927 (5687) The students in Israel print the *Etz Chaim* of the Ari z'l with the commentary, the *Panim Meirot uMasbirot*.

- 1928 (5688) Rabbi Ashlag returns to Israel, initially to Givat Shaul and then moves to Batei Warsaw near the Mintzberg family. Rabbi Ashlag then moves, alone, to Tel Aviv, Achad HaAm Street, while the Rabbanit stays in Jerusalem with all the children. This was because it was not a permanent lodging.

- 1932 (5692) The Sage moves to the Neveh Shalom district, close to the city of Jaffa. There the rest of his family joins him.

- 1933 (5693) Rabbi Ashlag composes the book *Matan Torah* and starts writing the *Talmud Eser haSephirot*, his major commentary on the writings of the Holy Ari. He then adds the work, *Sha'ar haKavanot*, also a commentary on the writings of the Ari.

- 1936 (5696) Rabbi Ashlag and family move to Bnei Brak, living in the same neighborhood as the Chazon Ish. They then return to Jerusalem, to Ben David Street/corner of Yoel Street. They move again to Yechezkel Street/corner of Avinoam Yellin Street.

- 1940 (5700) The family moves to Mayesof Street in the Bukharian Quarter, Jerusalem, and lives there throughout World War II.

- 1943 (5703) Rabbi Ashlag begins to write the *Perush haSulam*.

- 1946 (5706) The family returns to Tel Aviv, Rechov Yavneh, where they stay during the War of Independence.

- 1952 (5712) The Rabbi and family move to his last lodging, Balfour Street/corner of Sderot Rothschild in Tel Aviv.

- 1953 (5713) The Baal HaSulam completes writing the *Perush haSulam* on the Zohar.

- 1954 (*Tishrei* 10, 5715) Rabbi Yehudah Leib Ashlag, the Baal HaSulam, passes away, Yom Kippur, 7th October.

- 1954 (*Tishrei* 28, 5715) Rabbi Baruch Shalom Halevi Ashlag is requested by the other students to succeed his father as sage.

References

Chapter Two: The Work Begins

1. See also *Perush haSulam, Parshat Tazriah* paragraph 1.
2. *Beit Sha'ar haKavanot.*
3. *Igarot HaSulam, Igeret* 25 (Or HaSulam)
4. Letter to Rabbi Brandwein *Igarot HaSulam, Igeret* 14 (Or HaSulam).
5. *Succah* 52a.
6. Poem from the prayers at the close of Yom Kippur.
7. *Rashi* on Ps. 36:7.

Chapter Three: From Warsaw to Jerusalem

1. Reported by Rabbi Azriel Chaim Lemburger.
2. Reported by Rabbi Azriel Chaim Lemburger.
3. Reported by Rabbi Avraham Brandwein.
4. *Sanhedrin* 101a.
5. Rabbi Y. L. Ashlag, unpublished writings.
6. Zohar, *Perush haSulam Beha'alotecha* paragraphs 58-64.
7. *Igarot Pri Chacham, Igeret* 41 (Or HaSulam).

Chapter Four: The First Band of Pupils

1. To listen to the recordings, see Rabbi Ashlag's Works.
2. *Pirkei Avot* (Ethics of the Fathers) 1, 6.

Chapter Five: The Path

1. *Bircat Shalom, Sefer haMa'amarim* vol. 3.

Chapter Six: Treading the Path

1. *Igarot HaSulam, Igeret* 62 (Or HaSulam).
2. *Sotah* 14a.
3. Grace after Meals.
4. *Igarot HaSulam, Igeret* 12 (Or HaSulam).
5. *Igarot HaSulam, Igeret* 59 (Or HaSulam).
6. *Berachot* 61b.
7. *Bava Batra* 98a.

References

Chapter Six: Treading the Path (cont.)

8. *Pesachim* 119b.
9. *Igarot HaSulam, Igeret* 6 (Or HaSulam).
10. Zohar, *Parashah Acharei-mot, Perush haSulam* paragraph 299.
11. *Kiddushin* 30b.
12. *Etz Chaim, sha'ar* 1, *anaf* 1.
13. Zohar, *Parashat Emor, Perush haSulam* paragraph 188.
14. *Etz Chaim, Talmud Eser haSephirot* part one, chapter one.
15. Zohar, *Parashat Kedoshim, Perush haSulam* paragraph 44.
16. *Midrash, Song of Songs* 5:2.
17. *Igarot HaSulam, Igeret* 20 (Or HaSulam)
18. *Pesachim* 22b.
19. *Pesachim* 112a.
20. *Berachot* 7a.
21. *Igarot HaSulam, Igeret* 51 (Or HaSulam)
22. Zohar, *Parashat Pinchas, Perush haSulam*, paragraph 372.

Chapter Seven: Emphasis on the Inner

1. *Pirkei Avot (Ethics of the Fathers)* 1, 15.
2. Rabbi Y. L Ashlag, *Hakdamah l'Sefer haZohar*, paragraph 66.
3. Rabbi Y. L. Ashlag, *Hakdamah l'Talmud Eser haSephirot*, paragraph 19
4. *Meir Einei haGolah*, paragraph 647.
5. *Tzavat haRibash*
6. Zohar, *Parashat Metzorah, Perush haSulam* paragraph 20.
7. Rabbi Meshulam Feibush HaLevi Heller, *Yosher Divrei Emet*.

Chapter Eight: Kabbalah and Redemption

1. *Yerushalmi Yoma* 5a.
2. *Tikkunei haZohar tikkun* 30, brought here in the *Introduction to the Etz Chaim* of the Ari.
3. *Yebamot* 63a.
4. *Baba Kama* 60.
5. Zohar, *Parashat Naso, Perush haSulam* paragraph 90.
6. Rabbi Y. L. Ashlag, *Hakdamah l'Sefer haZohar* paragraph 70.
7. *Meir Einai haGolah* paragraph 479.
8. *Tikkunei haZohar, end Tikkun* 6.
9. Unpublished writings.
10. Oral teaching of the Beth Yisrael, *Parashat Shmot* 1949.

Chapter Nine: Writing the Books

1. *Igarot HaSulam* 54 (Or HaSulam).
2. *Berachot* 61.
3. As is brought in the *Pesikhtah*
4. *Sha'ar haGilgulim, Sha'ar* 8, page 49.
5. *Sha'ar haGilgulim, Sha'ar* 8, page 71.
6. *Igarot HaSulam, Igeret* 48 (Or HaSulam).
7. *Yad Benyamin* page 205.
8. *Torat haKabbalah u'Mahuta, Pri Chacham Ma'amarim* page 165.
9. Zohar, *Parashat Mishpatim, Perush haSulam* paragraph 122.
10. Zohar, *Parashat Vayetzeh, Perush haSulam* paragraph 257.
11. *Succah* 5a.
12. Rabbi Y. L. Ashlag, *Hakdamah l'Talmud Eser haSephirot* paragraph 156.
13. Rabbi Y. L. Ashlag, writings

Chapter Ten: Why Should We Study Kabbalah?

1. *Hakdamah l'Talmud Eser HaSephirot*, paragraph 2
2. *Leviticus Raba* 13
3. *Sifre, Parashah Kedoshim*, on 20:26
4. *Kiddushin* 30b
5. *Gittin* 28b.
6. Rabbi Y. L. Ashlag, *Torat haKabbalah u'Mahutah, Pri Chacham, Ma'amarim.*
7. *Chullin* 24a
8. Rabbi Y. L. Ashlag, *Hakdamah l'Talmud Eser haSephirot* paragraph 22.
9. *Hakdamah l'Talmud Eser haSephirot* paragraph 155.
10. Introduction of Rabbi Chaim Vital to *Sha'ar Hakdamot* of the Holy Ari, brought in the *Hakdamah l'Talmud Eser haSephirot* paragraph 19.
11. Zohar, *Parashat Naso, Perush haSulam* paragraph 90.
12. *Midrash* Lamentations, *Peticah* b
13. *Sanhedrin* 98a.
14. *Sotah* 49b.
15. *Hakdamah l'Panim Meirot uMasbirot* paragraph 5.

Chapter Twelve: The Synagogue in the Bukharian Neighborhood

1. All these conversations are recorded in the volume, *Yad Binyamin*, volume 4 *HaShem Shamati Shimecha* (Bircat Shalom)
2. Zohar, *Parashat Vayera, Perush haSulam* paragraph 381.
3. *Pesachim* 109a.

References

Chapter Thirteen: The *Perush haSulam* on the Zohar

1. Rabbi Y. L. Ashlag, *Mavo l'Zohar* 1.
2. Rabbi Y. L. Ashlag, *Hakdamah l'Sefer haZohar* paragraphs 59-60.
3. ibid. paragraph 58.
4. Rabbi Y. L. Ashlag, *Torat haKabbalah u'Mahutah, Pri Chacham Ma'amarim*
5. Rabbi Y. L. Ashlag, *Zohar, Parashah Acharei Mot, Perush haSulam* paragraph 199.
6. Rabbi Y. L. Ashlag, *Zohar, Hakdamat Sefer haZohar, Perush haSulam* paragraphs 182-184
7. Rabbi Y. L. Ashlag, *Zohar, Parashah vaEtchanan, Perush haSulam* paragraph 11.
8. Weekday *Amidah*.
9. *Pirkei Avot* (Ethics of the Fathers) 5, 13.

Chapter Fourteen: In the Presence of the Sage

1. Rabbi B. Sinkovsky *Yad Binyamin* article 20 vol. 4 *HaShem Shamati Shemecha* (Bircat Shalom).

Chapter Fifteen: The Real Miracle — The Inner Transformation

1. Introduction to *Yalkut Yoseph, HaShem Shamati Shemecha (Bircat Shalom)*

Chapter Sixteen: The Foundation of a Just Society

1. Marx, K. *Critique of the Gotha Program*, 1875. Earlier socialist philosophers who articulated this idea were: August Becker, 1844; Louis Blanc, 1851.
2. Rabbi Y. L. Ashlag, *Matan Torah*, article *haShalom*.
3. Rabbi Y. L. Ashlag, unpublished writings.

Chapter Seventeen: The Establishment of the State of Israel

1. *Sotah* 4b.
2. Rabbi Y. L. Ashlag, *Hakdamah l'Panim Meirot uMasbirot*
3. Rabbi Y. L. Ashlag, *Ma'amar l'Siyum haZohar* 1953, published in *Matan Torah*.
4. after *Sotah* 12a.
5. Rabbi Y. L. Ashlag, *Hakdamah l'Sefer haZohar* paragraph 67.

Chapter Eighteen: *Dvekut*

1. after *Succah* 51b.
2. *Sotah* 14a and *Shabbat* 133b.
3. *Pesachim* 50b.
4. end tractate *Uzkin*.
5. *Bava Batra* 12a.
6. Rabbi Y. L. Ashlag, *Ma'amar l'Siyum haZohar* (Article on finishing the Zohar,) Meron 1953, published in *Matan Torah*.

Chapter Nineteen: "My Father! My Father!"

1. *Yad Binyamin, Shamati Shemecha* vol. 4 (Bircat Shalom)
2. Neilah Service, Yom Kippur

Chapter Twenty: Swifter than Eagles, Stronger than Lions

1. *Pesachim* 112a.
2. *Pirkei Avot* (Ethics of the Fathers) 3, 10.
3. *Pirkei Avot* (Ethics of the Fathers) 4, 26.

Afterword: The Love of Companions

1. Rabbi Y. L. Ashlag, *Igarot HaSulam, Igeret* 57 (Or HaSulam).
2. Rabbi Y. L. Ashlag, *Igarot HaSulam, Igeret* 14 (Or HaSulam).
3. Rabbi Y. L. Ashlag, *Igarot HaSulam, Igeret* 16 (Or HaSulam).
4. Rabbi Y. L. Ashlag, *Matan Torah: Ma'amar l' Siyum haZohar*
5. Rabbi B. S. Ashlag, *Sefer haMa'amarim* vol. 1 article 1.
6. Rabbi B. S. Ashlag, *Sefer haMa'amarim* vol. 1 article 2.
7. Rabbi B. S. Ashlag, *Sefer haMa'amarim* vol. 1 article 3.
8. *Berachot* 5a.
9. Rabbi B. S. Ashlag, *Sefer haMa'amarim* vol. 1 article 4.
10. *Sanhedrin* 39a.
11. Rabbi B. S. Ashlag, *Sefer haMa'amarim* vol. 1 article 5.
12. *Bereishit Raba, Perush* 24.
13. *Berachot* 6b.
14. *Makot* 24a.
15. *Midrash Raba v'Zot haBracha* 11,6 quoted in *Hakdamah l'Talmud Eser haSephirot* paragraph 21.
16. Rabbi Y. L. Ashlag, *Hakdamat haZohar, Perush haSulam*, vol. 1 paragraph 189
17. Rabbi Y. L. Ashlag, *Hakdamat haZohar, Perush haSulam*, vol. 1 paragraph 203
18. Rabbi B. S. Ashlag, *Sefer haMa'amarim* vol. 1 article 6.

Rabbi Ashlag's Work and Bibliography

1. Zohar, *Parashat Pinchas* Paragraph 488 and other texts
2. *Berachot* 17a

Glossary

The purpose of this glossary is threefold: (1) to provide translations and definitions of words that originate in the Hebrew language, (2) to provide short explanations of words whose usage in the language of Kabbalah differs from our everyday usage, and (3) to give the Hebrew equivalents for those who know Hebrew but may not be familiar with the specific terms that Rabbi Ashlag uses. All terms are either Hebrew or English unless stated otherwise.

above לְמַעְלָה **and below** לְמַטָה: That which tends toward affinity of form with the Creator, who is all-giving, is considered "above"; that which tends to oppose the desire of the Creator is considered "below." Thus the phrase, "faith above knowledge" אֱמוּנָה מֵעַל הַדַעַת implies that the consciousness of faith is more in affinity of form with the Creator than is the consciousness of knowledge.

affinity of form הַשְׁוָואַת הַצוּרָה: When two spiritual entities act with a similar desire they exhibit affinity of form. Since God is all giving, if we act with a similar desire of giving unconditionally, either to God or to our fellow, we exhibit affinity of form with God. Such affinity of form leads to *dvekut*, unity with the Creator.

aliyah laTorah עֲלִיָה לַתּוֹרָה pl. *aliyot*, lit., ascent to the Torah: An honor given in the synagogue, when a person is called up to participate in the reading of the Torah scroll. In many communities, these *aliyot* are "sold" as a means of providing financial support for the synagogue and its institutions.

amidah עֲמִידָה lit., standing: This is the central prayer of all three daily prayer services and of the Shabbat and festival prayers. Each part of the daily prayers is associated with a particular spiritual world. The *Amidah*, which is said standing, in a silent whisper, with the feet together, is associated with the highest of the spiritual worlds, the world of Atzilut.

attainment הַשָּׂגָה: When a person merits to attain a certain level of spiritual consciousness, it implies that he has perfected his consciousness at that level, in affinity of form with the Creator. This includes intellectual, emotional, and behavioral attainment. Such attainment enables the person to perceive processes within these consciousnesses.

Atzilut אֲצִילוּת: This is the highest spiritual world whose consciousness the human being can attain. See "world." See also Rabbi Ashlag's Works page 340

beit knesset בֵּית כְּנֶסֶת lit., meeting place: Term for synagogue.

beit midrash בֵּית מִדְרָשׁ: The study hall attached to a synagogue or to a private home for the purpose of Torah study.

body גּוּף: In Kabbalah, the word "body" refers to the will to receive. This includes all aspects: physical, emotional, intellectual, and spiritual. It often refers to the ego.

chasidut חֲסִידוּת lit., piety: This term refers to the form of Jewish practice and thought founded by the Baal Shem Tov in the eighteenth century in Eastern Europe. Many different schools of chasidut developed according to the different emphasis placed on its ideas by its great teachers. Its adherents are called "chasidim."

chametz חָמֵץ lit., that which leavens: This term refers to products that are made from the five species of grain: wheat, barley, oats, spelt, and rye, which, when combined with water for eighteen minutes constitute *chametz*. *Chametz* is completely forbidden to see or to have within one's possession, let alone eat of it, during the week of Pesach. In Kabbalah, *chametz* is equated with the will to receive for oneself alone. On Pesach, unleavened bread, matzot, is eaten instead.

chol hamoed חוֹל הַמּוֹעֵד: These are the intermediate days of the festivals of Pesach and Succot which retain the holiness of the festival, but on which essential work is permitted. The holiday atmosphere prevails everywhere, businesses are often closed and the days are used by the religious as a time for visiting and learning Torah in an atmosphere of joy.

counting the *Omer* סְפִירַת הָעוֹמֶר: This relates to the mitzvah of counting seven full weeks starting on the second night of Pesach until the night of the festival of Shavuot on which we celebrate the Receiving of the Torah on Mount Sinai. According to Kabbalah, each day represents another vessel within ourselves that we rectify in order to come to affinity of form with the Creator, in order that we will be prepared to receive the great light of Torah in an appropriate way.

***Da'at* דַּעַת (Heb.) also *De'ah* דֵּעָה:** Often translated as knowledge; these words are better translated as connection or connective knowledge. The Sephirah *Da'at* encompasses intuitive, emotional, and intellectual knowledge. When we strive to attain affinity of form with the Creator, either through prayer or through the performance of good deeds, then we are associated with the Sephirah *Da'at*. The Sephirah *Da'at* connects the Sephirah Chochmah חָכְמָה with the Sephirah Binah בִּינָה in the higher worlds. Thus our good deeds enable the goodness of God to flow to all the created beings.

day יוֹם and night לַיְלָה: The state of consciousness that arises within us when God's light—His goodness— is openly revealed to us, is called "day." In this state, we experience the goodness of God. It is also called "the revelation of God's face," *gilui panim* גִּילוּי פָּנִים.

"Night" refers to states of consciousness in which God's goodness is hidden from us, *hester panim* הֶסְתֵּר פָּנִים.

Both states of consciousness, day and night, are necessary for our full development as human beings so that we can come to a full desire for God's light, and to the awareness that God is good and gives good to all.

difference of form שִׁינוּי צוּרָה: Two spiritual entities that are acting with different interests or different desires are said to exhibit difference of form or even opposition of form. Such difference of form leads to separation. When a person uses his desire to receive for himself alone he is completely separated from the Creator, as now he is in opposition of form הִיפּוּךְ צוּרָה from the Creator.

Divine Providence הַשְׁגָחָה: This is the belief that God is Good and does good, and that all that happens to us is by His will alone. God is the one ruling force that governs all that occurs in our lives, both as individuals and as part of the collective.

dvekut דְּבֵקוּת: This term is usually translated as cleaving to the Creator, which implies unity with Him. We come to *dvekut* with the Creator through performing acts of unconditional giving, as these lead to affinity of form with the Creator and hence unity with Him.

Ein Sof אֵין סוֹף lit., without end, or The Infinite: The Ein Sof is the spiritual stage at which the Purpose of Creation is manifest. It is the spiritual stage at which the highest light of God emanates from the *Atzmut* עצמות (God's Essence). This light includes within it the Malchut מַלְכוּת (the vessel) of the Ein Sof, from which all created beings come.

Elul אֱלוּל: The Hebrew month that is associated with the work of *teshuvah* (repentance). It is the month that precedes the festivals of Rosh HaShanah ראש הַשָׁנָה and Yom Kippur יוֹם כִּפּוּר.

emunah אֱמוּנָה faith: The term implies faith in God's existence, faith in Divine Providence, and faith that God is good and does good to all. When we think, speak, and act in faith we are in the consciousness of giving. Thus faith belongs to a paradigm of consciousness that is more in affinity of form with the Creator than is that of knowledge or of experience, which, in contrast, are states of consciousness associated with receiving. Faith in God is developed when God's light is concealed from us. But when God's light is revealed to us, faith is a state that may be freely chosen.

evil: See will to receive for oneself alone.

framework of holiness מַעֲרֶכֶת הַקְדוּשָׁה: This is a whole system based on the desires of the soul, which is in affinity of form with the Creator. It is associated with the consciousness of using vessels of receiving or of giving, but only for the sake of giving unconditionally.

framework of uncleanness (evil) מַעֲרֶכֶת הַטּוּמְאָה: This is any system that uses the will to receive for itself alone as its guiding consciousness.

giving unconditionally הַשְׁפָּעָה: Giving with our focus on what the other needs, without any thought as to what we would like to receive in return. Such giving is not in our inborn nature; our inborn nature being one of self-centeredness. Only through the light of the Torah or through the experience of suffering brought about by using our will to receive for ourselves alone, do we gradually acquire a new vessel of unconditional giving. This vessel is in affinity of form with the Creator.

gmar hatikkun גְּמַר הַתִּקּוּן: The perfected state of the Creation. This will take place when all the souls will together have completely recti- fied the will to receive for oneself alone implanted in them since the sin of Adam. The *gmar hatikkun* is also known as the final redemption.

halachah הֲלָכָה: This term refers to the great body of Jewish law that determines how the mitzvot are carried out in practice.

hakafah הַקָּפָה lit., encircling: In the synagogue, on the festivals of Succot and Simchat Torah, we conduct a conscious reenactment of the encircling of the altar in the Temple that took place on these holidays.

holiness קְדוּשָׁה: That which is set aside and is in affinity of form with the Creator, that is to say, giving for the sake of giving.

heart and mind מוֹחָא וְלִיבָּא: The will to receive for oneself alone expresses itself through the heart as the sensual will to receive pleasure, and through the mind as the desire for certainty. The tikkun of the heart is through service, and the tikkun of the mind is through faith.

intentions כַּוָונוֹת: Our acts are open and revealed to all, but our inten- tions that inspire the acts are not. They are hidden, sometimes even from ourselves. Kabbalah is called the hidden part of the Torah, *Torat haNistar*, because it deals with intentions.

Kiddush קִידוּש lit., sanctification: The ceremony over wine conducted at home with which the head of the family formally welcomes in the Sabbath. In the Zohar, the Kiddush has profound significance: its text is composed of the names of God, and the wine is a physical representation of the *Or d' Chochmah*—the light associated with the fulfillment of the Purpose of Creation.

klipot קְלִיפּוֹת lit., shells: These are the lights given over to the framework of uncleanness that entice a person to receive for oneself alone. As the klipot provoke the development of a person's desires to receive for himself alone they thus force the soul to grow as the person now needs to overcome these desires. They thus have a protective function, in that they encourage the soul to grow until it matures enough to be able to receive the real lights of holiness. The *klipot* are the lights that sustain physical reality. They move, as needed, between the frameworks of evil and of holiness, according to the deeds and consciousness of the human as an individual and of humankind in general.

knowledge דַּעַת: Knowledge refers to that which we experience as well as that which we know intellectually. It fulfills the will to receive certainty. Knowledge belongs to the consciousness of receiving and is therefore considered as less in affinity of form with the Creator than is the consciousness of faith, which is a state of giving.

kolel כּוֹלֵל lit., a gathering: An institute for full-time, advanced study of the Torah, usually for married men.

lack חִסָּרוֹן: Lack causes us suffering because our origin is in the Ein Sof, where the vessel, the Malchut of the Ein Sof, is filled with light. Thus we find any state of lack unsatisfactory and painful. The state of lack thus arouses us to prayer.

Lag b'Omer לַ"ג בָּעוֹמֶר: This is the 33rd day of the Omer period between Pesach and Shavuot. On this day, Rabbi Shimon Bar Yochai gave over some tremendous teachings in the Zohar just before he passed from this life. It is a day of celebration and rejoicing when many thousands visit the grave of Rabbi Shimon in Meron. It is also the day on which the plague that killed 24,000 students of Rabbi Akiva finally ceased.

lashon hara לָשׁוֹן הָרַע lit., evil speech: This is negative speech about another person even when what is said is objectively true. The term also applies to grumbling against God and His providence. Such grumbling is considered *lashon hara*.

left-hand line: See right-hand line and left-hand line.

light אוֹר also שֶׁפַע: God's bounty. The light of God is ever-present, but we can only experience it when our desires, which are the vessels for the light, are in affinity of form with the Creator. The light is one, but it appears differently according to our spiritual state.

Malchut מַלְכוּת lit., governance: The Malchut is the vessel, that is the desire to receive, that is created by the light of God in the Ein Sof as a consequence of God's purpose in creation, which is to give pleasure to all created beings. As the worlds devolve from the Ein Sof, the vessels separate from the light, ultimately reaching a point at which they can receive for themselves alone. At each point on the devolution of the worlds, and at their subsequent rectification, the name of the vessel is the Malchut. So in order to understand the meaning of the term "Malchut" at any point in our learning of Kabbalah, we need to know at which spiritual level the text is speaking. The fully rectified Malchut that is in affinity of form with the Creator is called "the Shechinah" and represents the collective soul of humanity.

Malchut Shamayim מַלְכוּת שָׁמַיִם lit., the rule of Heaven: The term implies acceptance of the crucial role that Divine Providence plays in our individual and collective lives, and the acknowledgment that the Divine Providence is inherently good.

masach מַסָךְ lit., a screen or barrier: Although the vessel of the spiritual entity desires to receive the light, the spiritual entity, nevertheless, prefers to remain in *dvekut* rather than receive the light for itself. Thus the spiritual entity exerts itself to overcome its desire to receive, and it returns the light. An example of this is fasting on Yom Kippur. Even though our vessel is hungry and desires to receive food, we prefer to remain in affinity of form with the Creator and obey the mitzvah of fasting on Yom Kippur. This restraint sets up a new dynamic, which ultimately leads the spiritual entity to receive the light only for the sake of giving pleasure to the Giver.

mitzvah מִצְוָה pl. *mitzvot* מִצְוֹת lit., that which is commanded: The word mitzvah refers to actions that we are specifically prescribed to do or those we are specifically proscribed from doing by the Torah, as handed down by Moses from Sinai, and whose practical observance has been formulated through the ages by the sages. There are mitzvot which are conducted between ourselves and God and between ourselves and our fellows.

names of God: The names of God are ways in which we perceive His light. They may be looked at as specific vessels for His light. For example, God may be called "King מֶלֶךְ," or the "King of Kings מֶלֶךְ מַלְכֵי הַמְּלָכִים," which implies God as the ultimate source for Good. In other circumstances, He may be referred to as *Ribono Shel Olam,* רִיבּוֹנוֹ שֶׁל עוֹלָם "the Master of the world." Thus a name of God refers to the light of God as received through a specific vessel for the light, not to God as He is in Himself, who, as the Holy Ari teaches, has no border and no name.

Or d'Chassadim אוֹר דְּחֲסָדִים lit., the light of loving-kindness: This is the light we attract to ourselves through our desire to give unconditionally to God or to our fellow. It is the joy of giving.

Or d'Chochmah אוֹר דְּחָכְמָה lit., the light of wisdom: This is the great light that God wants to give us according to the Purpose of Creation.

Or Elyon אוֹר עֶלְיוֹן lit., the highest light: This is a term for the light of the Ein Sof. It is also referred to as the *Or d'Chochmah.*

Parashah פְּרָשָׁה lit., section: The weekly Torah portion. Each *parashah* is read on its specific week. The Torah is read consecutively, the cycle starting and finishing on Simchat Torah שִׂמְחַת תּוֹרָה when the cycle begins again.

Pesach פֶּסַח Passover: The festival of redemption of the Children of Israel from Egypt. In Kabbalah, it also has the meaning of redemption from our wills to receive for ourselves alone.

Purpose of Creation מַטְרַת הַבְּרִיאָה also called the Thought of Creation מַחְשֶׁבֶת הַבְּרִיאָה: The Ari teaches that God's purpose in creation is to give goodness and satisfaction to all the created beings. The Purpose of Creation is manifested by the light of the Ein Sof and will be fulfilled at the *gmar hatikkun*, the redemption.

redemption הַגְּאוּלָה הַשְּׁלֵמָה: Following the completion of the tikkun, the consciousness of humanity and of all the worlds will ascend to a level at which we will all be able to receive only for the sake of giving, acting as infinite channels for the love of God in affinity of form with Him.

right-hand line קַו יָמִין **and left-hand line** קַו שְׂמֹאל: The Sephirot, which are the vessels with which we receive the divine light, are either those whose qualities are of giving (right-hand line) or of receiving (left-hand line). Accordingly, our work for God may be similarly divided along these two lines:

The **right-hand line** קַו יָמִין is the conscious state of giving unconditionally in which we give our confidence and faith to God that the way the world is—including ourselves—is just the way He wishes it to be. This is the attitude we need to adopt for the greater part of the day. It is the line of joy which we endeavor to maintain, no matter what our rationale or our senses are telling us, as it is based on the belief that God is good and does good.

The **left-hand line** קַו שְׂמֹאל comprises the aspect of truth, wherein we examine where we are truly standing in our love of our fellows and in our service to God. When we see our lacks in these areas, we feel sorry and thus our prayer to God to help us naturally arises in this line of consciousness.

root and branch שׁוֹרֶשׁ וְעָנָף: Every element of a lower world stems from its root in the higher spiritual world above it. It is on this fact that the "language of the branches" שְׂפַת הָעֲנָפִים of the Zohar and of the other works of Kabbalah is based.

sadness עַצְבוּת: Since God, the Master of the world, is good and does good, then, despite our experiences, we need to be thankful and maintain our equanimity and happiness at all times. This high spiritual state was emphasized by Rabbi Ashlag and his son Rabbi Baruch Shalom Ashlag who taught that dwelling on one's sadness is considered as *lashon hara* לָשׁוֹן הָרַע (slander) against the Creator.

sage אַדְמוֹ"ר an acronym for אֲדוֹנֵנוּ מוֹרֵנוּ וְרַבֵּנוּ, our master, our teacher and our rabbi: A sage is one who not only has the highest moral and ethical standards and keeps all the Torah, written and oral, but also has direct perception of the higher worlds, as he is in affinity of form with the Creator. Each individual sage has a unique role and unique vessels of receiving, which he uses only for the sake of giving, thus being a channel of good for all.

Second *Tzimtzum* צִמְצוּם ב': lit., the second contraction. The joining of Compassion (the Sephirah Binah) with Judgment (the Sephirah Malchut). This is an event in the spiritual worlds that allows for the creation of the human being. The human being is unique of all created beings in that he is made up of both the soul, which comes from the framework of holiness and the body, which stems from the framework of evil. This allows him to fulfill the purpose for which he was created, namely the moving of elements from the framework of evil to the framework of holiness.

seder night לֵיל הַסֵּדֶר: This is the first night of Passover, when Jews all over the world sit together in family groups and relate the story of the deliverance of the Children of Israel from Egypt. It is a unique night of the year in which the great light of redemption, the *Or d'Chochmah*, is present in the world.

Sephirah סְפִירָה pl. *Sephirot* סְפִירוֹת lit., one that shines: The Ten Sephirot are also known as the Tree of Life and are the most subtle vessels for the light of God.

Shabbat שַׁבָּת pl. *Shabbatot* שַׁבָּתוֹת: lit., He ceased (work): The Sabbath has the essence of the light of the final redemption. It is a holy day that occurs each week in which the essence of the redeemed world permeates our ordinary existence. It is ushered in with the sanctification over the wine, Kiddush, which represents the *Or d'Chochmah*, the light that God wants to give us in His Purpose of Creation.

Shechinah שְׁכִינָה: The indwelling presence of God. The Shechinah is the term for the collective soul, also called the Malchut or the *Knesset Yisrael*. It is the vessel for the light of God that resides within us.

shechitah שְׁחִיטָה: Slaughter of a kosher animal for food in accordance with halachah. The person who carries out the slaughter is called the *shochet*.

shiur שִׁיעוּר pl. *shiurim* שִׁיעוּרִים lit., measure: A *shiur* is a formal lesson given by a sage or another teacher based on a sacred text.

shofar שׁוֹפָר: The ram's horn blown on Rosh HaShanah to awaken us to *teshuvah*, repentance. According to the Zohar, the shofar's call awakens the sound of compassion in ourselves and in the world, and is related to the joining of the Sephirah Malchut, the attribute of judgment, with the Sephirah Binah, the attribute of compassion.

sitra achra סִתְרָא אָחֳרָא (Aram.) lit., the other side: The framework of evil: in which evil exists not just as a solitary act but as a system with its own rules and behaviors. It is sustained by the Creator and fed by our own individual wills to receive for ourselves alone, which act synergistically to create an entire framework.

soul: The aspect of God's essence within us. The desire of the soul is to be in affinity of form with the Creator via giving unconditionally, or through receiving only for the sake of giving. The collective soul of humanity is called the Shechinah, and the soul within the individual is designated as the aspect of Israel within him. The lights of the soul are called *Nefesh* נֶפֶשׁ, *Ruach* רוּחַ, *Neshamah* נְשָׁמָה, *Chayah* חַיָּה, and *Yechidah* יְחִידָה, which the person acquires by gradually transforming his desires from receiving to giving unconditionally.

spiritual vs. material: That which is in affinity of form with the Creator is called "spiritual" רוּחָנִי; that which is in opposition of form to the Creator is called "material" גַּשְׁמִי. See also "above and below."

Succot סוּכּוֹת lit., booths: This festival follows immediately after the holidays of Rosh HaShanah and Yom Kippur. It is a festival in which we shelter in the light of faith, symbolized by the roof of the succah, called the *sechach* סְכָך. In this festival, each family builds a succah סֻכָּה (a temporary dwelling) that takes the place of the home during these seven days. We also take hold of the four species: the lulav, the etrog, the myrtle, and the willow, which together represent the four-letter name of God.

Tanach תנ״ך: This is an acronym formed from the first letters of the written Torah תּוֹרָה (The Five Books of Moses), Nevi'im נְבִיאִים (Prophets), and the Ketuvim כְּתוּבִים (Writings) that, together, make up the three sections of the Hebrew Bible.

Targum תַּרְגּוּם (Aram.): The first translations of the Torah were in Aramaic by Onkelos and by Yonatan Ben Uziel.

tikkun תִּקּוּן pl. *tikkunim* תִּקּוּנִים repair or rectification, also Tikkun **of Creation** תִּקּוּן הַבְּרִיאָה: The tikkun is the work that the soul is brought down to this world to do. It involves taking elements from the framework of evil that manifest within us as the will to receive for ourselves alone, and changing their direction, so that these desires will now be used only to give benefit to God or to our fellow, in affinity of form with the framework of holiness.

We each need to do our own individual tikkun and thus we participate in the collective Tikkun of Creation. When this is complete, we will all be able to receive from God all that He wants to give us, because our receiving then will be only for the sake of giving to God. All souls participate in the Tikkun of Creation until the *gmar hatikkun*, the full redemption, when the one soul of Adam, of which we all form a part, will be fully rectified.

teshuvah תְּשׁוּבָה lit., returning, often translated as repentance: *Teshuvah* is closely associated with the idea of tikkun, in which we regret having used our will to receive for ourselves alone, thereby becoming separated from the Creator, and we turn again to use the vessels of the soul, the vessels for giving unconditionally, with which we are in affinity of form with the Creator.

tisch (Yiddish): A meal eaten by chasidic students together with their sage on a Shabbat or festival at which the inner meaning of the holiness of the day is elucidated by the sage.

Torah (Heb.) תּוֹרָה lit., instruction: This refers to both the written Torah and the oral Torah that were given to Moses at Mount Sinai through divine revelation. It also refers to the ongoing development of the oral Torah throughout the ages. The term includes The Five Books of Moses, the Prophets, the Writings, Talmud, Responsa, Halachah, Midrash, and Kabbalah.

Torah and *mitzvot* תּוֹרָה וּמִצְווֹת: This phrase implies the study and conscious application of the divine wisdom as received through Moses and interpreted for every generation by the sages. The phrase, as used in Kabbalah, applies both to our actions in accordance with the *halachah*, and to our inner work conducted between ourselves and the Creator, and between ourselves and our fellow.

Torah *l'shmah* תּוֹרָה לִשְׁמָהּ: the practice of Torah and mitzvot carried out for its own sake, that is to say without motives of self-interest mixed in.

Torah *shelo l'shmah* תּוֹרָה שֶׁלֹּא לִשְׁמָהּ: Torah that is practiced not for its own sake. This phrase has two different meanings in Kabbalah:

(1) The practice of Torah and mitzvot that is carried out for self-interest or gain. The sages of the Talmud condemn such practice and say such practice causes the Torah to become a drug of death because this type of practice increases one's ego.

(2) The term also refers to an intermediate stage, wherein a person begins his practice of Torah and mitzvot endeavoring to come to the complete form of the practice of Torah, *Torah l'shmah*. But since we are all born and grow for the first 12-13 years of our life under the influence of the framework of evil, we have no choice but to begin our practice of Torah with motives of self-interest mixed in. In this case, our practice of *Torah shelo l'shmah* is considered a valued and necessary step towards our practice of *Torah l'shmah*, on condition that we remember that, in itself, it is not a complete form of practice, but one that needs

purifying. Thus, such practice of *Torah shelo l'shmah* is associated with the framework of holiness, even though it is not complete.

tzaddik צַדִּיק pl. *tzaddikim* צַדִּיקִים: A righteous person. A tzaddik is one who has attained affinity of form with the Creator. A person who desires and labors to become a tzaddik but has not yet attained this spiritual stage may also be referred to as a tzaddik.

vessel כְּלִי: A desire for the light of God. Some vessels manifest the desire to receive the light of God, thus attracting to themselves the *Or d'Chochmah*, the light that God wants to give according to the Purpose of Creation. Other vessels manifest the desire to give and to be in affinity of form with the Creator, thus attracting light from the Creator called the *Or d'Chassadim*, experienced as the joy of giving. According to the nature of the vessel so is the light within it perceived.

Our vessels develop through our spiritual work from those distanced from the Creator to those that fulfill the Purpose of Creation as follows:

- **the will to receive for oneself alone** רָצוֹן לְקַבֵּל לְעַצְמוֹ also known as רָצוֹן לְקַבֵּל עַל מְנַת לְקַבֵּל receiving for the sake of receiving: This is the vessel most removed from God, as it is in opposition of form with respect to the Creator. The phrase, the "will to receive for oneself alone" refers to every action and every intention of action that is directed to fulfilling one's own egoistically directed demands. Other synonyms for this phrase are "selfish love" אַהֲבָה עַצְמִית; "the evil inclination" *yetzer hara*, יֵצֶר הָרַע; "the angel of death" מַלְאַךְ הַמָּוֶת; "Satan" הַשָּׂטָן; "the ego." The light that is received in this vessel is extremely limited and is called *nehiro dakik* נְהִירוֹ דַּקִיק a tiny light, which fades very soon after it is received.

- **the will to give for the sake of receiving** רָצוֹן לְהַשְׁפִּיעַ עַל מְנָת לְקַבֵּל: This is an intermediate stage in which the person does actions of giving, but his underlying intention in his action of giving is to receive some benefit for himself. Therefore, although this is immeasurably better than receiving for oneself alone, such giving is still in service of one's selfish love. However, this is a necessary intermediate stage one needs to go through in order to progress to the framework of holiness. See *Torah shelo l'shmah.*

+ **the will to give for the sake of giving, also called the will to give benefit or the will to give unconditionally, or the attribute of altruism** רָצוֹן לְהַשְׁפִּיעַ עַל מְנַת לְהַשְׁפִּיעַ: This is the stage of the tzaddik. He has completely let go of his will to receive and is only focused on what he can do for others in order to benefit them. Vessels of giving unconditionally attract the light of God called the *Or d'Chassadim*, the experience of the joy of giving. A person who attains the will to give for the sake of giving is in the framework of holiness and is in affinity of form with the Creator. This is the spiritual level called the Tikkun of Creation and is actualized in the practice of *Torah l'shmah.*

+ **the will to receive for the sake of giving** רָצוֹן לְקַבֵּל עַל מְנַת לְהַשְׁפִּיע: This is the transformed vessel in which the will to receive is only used to receive when it pleases the Giver that we do so. It attracts the light that God wishes to give according to the Purpose of Creation, the *Or d'Chochmah*. Now the will to receive is used only to give pleasure to the Giver, and thus transforms from a finite vessel to an infinite channel for the light of God used to benefit all. It is this vessel that fulfills the Purpose of Creation.

will to receive רָצוֹן לְקַבֵּל: This is the vessel for the *Or Elyon*, the Highest Light. It came forth in the Ein Sof, where it is known as the Malchut of the Ein Sof. The will to receive characterizes all created beings. It is the basic vessel for the light, and it is through the rectified will to receive that all created beings will receive the light of God at the *gmar hatikkun.*

world עוֹלָם: a complete level of consciousness characterized by a specific type of desire. A spiritual world in the framework of holiness has an overriding consciousness of giving in which all its components are elements or expressions of that consciousness, whereas a spiritual world within the framework of evil has elements that all express the desire to receive for oneself alone. The spiritual worlds are called,

Atzilut אֲצִילוּת, Briyah בְּרִיאָה, Yetzirah יְצִירָה, and Assiyah עֲשִׂיָּה. While physically present in this world, we can connect with the higher spiritual worlds of holiness through our acts and our consciousness.

Yirah יִרְאָה; *yirat HaShem* יִרְאַת ה'; *yirat shamayim* יִרְאַת שָׁמַיִם reverence for God, or awe of God. The attribute of *yirah* means to be concerned not to do anything that will separate ourselves from God. This, therefore, encompasses keeping the "don't do's," the 365 negative commands. But the concept has also the idea of valuing and revering God in both good times and in bad, recognizing Him and having reverence for Him as the Source of all. *Yirat HaShem* is the foundation of faith and trust in God.

yeshivah יְשִׁיבָה: A seminary for Torah learning.

yetzer hara יֵצֶר הָרַע: See the will to receive for oneself alone.

Rabbi Ashlag's Works and Bibliography

Panim Meirot uMasbirot (Illuminating and Welcoming Revelations)
This is the first commentary that Rabbi Ashlag wrote on the writings of the Ari. In this book, Rabbi Ashlag organizes the teachings of the Ari according to cause and effect. This gives rise to a logical flow in the dynamics of light and vessels from the Ein Sof through the spiritual worlds until the creation of this world.

The *Panim Meirot uMasbirot* is made up of two commentaries: the *Panim Meirot*, which is a detailed explanation of the terms used by the Ari in the text of the *Etz Chaim*—the main work of the Ari that was set down by Rabbi Chaim Vital; and the *Panim Masbirot*, which is a broad explanation of the processes and principles found in the Ari's teaching.

The publication of the *Panim Meirot uMasbirot* was revolutionary in its day, as it was the first book ever to explain the teachings of the Ari in a clear and logical way. Its study has largely been superseded by a more detailed work, the *Talmud Eser haSephirot* that Rabbi Ashlag wrote subsequently as a result of his pupils' difficulties in understanding this work.

The Talmud Eser haSephirot (The Study of the Ten Sephirot)
This is a sixteen-volumed work, in which Rabbi Ashlag enlarges on the *Panim Meirot uMasbirot*. Its content deals with the flow of the dynamics of light and vessel as they devolve from the Ein Sof to this world. Here is a brief outline of this flow for the interested reader:

The *Talmud Eser HaSephirot* opens with the first spiritual state, the Ein Sof. The Ein Sof consists of the Highest Light, the *Or Elyon*, which emanates from the Creator's essence (the *Atzmut*). This light is God's goodness. The light has one constant desire, which is to give pleasure to all created beings. This desire is called the Purpose of Creation. The pleasure the Creator wishes to give is the light itself, His goodness.

In order to actualize this desire of giving of itself, the light creates something new. This new creation is a desire for the light, known as "a vessel." This desire to receive the light of God forms the basic nature of all created beings, which are composed both of vessels and of the light that is received within these vessels.

In the Ein Sof, the vessel is designated, "the Malchut of the Ein Sof." At this level, the Malchut is filled entirely with light in a state of complete wholeness and perfection. It is the Malchut of the Ein Sof that constitutes the collective of all the souls. In the Ein Sof all the souls are already perfected, receiving all the goodness and joy that will become manifest to us at the end of the tikkun of creation. This is because the Creator needs no process as we do, but at the very moment He thought to give pleasure to the created being, it instantly occurred.

As all developments of the spiritual worlds are additional to previous states and do not replace previous states, so the state in the Ein Sof, in which the souls are already perfected, exists in parallel to our current experience and will manifest again in the future at the end of the tikkun, according to the inner meaning of the phrase from the Zohar, "The end of an action is implicit in its original thought."[1]

Although the light of the Ein Sof and the vessel of the Ein Sof, the Malchut, are in complete harmony, according to the inner meaning of the verse (Zech. 14:9), "He and His Name are One," in which "He" refers to the light, and "His Name" refers to the Malchut," nevertheless the Malchut awakens to desire extra *dvekut*, super-*dvekut*! This occurs because there is a spiritual rule that every branch wants to be like its root. Therefore, since the Malchut of the Ein Sof is a branch of the light of the Ein Sof, it desires to become like the light—to become a giver, just as its root, the light, is giving. The fulfillment of this desire would add a further dimension of the Malchut's *dvekut* with the Highest Light as it would then be in affinity of form with the light of the Ein Sof.

This new desire of the Malchut, that of wanting to give in order to acquire affinity of form with the light, leads to the creation of all the worlds.

The Hebrew word for "world" is עולם. It derives from the word עלם which means "hidden." The worlds are states of consciousness in which the light of God is progressively more hidden until we reach this physical world in which it is perfectly possible to live without being aware of the Creator at all. All these worlds unfold in order for the Malchut, the collective of all the souls, to achieve its desire of becoming a giver as well as a receiver.

Thus, from this decision of the Malchut of the Ein Sof to desire "super-*dvekut*" with the light, comes forth the first stage of spiritual development, the creation of the world of *Tzimtzum*.

In this world of *Tzimtzum*, the Malchut of the Ein Sof starts to implement its decision. It first decides that it does not wish to receive from the light. It reduces its will to receive pleasure and joy to an absolute minimum. The first consequence of this decision is that the light, which in the Ein Sof filled the Malchut completely, withdraws.

For the first time, the Malchut is empty. Now that it is empty it can realize two things it could not realize while filled with the light: (1) that it is a vessel and that it has a great desire to receive the light of the Creator, and (2) it can apprehend what it is composed of. Now that the Malchut is empty, it can see that it developed from the Highest Light in four gradations of will, culminating in a complete will to receive. This complete will to receive is the essence of the Malchut.

These gradations of will that develop from the light form the Sephirot. The Sephirot are the most delicate and subtle vessels that receive the light of the Creator. They are the basic building blocks that make up all beings. Some of the Sephirot embody more of the will to give, others embody more of the will to receive. The complete will to receive is embodied by the Malchut itself.

Since this choice to reduce the will to receive to an absolute minimum, is a choice the Malchut makes freely, there is no hierarchy in this world of *Tzimtzum*; no better or worse, no higher or lower. All elements in this world are equal to each other. Therefore this world is also designated as "The world of the *Sephirot Igulim* (circular Sephirot)"— the term circular being a term borrowed from this world, as a circle implies equality.

There is, however, a spiritual principle that a choice made at a higher level becomes obligatory for all lower levels. So although the initial choice made by the Malchut of preferring to give rather than to receive is a decision made freely, this decision becomes binding on all subsequent worlds that develop.

The Highest Light never changes its desire of giving to the Malchut, "I am the Lord, I do not change" (Mal. 3:6), so the Highest Light comes again repeatedly to the Malchut. On its part, the Malchut of the world of *Tzimtzum* has now realized that it really does have a will to receive the light, yet it still wants to remain true to its desire to give. These two contradictory desires lead to the development of the next spiritual world, the world of Adam Kadmon.

When the Highest Light comes again to the Malchut, it now erects a *masach* (barrier) over its own desire to receive, giving the light back to the Creator. This action demonstrates, both to itself and to the Creator, that despite its desire to receive the light, it nevertheless is staying true to its decision of being a giver. The Malchut prefers giving, thus allowing it to be in affinity of form with the Creator, rather than using its vessel of receiving, as to use it now would cause opposition of form between it and the Creator and thus separation from the Creator. This is because the decision that was made at a higher level is now binding on it.

Eventually, when the Malchut sees that the Highest Light comes to it repeatedly, "hitting" at the barrier it has erected over its own desire to receive, it comes to understand that by receiving the light it would actually be giving pleasure to the Giver. Thus, there comes into being a new way of receiving: **receiving, only for the sake of giving pleasure to the giver.**[*]

This type of receiving is not unlimited, but is determined by the ability of the Malchut to give. Thus the world of Adam Kadmon is designated "the line." This is for two reasons: (1) it has direction. Aspects of spiritual reality that are closer to the aspect of giving are considered as higher or purer, whereas those that are closer to the aspect of receiving are considered lower or more dense. (2) The ability of the worlds to receive light is limited to the ability of the *masach* to return the light. Now the vessel will accept only that which it is able to receive for the

---

[*] For a full discussion of this process, see A Tapestry for the Soul, (Nehora Press) Lesson Eight.

sake of giving, but no more. So instead of receiving infinite light, as in the Ein Sof, the vessel now receives only a very limited amount of light.

Spiritual entities that act in consonance with this choice of giving constitute the framework of holiness. Those that act against this choice of giving constitute the framework of evil. Since, in the world of Adam Kadmon, the Malchut acts only to receive that which it is able to receive for the sake of giving pleasure to the Creator, and does not receive for itself, this world is in the framework of holiness.

The next spiritual world is designated *Olam haNikkudim*. In this world, the *Second Tzimtzum* first appears. This is the joining of the attribute of compassion with the strict rule of not receiving solely for the pleasure of receiving.* Now the Malchut acquires an additional desire, that of giving for the sheer delight of giving. This desire attracts to itself the *Or d' Chassadim*, the light caused by loving-kindness.

However, this development of the *Second Tzimtzum* also led to a situation in which, for the first time, the created being used its will to receive for its own pleasure, leaving the framework of holiness and entering the framework of evil. This event is referred to as *Shvirat haKelim*, "the breaking of the vessels."

The next spiritual world is designated the world of Atzilut of the framework of holiness. This world has the quality of complete divinity, according to the inner meaning of the statement of the sages of the Zohar, "He, His light, and His vessels are all One." [14] To some extent, the world of Atzilut repairs the previous world, whose vessels shattered. This world is the highest spiritual level that the tzaddik achieves. Atzilut is the consciousness of loving God eternally, for at this level the tzaddik attains that God's providence over all his creatures is of the ultimate good. The tzaddik actually perceives the Creator's goodness and that He does good to all, to the wicked and to the good.

Opposing this consciousness is the world of Atzilut of the framework of uncleanness, which tries to disturb this love.

The next spiritual world is the world of Briyah, the world that is designated "the quarry of the souls." In this world, the souls become recognizable as individual created beings, separate from the Creator.

---

* This is termed "the joining of Compassion with Judgment."

When we are in affinity of form with this world, we attain the consciousness of unconditional love and perceive God as being Good and as acting beneficently to ourselves, personally, but we can't see it with regard to the rest of the world. Opposing this world is the world of Briyah of the framework of uncleanness, which tries to oppose this love.

The next spiritual world is the world of Yetzirah. When we are in affinity with the consciousness of this world we attain the revelation of seeing clearly the consequences of our actions, in that we perceive that the reward for a mitzvah performed unconditionally is closeness to God, and the consequence of a sin is separation from God. We merit a revelation of the light of God according to the inner meaning of the saying of the sages of the Talmud: "You will see your reward in your lifetime."[2] This is the level of conditional love. Opposing this consciousness is the world of Yetzirah of the framework of uncleanness, which tries to disturb the factor on which our love depends.

The next spiritual world is the world of Assiyah. This is the lowest of all the spiritual worlds. In this world, the Divine Providence is concealed. It is in the consciousness of this world that our spiritual work consists of attaining *emunah* (faith in the Creator.)[*] *Emunah* is in greater affinity of form with the Creator than is the paradigm of knowledge. Opposing this consciousness is the world of Assiyah of uncleanness, which tries to impose the thought that the Divine Providence is not good, or that the Creator does not exercise any watchfulness over His creatures.

The final world is this world, the world of materialism. This does not refer to its physicality, but to the conscious state in which we consider only that which will benefit our own selfish love. This is the state of consciousness known as egoism, the evil inclination or the angel of death.

---

* *Emunah*, faith in the Creator, implies belief in His existence and faith that He is good and does good. When *emunah* informs our thoughts, speech, and actions it brings us into affinity of form with the Creator because it constitutes an act of giving, whereas knowledge is received.

The main states of consciousness as described in the spiritual worlds of holiness are represented by the four letters in the name of God, יהו'ה (Y-H-V-H):

+ The world of Adam Kadmon by the tip of the first letter י
+ The world of Atzilut by the letter י
+ The world of Briyah by the letter ה
+ The world of Yetzirah by the letter ו
+ The world of Assiyah by the letter ה

Beit Sha'ar haKavanot (The Gate of Intentions)

Rabbi Ashlag wrote this work following the completion of the *Talmud Eser haSephirot* as a further commentary on the teachings of the Ari. It differs from the *Talmud Eser haSephirot* in that it focuses primarily on the souls, beginning with their work while they are here in this world, and delineating their progress as they ascend in spiritual consciousness. Thus this book adds much clarification on the work of the human being with respect to the Creator.

The Petichah l'Chochmat haKabbalah (The Gateway to the Wisdom of Kabbalah)

A *tour de force* of spiritual insight, this work comprises a broad overview of the development of consciousness from the Ein Sof to this world. It opens with the Purpose of Creation—the desire of the Creator to give good to all created beings. It is this desire that creates the whole of existence right up to, and including, the consciousness of this world.

This essay is an essential text for the serious student as it provides an outline of the development of the vessels and introduces the student to the language of Kabbalah. As its name suggests, its text provides a gateway to understanding the works of the Ari and to the *Perush haSulam*, Rabbi Ashlag's great commentary on the Zohar. For the advanced student, it gives a summary of the main features of the spiritual landscape.

Perush haSulam on the Zohar (The Ladder Commentary on the Zohar)

The commentary on the Zohar, the main book of Kabbalah, for which Rabbi Ashlag was named Baal HaSulam. See Chapter Thirteen, page 175.

Petichah l'Perush haSulam (The Gateway to the *Perush haSulam*)
This is a complementary work to the *Petichah l'Chochmat haKabbalah*, focusing particularly on the world of Atzilut. In this work, Rabbi Ashlag explains the way the Sephirot function with respect to the three lines: the right-hand line, the left-hand line, and the middle line.

Or haBahir (The Clear Light)
This is a lexicon that Rabbi Ashlag compiled of all the technical terms found within the writings of the Zohar and in the Kabbalah of the Ari. It has over a thousand entries.

The Introductions and Essays
Hakdamah l'Sefer haZohar (The Introduction to the Zohar) opens with the question, "What is our essence?" This question and its answer form the central theme of this introduction in which Rabbi Ashlag discusses the makeup of the human being, the origin of the ego, the incarnation of the soul, the paradoxical association of soul and body and their subsequent development through the work given to a person in this world.

Hakdamah l'Talmud Eser haSephirot (The Introduction to the Study of the Ten Sephirot) consists of two separate articles that were later joined together. In the first, Rabbi Ashlag discusses the questions: What is the essence of the Torah? and What is the path of Torah? In the second, Rabbi Ashlag considers the four worlds of spiritual consciousness: Atzilut, Briyah, Yetzirah, and Assiyah, in terms of an individual's development: that is, the extent to which the person has attained a true appreciation of the Divine Providence and has clarified his love for the Creator.

Hakdamah l'Panim Meirot uMasbirot (Introduction to the *Panim Meirot uMasbirot*): In this introduction, Rabbi Ashlag deals with the history of the writings of the Ari and looks at why the teachings of Kabbalah were concealed until this generation. He goes on to discuss the development of the opposing frameworks of holiness and of uncleanness and the balance between them, both in the life of society and in the life of the individual. This introduction includes a fascinating discussion on the causes and consequences of the events in the Garden of Eden and their implications for us today.

Mavo l'Zohar (Prologue to the Zohar): In this further introduction to the Zohar, Rabbi Ashlag considers the composition of reality and the boundaries within which the Zohar confines its discussion.

Matan Torah (The Gift of the Torah)
This work was written for the secular world. See page 138. The articles that presently constitute *Matan Torah* are:

- *Et La'asot* (A Time to Act)
- *Gilui Tephach v'Kisui Tephachayim* (Revealing One Handbreadth, Concealing Two)
- *Matan Torah* (The Gift of the Torah)
- *haArevut* (Mutual Responsibility)
- *Mahut haDat u'Mataratah* (The Essence of Religion and its Purpose)
- *Mahut Chochmat haKabbalah* (The Essence of the Wisdom of Kabbalah)
- *haChomer v'haTzurah b'Chochmat haKabbalah* (Substance and Form in the Wisdom of Kabbalah)
- *haShalom* (Peace)
- *Ma'amar haCherut* (Article on Freedom)
- *Ma'amar l'Siyum haZohar* (Article on the Conclusion of the Zohar)
- *Sechel haPoel* (Active Intelligence)
- *v'Zot l'Yehudah* (This is Yehudah's: A Commentary on the Passover Haggadah)

Much of Rabbi Ashlag's writing has lain hitherto hidden and unpublished. Due to the efforts of the Or HaSulam organization, further articles that were originally written for the secular world are now coming to light and are gradually being published.

Pri Chacham (Fruit of the Wise)
These three volumes consist of the collected letters that Rabbi Ashlag wrote to his students, various essays on the nature of the wisdom

and the language of Kabbalah, and many personal notes found in his writings after his death. This collection was first assembled by Rabbi Avraham Yechezkel Ashlag, a grandson of the Baal HaSulam. As more and more unpublished material is coming to light this collection is being enlarged.

Bibliography for this Work

The main resource for this book was *HaSulam: Pirkei haChaim u'Mishnatam shel Raboteinu haKedoshim, haAdmorim l'beit Ashlag u'Talmideihem.* (The Ladder: The Biography and Teachings of Rabbi Yehudah Leib Ashlag and Rabbi Baruch Shalom Ashlag and of their Students). Rabbi Avraham Mordecai Gottlieb (Or Baruch Shalom 1997)

Further materials were added to this English edition: The main additions came from:

HaShem Shamati Shemecha (Oh God, I have Heard of Your Fame): A collection of the notes and writings compiled by the students of the Baal HaSulam following the discussions and oral talks they heard from the Sage on the way of serving God. (Or Baruch Shalom 2009)

Igarot HaSulam (Letters of the Baal HaSulam) (Or HaSulam 2014) The letters of the Baal HaSulam were first published by Rabbi Avraham Yechezkel Ashlag as *Pri Chacham* vol. 2 *Igarot Kodesh*. However, the version used for this book, the Or HaSulam edition, is a more recent one that includes many not previously published. (The numbering of the letters differs between publishers.)

Sefer Hakdamot l'Chochmat haEmet im haBeorim Or Baruch v'Or Shalom (A collection of the Introductions to the Wisdom of Kabbalah) (Or Baruch Shalom, second edition 1996)

Perush haSulam (The Sulam Commentary on the Zohar) (M. Claar, 1998)

Excerpts from Rabbi Ashlag's philosophical writings came from *Matan Torah* (the Gift of the Torah) (Or haGanuz 1995); *Pri Chacham 1 Ma'amarim* (edited and published by Rabbi Avraham Yechezkel Ashlag 1999); from unpublished manuscripts.

Translations of excerpts from the *Hakdamah l'Sefer haZohar* (Introduction to the Zohar) and the *Hakdamah l'Talmud Eser haSephirot* (Introduction to the Study of the Ten Sephirot) were taken from, *In the Shadow of the Ladder: Introductions to Kabbalah by Rabbi Yehudah Lev Ashlag* by Mark and Yedidah Cohen (Nehora Press 2003)

Songs and Poems by Rabbi Yehudah Leib Ashlag have been published by the organization Or haSulam which is working to collect, digitalize, and archive the many thousands of pages of unpublished manuscripts written by the Baal HaSulam. Recordings of the shiurim by the Baal HaSulam are similarly available on the Or HaSulam website.

The essays on the Love for Companions that form the Afterword are taken from *Bircat Shalom Ma'amarim* by Rabbi Baruch Shalom Ashlag, Volume One (Or Baruch Shalom 1996)

Commentaries by Rabbi Avraham Mordecai Gottlieb: The commentary on the teaching of the Rabbi of Belz to Rabbi Ashlag (page 16) was written by Rabbi Gottlieb especially for this volume. The commentary on the letter to Rabbi Joshua Horovitz was translated from *Pri Chacham Igarot Kodesh im He'arot uBeorim* by Rabbi Avraham Mordecai Gottlieb (Or Baruch Shalom 2009)

Many thanks to Ofer Shneider of the Bircat Shalom Institute for the music on page 136.

Rabbi Avraham Mordecai Gottlieb

Avraham Mordecai Gottlieb was born in 1963 in Bnei Brak into a chasidic family. His father, Rabbi Shraga Gottlieb, used to take his young son with him when he went to study at the beit midrash of Rabbi Shlomoh Binyamin Ashlag, a younger son and student of the Baal HaSulam. There, the young Avraham would play with the Baal HaSulam's grandchildren, unconsciously absorbing the words of Kabbalah. When he was only seven years old, his father started to study with him, choosing one of the complex works of the Baal HaSulam, the *Petichah l'Chochmat haKabbalah*. At that time the child could not understand his father's words, but they made a lasting impression on him.

As he grew, the young Avraham Mordecai began to ask his own questions on the way of serving God. Soon after his bar mitzvah, he became a student of Rabbi Shlomoh Binyamin in his own right. He matured rapidly, learning constantly, and in the following year, at the young age of fourteen, he entered the beit midrash of Rabbi Baruch Shalom Ashlag.

This was a most unusual move. At that time, the other students in the beit midrash were all mature men; many had been students of the Baal HaSulam. Some were old enough to have been Avraham Mordecai's grandfather. They were men of exceptional spiritual stature; the studies and demands they made on themselves were serious and intense. They did not view the entry of the youngster in their midst favorably. But Rabbi Baruch Shalom sensed the young lad's true dedication and allowed him to stay.

Thus, Rabbi Baruch Shalom Ashlag became Avraham Mordecai's guide and mentor. At his teacher's behest, he studied at the Lithuanian Yeshivah, Beit Meir, in order to gain proficiency in the Talmud while simultaneously continuing his studies at the beit midrash of Rabbi Baruch Shalom. Thus, in the realm of Talmud, Avraham Mordecai learned from the tradition of the Chofetz Chaim, whereas his knowledge of Kabbalah and its application in serving God, he gained from the tradition of the Baal HaSulam.

Rabbi Avraham Mordecai eventually became very close to Rabbi Baruch Shalom, acting as his assistant, and being present at all his shiurim; sometimes for as much as ten hours a day. In his later years, Rabbi Baruch Shalom asked Rabbi Avraham Mordecai to teach the younger students who were then entering the beit midrash. It was at that time that Rabbi Avraham Mordecai started what was to become his life's work—editing and arranging the books of the Baal HaSulam including the oral teachings of Rabbi Baruch Shalom Ashlag Rabbi Avraham Mordecai served Rabbi Baruch Shalom devotedly until the Sage's death in 1991.

It was time for a new beginning. Rabbi Avraham Mordecai moved to Kiryat Ye'arim where he established the beit midrash, Bircat Shalom. Many families joined him there, making a vibrant Orthodox community that conducts itself according to the principles of the inner aspect of the Torah. There, Rabbi Avraham Mordecai teaches the writings of the Baal HaSulam morning and evening and compiles the commentaries on his works collated from the oral shiurim of Rabbi Baruch Shalom, many of which are preserved on tape. To this date, Rabbi Avraham Mordecai has published thirty-seven books of the teachings of the Baal HaSulam and of Rabbi Baruch Shalom Ashlag.

In 1986, Rabbi Avraham Mordecai married Rabbanit Chana Matel Zilberfeld and they are blessed with three children and grandchildren.

Yedidah Cohen lives in Tsfat, the mother of four children. She translates into English and collates the works of the Baal HaSulam and of Rabbi Baruch Shalom Ashlag in both Hebrew and English. She teaches in both languages to small groups and to individuals wanting to learn. She loves seeing how her own and other peoples' perspectives change as a direct result of this learning. Yedidah's other interest is helping people of all backgrounds and levels develop a deep spiritual connection through the Hebrew language. She can be contacted through Nehora Press.

Endorsements (*Haskamot*) of Rabbi Avraham Mordecai Gottlieb's work by prominent *Talmidei Chachamim**

Beis Din Zedek
of Kahal Machzekei Hadas E. Israel

בית דין צדק
קהל מחזיקי הדת בארץ ישראל

בס"ד ז' טבת תשע"ד לפ"ק, פעיה"ק ירושלים תובב"א

1670

מצוה גדולה וחשובה לסייע ולתמוך בידיו האמונות של מעלת כבוד הרב הצדיק
המופלא ומופלג ידיו רב לו בנגלה ובנסתר כש"ת רבי **אברהם מרדכי גוטליב** שליט"א,
תלמידו הנאמן והחביב של כ"ק הרב הגאון הצדיק המר"מ בנגלה ובנסתר כש"ת רבי
ברוך שלום אשלג זצללה"ה בנו של הרה"ק בעל ה**"סולם"** זצוק"ל, אשר לקח על עצמו
משימה קדושה לערוך את ספרי רבו זצ"ל, הסובבים על ספרי אביו הגדול זי"ע, ולהוסיף
בהם הערות, הארות וביאורים, ואך למותר הוא להרבות בשבח העוסקים בתורת הנסתר
לשם שמים ובלימוד ספרי מוהר"ר הזוהר הקדוש, כידוע מספרים וסופרים, ובזכות זה תהי' גאולתם
של ישראל מגלות החל הזה ברחמים וחסדים, כדאיתא בזוה"ק.

אשר על כן ידינו תכון עמו להוציא לאור תורות רבו בנסתר ובנגלה, עם הערותיו
וביאוריו שנערכו במתוק טעם ודעת, אשר רבים ימצאו בהם חפץ, הן בספרים העוסקים
בתורת הקבלה, והן בספרי האגדה על דרך העבודה וההחסידות לעורר לבבם לתורה
ולעבודת השי"ת.

וברכתנו צרופה בזה שחפץ ה' בידו יצליח לזכות את הרבים בהפצת אורה וזו תורה
מתוך נדת הרחבת הדעת, ויזכה לראות בישועתם של ישראל בביאת משיח צדקנו
במהרה בימינו.

הכו"ח לכבוד התורה ולומדי', הביד"ץ דקהל מחזיקי הדת בארץ ישראל

נאם: נאם: נאם: נאם:

לשכות הביד"ץ
ירושלים:
רח' יצחק שולל 4
טל. 02-5019888
פקס. 02-5019860
ת.ד. 6712 מיקוד 91006

בני ברק:
רח' האדמו"ר מבעלזא 6
טלפקס. 03-5786762

אשדוד:
רח' מבוא החננים 3
טלפקס. 08-8664843

Chambers Badat'z:
Jerusalem:
4 Itzhak Sholal St.
Tel. 02-5019888
Fax. 02-5019860
P.O.B. 6712 Zip 91006

Bnei-Brak:
6 Haadmor Mi'Belz St.
Telefax. 03-5786762

Ashdod:
3 Mevo hananim St.
Telefax. 08-8664843

---

* The Baal HaSulam's work was endorsed by prominent sages of his own generation. See Chapter Eleven, Connections with the Great Sages of Israel, page 159.

Rabbi Y.M. Morgenstern

Rosh hayeshiva of

"Toras Chochom"

Yerushalaim

יצחק מאיר מארגנשטערן

רב ור"מ דק"ק "תורת חכם"

לתורת הנגלה והנסתר

פעיה"ק ירושלים תובב"א

אור ליום ט"ז כסלו תשע"ד לפ"ק, פעיה"ק תובב"א

כבר נודע בשערים קדושת הגה"ק האלקי בוצי"ק מרן בעל הסולם זיע"א, וקדושת
ספריו שזכה להאיר על ידם לארץ ולדרים פנימיות חכמת הקבלה עפ"י דרכי
העבודה דמרנא ורבנא אור שבעת הימים הבעש"ט הק' זיע"א, וכבר אמר הוא הק'
זצוק"ל שבדורותינו אלה שוב אין צורך לתעניתים וסיגופים, אלא עיקר העבודה הוא
העסק בתורת רבינו האריז"ל עפ"י עומק תורת הבעש"ט הק', ועי"כ יזכה ממילא
להשיג הדרך הנכון והאמיתי בעבודת ה', וקבלתי בזה מח"א ששמע מרבו שהיה
מגדולי מיוחדי תלמידי בעל הסולם, ששמע בעצמו מפי"ק דרבו, דכוונתו בחיבורו על
הזוהר היתה להשלים הגילוי דבעל התניא, דמאחר ולא השלים הגה"ק בעל התניא
בחיים חיותו הביאור על ספר הזוהר, זולת מעט מאמרים לפי ערך, עלה ברצון
הגה"ק בעל הסולם להשלים זה הגילוי ולהמשיך האור דמרנן האר"י והבעש"ט לתוך
ספר הזוהר, וזכה בזה כנודע לכל באי ספריו בקדושה המתעמקים בחיבוריו הק',
שעל ידם יוכל להשיג האיך כל תורת האר"י והזוהר אינם אלא דרכי עבודת ה'.
ואחריו ל"ו קם ברא כרעא דאבוה ה"ה בנו הגאון הרה"ק המקובל חו"פ ונהרא
נפישא מישיש צדיקי הדור כמ"ע רבי ברוך שלום הלוי אשלג זצוק"ל, וכל ימיו
דרש לרבים בתורת אביו הקוה"ט ברביה והמשכה בעומק העיון בהשכל ודעת,
ולפרש דברות קדשו העמוקים מני ים במקומות הרבה, וכל ימיו חתר חתירה לגלות
עומק תורת אביו הקדוש ז"ל על פי דרכי עבודת ה' האמיתית שהמשיך וגילה מרן
הבעש"ט הק' נגב"ם.
והנה זה שנים רבות שזכה תלמידו המובהק ה"ה ידידנו המופלג הרה"צ חו"פ אדמו"ר
כמוהר"ר אברהם מרדכי גוטליב שליט"א לייסד בית המדרש על שמו, ולהעמיד
תלמידים הגונים, ונוסף על אלו זכה לחבר ספרים קדושים יקרי ערך בעומק רום
ועומק תחת הן בתורת הגה"ק בעל הסולם זיע"א בספרי תלמוד עשר הספידות,
ובתורת רבו הק' ושיחותיו העמוקים מני ים בדרכי עבודת ה' שנדפסו בספרי ברכת
שלום, ונתקבלו ברצון לפני רבנן ותלמידיהון, וכבר עלו עליהם בהסכמה חכמי הדור
שליט"א, ואף אנא אצטרפנא עמהון, כי ודאי יועילו לקרב נפשות ישראל לתורת
אמת ולדרכי עבודה, ויהא רעותא שיזכה עוד רבות בשנים להגדיל תורה ולהאדירה
עדי יקויים בנו מהרה מאמה"כ "ומלאה הארץ דעה את ה' כמים לים מכסים".

בברכה נאמנה

Shlomo Moshe Amar
Rishon Lezion Chief Rabbi Of Israel
President of the Great Rabbinical Court

שלמה משה עמאר
ראשון לציון הרב הראשי לישראל
נשיא בית הדין הרבני הגדול

בס"ד, י"ד תמוז, תשע"ב

ב/701-5ע"ב

ה מ ל צ ה

הנני בזה להמליץ אודות מוסדות **"ברכת שלום"** ע"ש האדמו"ר רבי ברוך שלום אשלג זצוק"ל
בראשות הגה"ח רבי **אברהם מרדכי גוטליב** שליט"א, אשר זכה להיות גדול ומשקה מתורת
רבו העובדהק הגה"ק רבי ברוך שלום זצוק"ל הנ"ז, ונתאספו סביבו חברים מקשיבים לקולו,
ועוסקים בפנימיות התורה ועילים כמסילה העולה בית אל, וכבר זכה להוציא כמה ספרים יקרים
וחשובים מאד. על כן הנני לברכו כי ימשיך בכפעליו הכבירים, לחזק ידים רפות ולאמץ ברכים
כושלות, להרבות פעלים לתורה כפליים לתושיה.

ואל אחב"י נדיבי הלב הנני קורא לתמוך במוסדות היקרים הללו, ילחזק את האהל לבל יצען
ולבל יתרופפו יסודותיו, וכל המסייעים והעוזרים לדבר מצוה יזכו לברכת ה' בכל מעשי ידיהם,
מתוך שובע שמחות וברכה וחיים עד העולם, אכי"ר.

כברכה מהררי קודש ציון וירושלים,

שלמה משה עמאר
ראשון לציון הרב הראשי לישראל

Index

cont.

cont.

cont.

Index

cont.

cont.

cont.

Index

cont.

cont.

Index

cont.

 Nehora Press

presents further translated works of Rabbi Ashlag into English:

In the Shadow of the Ladder: Introductions to Kabbalah by Rabbi Yehudah Lev Ashlag

Translated from the Hebrew with additional explanatory chapters
by Mark Cohen and Yedidah Cohen

"Through this book, readers will discover a fascinating path to inner harmony and growth through receptivity to the divine light that fills creation."
Rabbi Lord Jonathan Sacks

In the Shadow of the Ladder contains two main introductions to Kabbalah written by Rabbi Ashlag as well as explanatory chapters designed to help the reader.

The Introduction to the Zohar goes deeply into the questions: What is our essence? What is the meaning of the paradoxical association of body and soul? What is our purpose here on earth?

The Introduction to the Study of the Ten Sephirot considers questions we have about the Torah: What is the pathway of the Torah? What is its destination? It also examines human relations and how these impact our relationship with the Creator.

ISBN-13: 978-9657222089, paperback, 273 pages, 6 x 9 inches.
price 22:95

Available from www.nehorapress.com and all major virtual and brick retailers.

Distributed by IPG (Independent Publishers' Group)

A Tapestry for the Soul

The Introduction to the Zohar by Rabbi Yehudah Lev Ashlag explained using excerpts collated from his other writings.

Compiled by Yedidah Cohen

"I felt as if Rabbi Ashlag was sitting in the room with me!"

Rabbi Yonasson Gershom

Imagine having Rabbi Ashlag himself teaching you his own work! In this book Yedidah Cohen juxtaposes Rabbi Ashlag's own writings with the Introduction to the Zohar.

Experience Rabbi Ashlag teaching his own work; discover Rabbi Ashlag's wide range of thought; directly access more complex texts; use the text as an opportunity for inner work.

ISBN-13: 978-9657222041, paperback, 296 pages, 8.5 x 11 inches
price $24.95

Ma'arag l'Neshamah   מארג לנשמה

The Hebrew edition of "A Tapestry for the Soul."

Ma'arag l'Neshamah contains the original texts of Rabbi Ashlag, providing an authentic experience of Rabbi Ashlag's work. It may be used together with **A Tapestry for the Soul.** It is especially useful for those who have some Hebrew and wish to improve their skills.

"ספר זה מתאים לכל אדם ובע"ה יעזור לכל נפש להתקשרות אמיתית עם בורא עולם."

"This book will help everyone who is seeking to find a true connection with the Creator,"

Rabbi Shmuel Eliyahu, Chief Rabbi of Tsfat

ISBN-13: 978-9657222058, paperback, 264 pages, 6 x 9 inches
price $18.95

**All books available from www.nehorapress.com
and all major virtual and brick retailers.**

Distributed by IPG (Independent Publishers' Group)